Russian Narrative & Visual Art

Russian
Narrative &
Visual Art

VARIETIES OF SEEING

EDITED BY

Roger Anderson and
Paul Debreczeny

University Press of Florida

GAINESVILLE □ TALLAHASSEE □ TAMPA □ BOCA RATON

PENSACOLA □ ORLANDO □ MIAMI □ JACKSONVILLE

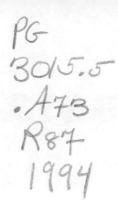
Copyright 1994 by the Board of Regents of the State of Florida

Printed in the United States of America on acid-free paper ∞

All rights reserved

99 98 97 96 95 94 6 5 4 3 2 1

Library of Congress Cataloging-in-Publication Data
Russian narrative and visual art: varieties of seeing / edited by Roger Anderson and
Paul Debreczeny.
p.   cm.
Includes index.
ISBN 0-8130-1255-4 (alk. paper)
1. Russian literature—19th century—History and criticism.   2. Russian literature—20th
century—History and criticism.   3. Art and literature—Russia.   4. Art and literature—
Soviet Union.   5. Art, Russian.   I. Anderson, Roger B.   II. Debreczeny, Paul.
PG3015.5.A73R87   1994
891.73'309—dc20   93-34786

The University Press of Florida is the scholarly publishing agency for the State University
System of Florida, comprised of Florida A & M University, Florida Atlantic University,
Florida International University, Florida State University, University of Central Florida,
University of Florida, University of North Florida, University of South Florida, and
University of West Florida.

University Press of Florida
15 Northwest 15th Street
Gainesville, FL   32611

Contents

Illustrations

Introduction

Roger Anderson
Paul Debreczeny

Late in his life Tolstoy was famous for denouncing the modern taste for mixing artistic media. When, for example, he laced the narrative of "The Kreutzer Sonata" with musical imagery and technique, he fitted a promiscuity of artistic categories to a promiscuity of moral categories. Wagner's *Gesamtkunstwerke* were emblematic of his open animosity for what he saw as the commingling of verbal with other artistic forms. The result for Tolstoy was inseparable from the self-indulgent sensuality he saw growing in modern European culture generally. Nor is Tolstoy's call to maintain the ramparts of discretion (in morals as in art) the only alarm raised on this count. Somewhat later Allen Tate sweeps together the late nineteenth and his own portion of the twentieth century to again equate mixed media with deeper questions of cultural values in crisis. In 1936 he writes:

> When the center of life disappears, the arts of poetry become the heart of poetry. And in an advanced stage of the evil, in the nineteenth century and today, we get the *mélange des genres*, one art living off another, that the late Irving Babbitt so valiantly combated without having understood the influences that had brought it about. Painting tries to be music; poetry leans upon painting; all the arts "strive toward the condition of music" till at last seeing the mathematical structure of music, the arts become geometrical and abstract, and destroy themselves.[1]

Quite beyond their moralism, Tolstoy's and Tate's conservative condemnation of mixed media gives rise to some broader and perhaps even more interesting questions. In a sense, the very harshness of their critique affirms the potential proximity of and interchange between visual and verbal domains. A common ground of discourse between visual and verbal forms both precedes and continues long after Horace's famous principle of *ut pictura poesis*. Western culture's long tradition of mingling and mixing these forms suggests deeper substrates of cultural thinking and image-making. In recent years Iurii Lotman's idea that a culture's given epoch is a "secondary modeling system," an integrated structure that can be described and analyzed, points toward exactly such articulation between artistic systems based on visual and verbal forms. For Lotman such aesthetic subsystems have a "need of each other in order to form the mechanism of culture and to be different according to the principle of semiosis, that is to say, on the one hand equivalent, and on the other hand not entirely mutually convertible."[2]

Verbal and visual art play off against and use one another in meaningful ways for Lotman, and that dialogue allows us to discern in part a culture's basic sense of the world and of itself at particular historical moments, along with underlying structural issues: what constitutes the norms and contradictions of representation; what kinds of values engage the imagination; what, after all, is reality like?

A few examples reflecting different historical eras illustrate Lotman's point. In the Russian Middle Ages we find an almost interchangeable certainty within verbal and visual art forms. Both were rooted in a theocentric order which was meant to celebrate a clear canon of religious belief. The fact that the majority of worshipers were illiterate strongly supported this integration of what the congregation saw and heard in the liturgy. The result was a singular semiotic confidence in both public speech and public vision, which together comprehended the entire community of their (Orthodox) Christian initiates. Here we find an extraordinary compaction and focus in how both a Rublev icon and readings from a saint's life could replicate and reinforce medieval Russian cosmology. Both drew on the same assumptions about man in nature and how standards of human behavior are ordered.

In seventeenth and eighteenth century Europe we find a secular, but still highly integrated, sense of human order shared by painting and poem. For example, we can recall the cool detachment and refined privacy which the period prized in the nature paintings of Claude Lorrain. He represented human activity amidst Arcadian landscapes, emphasizing a static, even remote visual order of dress, line, and color. Social privilege "naturally" merged with a refined, thoughtful mood for those who owned the natural scenery in which they reposed. In conception this message and technique of rendering man in nature was well matched to the period's popular topographical poetry of, say, James Thompson. His *Spring* (1749) features a manicured vocabulary, immovable scenic detail, richly muted color imagery, and a mood of relaxed, contemplative repose based on the confidence of ownership. Consequently he was much admired for his matching of language to pictorial scene. Lorrain and Thompson alike invite us into idealized landscapes to enjoy the proprietary rights depicted by brush and word alike. The unitary view of this era may no longer be theocentric, but we see again structural linkage, Lotman's "privileged" discourse between words and scene in declaring how life is, and should be, ordered.

G. E. Lessing's famous caution later in the century in *The New Laokoön* (1767) that verbal art is fixed in time while the fine arts are spatial by no means muted this deeply rooted discourse between word and brush. With the burgeoning Romantic movement the vocabulary of both media changed sharply, even as they again pursued the same direction. Gone were the visual and verbal renderings of aristocratic man at ease in class-owned nature typical of Lorrain's scenery or Thompson's poetry. In their place we find Byron and Lermontov mirroring Europe's penchant for private anxiety in scenes of turbulent nature. Correspondence between brush and word remains, even while embodied in the popular European literary themes of unfulfilled emotions and mood shifts paralleled by the stark contrasts of fire and air or water, strong colors, and mysterious shadows of, for example, Delacroix or Turner. In his own time Lermontov was far from unique in being a serious landscape artist who flooded his poetry, as well as several scenes in his *A Hero of Our Time*, with just these synesthetic connections of mood and natural scene from his visual palette.

An underlying associationalism between man and nature, in picture and poem alike, thus persists in the nineteenth century (in terms of strong emotion) as it did in the more staid Georgian eighteenth century (in terms of class and breeding). The breaks between aesthetic conceptions of successive ages, say between medieval, Georgian, and Romantic, can serve as examples of what Thomas Kuhn calls paradigmatic shifts distinguishing different historical ages or what Lotman has in mind in his "secondary modeling systems."

By the way, we can remember a younger Tolstoy as one of the more successful masters of that very *mélange des genres* he was later to denounce. Mario Praz has made the interesting observation that several scenes in *War and Peace*, for example, advance a rich dimension of visual imagery which so harmonizes with Tolstoy's authorial rhetoric that the reader's eye in fact takes over the narrative task. We explore whole scenes by "seeing" them rather than "hearing" their explanation.[3]

Symptomatic of the advent of the twentieth century, however, we find a more complex semiotic relationship between visual and verbal media. For example, Gauguin's idealized distortions of human forms in his "primitive" Tahitian figures in the late 1800s were quickly followed by Picasso's Cubist exploration of equally distorted, "primitive" African masks (e.g. his *Les Demoiselles d'Avignon* of 1907). Both imbued their canvases with an undertone of Europe's fascination with exotic and archaic cosmologies. In this sense both painters can be seen as intersecting with Joseph Conrad's fascination with the "primitive" in, for example, *Heart of Darkness* (1899). Considered together at the turn of the twentieth century, such visual and narrative texts can suggest something of Europe's search for invigoration in its late colonialist period.

If anything, the twentieth century has witnessed a progressive strengthening of relations between visual and verbal forms. Picasso's collages featured the playbills and notices of daily urban life as the base for "seeing" that world in a new light. In the 1940s Joseph Frank summarized a growing preference for literary compositions ordered about the visual-spatial over the narrative-sequential. Modern prose, he suggests, is distinguished by sets of "synchronic relations" whose physical echoing replaces diachrony (e.g., as found in the venerable Bildungsroman). The colors, visual images, points of architecture, and everyday details scattered through a modern novel such as Joyce's *Finnegans Wake* create visual gestalts which are held in memory until the reading ends. We must "see" such spatial wholes in order to conceptualize how characters think and act. It is only "after the pattern of synchronic relations ha[s] been grasped as a unity that the 'meaning' of the [work] can be understood."[4] The realist's unrolling of history, explained by the omniscient author, lost its compositional privilege and was supplanted by a grid of spatial balances, repetitions, and contrasts which sculpt meaning visually, quite independent of linear time.

Visual and verbal art can be considered, then, as rotating about a shared mimetic point. For much of the past, paintings and poems have produced a centripetal effect; they are complementary in reflecting core cultural assumptions in a particular period. Be it medieval Russia, the mid-eighteenth century, or the heyday of romanticism, disparate art forms contributed to the kind of maximum internal coherence which Thomas Kuhn and others consider as dividing history into discrete eras, recognizable paradigms of thinking and representation. This proximity of visual and verbal art—in technique as in similarity of theme—can yield the "constellational coherence"[5] Kuhn describes, approximately what Lotman means by the term "equivalence without being mutually convertible."

But this centripetal model of how belles-lettres and fine art reinforce one another gives us only a partial understanding of the matter at hand. To leave it at that is as narrow in its own way as is the moral geometry which Tolstoy and Tate used to separate verbal from all other art forms. Poems and pictures are iconic documents, cultural records which are open to discovery and rediscovery over time. Once produced, canvas and short story enter into a bank of forms which can take on new utility in unpredictable ways. To put it another way, when an artist or writer contemplates a predecessor's creations there can occur flashes of recognition, unexpected insight and reformulation which cross over chronological boundaries and give new definition to the earlier text. We see what we need to see and gain new, perhaps unintended, utility from older cultural icons. In this sense the relationship between visual and verbal art is highly unpredictable, or centrifugal, in contrast to Kuhn's centripetal model described above. With the passage of time disjunction and transformation can be found where repetition and continuity had first been discerned. This is perhaps especially the case given the acceleration of change over the past 150 years. An artistic document may start out as a distinctive statement (a *parole*) only to become part of the culture's *langue* and, in the process, opens to new use, new function in a later age. Meaning inevitably shifts with time; past and present take on unpredictable alignments of expression outside ordinary chronological boundaries. Picasso's African masks take on meaning quite apart from their original tribal uses or esthetic values. Nature untouched by European values as described by Conrad transforms the sentimental renderings of Chateaubriand or Rousseau even as it depends on just their preceding monuments to make its own statement. Discourse is no longer limited in time, just as Picasso's collage breaks the limits of visual representation.

The result is a more fluid sense of art and literary history in which old icons (*paroles*) are vitally open to new artistic reaction and use (the emergence of new *paroles*). In this regard it is moot to ask whether our cultural predecessors anticipated something of what the modern artist now sees or writes, or whether that modern artist has made something new out of the old. A more useful line of inquiry has to do with that intermingling of artistic forms which has accelerated over the past several centuries. Pictorial and poetic genres (as well as other artistic modes) are distinguished by a nonlinear discourse which moves ever more freely across ordinary boundaries of time and cultural experience. Material from other eras is made malleable, reemployed, as it is transformed, to represent a reality which the original era or place would perhaps find unrecognizable.

All the essays included in the present volume deal with interplay between verbal and visual art forms, revealing the internal tensions within the cultural matrix of different periods. The opening essay by James West brings into focus first of all what is characteristic for Russian culture in general during the last three centuries—an ambivalent attitude toward Western imports. We see an uneasy attempt by Russian landscape painters to reconcile the achievements of Western visual arts with Russian traditions. Iconography was so deeply rooted in Russian culture and was still such a vivid presence at the beginning of the nineteenth century that Russian painters, sometimes unconsciously, remained under its spell. Moreover, as James West shows, the slow pace of development in painterly techniques hindered the visual arts from expressing the ideological assumptions of the age as fully as some of the other artistic media were able to. Verbal art, with its capacity for indirect suggestion, lent itself more readily to expressing philosophical ideas. What is most interesting is that the principle of iconography—the arrangement of a landscape according to internal ideological imperatives rather than by external rules of perspective—influenced the vision of poets like Zhukovsky even more than it guided the hand of painters. In any case, even this early period of modern Russian culture reveals a breaking up of the full harmony between the verbal and the visual.

A divergence between the two art forms is manifest also in depictions of the country mansion, the subject of Priscilla Roosevelt's contribution. Visual representations of the dwellings of Russian nobility provide a rare example of an unmediated relationship between art and society. Since most painters during the first half of the nineteenth century were either serfs obliged to do the bidding of their masters or professionals whose livelihood depended on orders from noblemen, depictions of country mansions served the purpose, in most cases, of aggrandizing the nobleman's possessions. Here was an art form whose *raison d'être* was limited to social pretensions. By contrast, verbal representations of the country house tended to be more diversified, exposing class relationships and psychological tensions. It was to a large extent under the influence of literature that by the second half of the century visual representations of mansions took on the narrative function of showing disintegration and decay. Only at the beginning of the twentieth century do we see painting and verbal depiction occupying complementary positions, each attempting to recapture the fading beauty of the past.

As the essay by Gary Cox on Gogol's technique of montage demonstrates, the visual arts could also invade the territory of fiction writing. One would naturally assume that a novelist would borrow the painter's techniques in order to achieve clear vision. Not so in the curious case of Gogol. His devices of peripheral perspective and visual block serve to obscure rather than clarify the depicted object, anticipating twentieth-century techniques of the absurd. Cox contrasts Gogol's shifting perspective with Tolstoy's "central recording consciousness," and indeed the difference between the two writers could not be more manifest. Gogol, instead of moving along what Roman Jakobson called a horizontal, metonymic sequence of narration, enriches his text with vertical, metaphoric elements, some of them borrowed from the visual arts. In doing this, he comes very close to the kind of synthetic art Tolstoy was to condemn in connection with the moderns. The curious fact is, of course, that Gogol preceded Tolstoy. His writing did not replace the temporal-sequential, cause-and-effect narrative which we associate with the "realism" of Tolstoy and Turgenev: it came before. This chronological incongruity demonstrates once more, what James West also argued in connection with classicism and romanticism, that "-isms" do not yield themselves to neat packaging. Moreover, Gogol's example, violating accepted canons of aesthetic periodization, suggests that two hundred years of modern Russian culture can be split into chronological subdivisions only with reservations. This becomes even clearer if one focuses on more than one kind of artistic medium.

Tolstoy, as we mentioned above, also allowed the visual to invade his narrative. If in that sense *War and Peace* anticipates the twenti-eth-century novel, the same can be said even more convincingly of *Crime and Punishment*. Dostoevsky's novel, as Roger Anderson shows in his essay, does not portray life by the passage of time but arranges Raskolnikov's universe as a space of visual stimuli interact-ing with incoherent psychological forces. In order to understand it the reader needs to store its symbolic details in memory as though they were component parts of a picture; in other words, it experi-ments with the kind of spatial forms of urban life which Joseph Frank considers hallmarks of modernism. Like a Picasso painting, it tends to open up several perspectives on the same object. But a great deal of its "modernist" technique derives from iconographic com-positional principles. Its inverse perspective, two-dimensional de-scriptive plane, and pictorial frame are functions of an ideological center radiating outward.

Vertical, metaphorical enrichment of the text is as characteristic for Chekhov as it is for Gogol and Dostoevsky. As Paul Debreczeny argues in his contribution, "The House with the Mansard" is constructed on a principle of multiple coding. The reader is lured into accepting the artist's story as an impressionist painting with its patches of color, two-dimensional picture plane, blurred lines, and nostalgic atmosphere, but the narrative's jarring denouement is accessible only to a post-impressionist sensitivity. Playing not only on different trends in the visual arts but also on literary traditions, Chekhov creates a complex work that requires the reader's full participation. In his attempt to distance himself from the conven-tional reader brought up on Chernyshevsky and Pisarev, Chekhov erects semiotic barriers in much the same way as Gogol did half a century before. His example suggests that a strong tendency toward synthesizing different artistic media, involving as it does multiple coding and semiotic difficulties, may well signal a rupture in the cultural process. In any case the degree of syncretism observable in art forms seems to be a measure of cultural tensions.

The artist Valentin Serov, whose vision forms the subject of Alison Hilton's paper, also combined techniques of different genres in order to go beyond realistic representation. His greatest achieve-ment, which Hilton sees in portrait painting, would hardly have been possible if in his varied career he had not been involved with other forms of art, such as stage design and book illustration. If at the beginning of the nineteenth century painterly technique lagged behind societal consciousness, this was no longer the case a hundred years later. And such a development was brought about at least in part by an interaction among different artistic media.

The search for new forms observable around the turn of the century, revolutionary as it may have been, cannot be understood simply as a symptom of social change. It was dictated to a great extent by the internal development of the media involved, and its societal connections were subtle and complex. After the October Revolution, however, we see once more an unmediated link between political events and art forms. Marina Tsvetaeva's 1921 cycle of poems entitled *Separation*, argues Antonina Gove in her essay, is a direct response to the harrowing realities of war and revolution. Its striking stylistic innovations—indirection, fragmentation, elision— were brought about because the poet, whose child had died of starvation, could not linger in the traditional poetic attitudes of grieving. The existential despair and psychological displacement which inform the poems of the cycle called for continuities to be broken and representations to be distorted; clarity would have diminished the power of communication. These poems, Gove shows, are close in style to paintings of the same period by Pavel Filonov and to etchings and sculptures by Kaethe Kollwitz. The works of all three of these artists, complementary in their respective media, would have been considered iconoclastic before the Great War, but under the historical circumstances their stylistic innovations were simply a matter of necessity. Gove's choice of a German artist for a parallel with two Russian ones rests on the assumption, explicit in West's essay and implicit in the other contributors' discussions, that Russian culture is not an isolated system but one in constant interaction with other cultures.

No radical modernist, Mikhail Bulgakov did not set out to break images either; yet his *Master and Margarita*, argues Juliette Stapanian-Apkarian, represents an aesthetics of flux whose purpose is to challenge codified truths. Pre-Revolutionary artists, like Nikolai Ge whose 1890 painting "What Is Truth" provides a foil for Bulgakov's novel, sought to confound visual codes in order to distance themselves from convention. Ge, for example, subverts the traditional iconographic use of light in his picture, illuminating Pilate and shading Christ. The modernists' achievement—a whole new repertory of forms—had become tradition by the time Bulgakov was working on his novel, and he simply made use of it. By his technique of ironic stylistic shifts, inversion of roles, and blurring of temporal and spatial distinctions, he created a form which, like that of *Crime and Punishment,* can be understood only if taken in as a synchronic whole. We see these two great novels standing on either side of the abyss of the Russian Revolution, one anticipating, the other looking back, but both confronting history with ideas derived from medieval Russian iconography. The pervasive influence of the icon has thus been demonstrated in three contributions to the volume.

Consisting as it does of articles on specific subjects by different authors, the present volume cannot pretend to offer a comprehensive survey of the interaction between the visual and verbal arts in Russian culture. What it attempts is to draw attention to instances of semiotic systems in interplay that may not be manifest either to the literary scholar or to the art historian in isolation. It will have achieved its purpose if it stimulates further work in an area that has been relatively neglected until now.

Notes

Unless otherwise stated, all English translations of Russian sources in this volume are by the individual chapter authors.

1. Allen Tate, *Reactionary Essays On Poetry and Ideas* (New York: Scribner's Sons, 1936), 55.

2. Iurii Lotman, "Theses On the Semiotic Study of Cultures (As Applied to Slavic Texts)," in *Structures of Texts and the Semiotics of Culture,* ed. Jan Van Der Eng and Mojmir Grygar (The Hague and Paris: Mouton & Co., 1973), 22.

3. Mario Praz, *Mnemosyne* (Princeton: Princeton University Press, 1970), 22.

4. Joseph Frank, "Spatial Form: An Answer to Critics," *Critical Inquiry* 4 (1977): 231–52.

5. Thomas Kuhn, *The Structure of Scientific Revolutions* (Chicago: University of Chicago Press, 1975), 4.

ONE

The Romantic Landscape in Early Nineteenth-Century Russian Art and Literature

James West

It is a commonplace of European cultural history that no major period style took exactly the same form in all of the countries to which it spread. This is particularly true of romanticism, and one would hardly expect otherwise, given that one of the most fundamental traits of the romantic movement was to emphasize the individual, and to discern in every nation a unique historical and cultural identity. In the account of the Russian art historian V. S. Turchin: "England, for example, became renowned for landscape painting and for Byron's emotional love of liberty; France—for its school of historians, men of letters and dramatists, and for paintings of historical subjects; Germany—for philosophy, music and the creative use of its folklore heritage. . . . In Russia, [romanticism] expressed itself most strongly in portrait painting, in poetry, and even in politics, if we take into account the romanticism of the Decembrist movement."[1] The assertion (by no means confined to Turchin) that romanticism in Russian art manifested itself primarily in the portrait, and that landscape painting achieved maturity only in the 1820s, is broadly valid but somewhat misleading, and is to some extent contradicted by Turchin himself when he recognizes that landscape was developing in its own way in the early years of the nineteenth century.[2] While it is true that portrait painting reached unusual heights in Russia in the romantic period, landscape was in its way just as significant a component of Russian art in the late eighteenth and early nineteenth centuries, as is being increasingly recognized.[3] Its role has probably been obscured by the fact that the romantic landscape developed in literature as much as in painting, and differentiated itself relatively slowly and subtly from the neoclassical landscape. In point of fact, Russian landscape art is particularly interesting in this period because it reflects in one genre all of the varieties of romanticism that expressed themselves in portrait painting, poetry, and politics; it makes visible some of the national peculiarities of the assimilation of romanticism in Russia, especially its relationship to neoclassicism; and, most importantly, it illustrates some aspects of the process by which styles are generally propagated in both art and literature, and in the interaction of these two media.

The discussion of romantic landscapes that follows is rooted in the uncontroversial assumption that the portrayal of the external environment in art has always been conditioned by both the prevailing technical conventions of representation, and the prevailing philosophical view of the physical world (taking the word "philosophical" in its broadest possible sense). The two are interdependent: the media and techniques of art evolve in any given place and time in relation to some particular vision of the world, and a change in this vision will inevitably affect the representational conventions by which it is communicated. However, techniques of depiction tend to change more slowly than visions of the world. This is partly because representational techniques are perpetuated by artists through the exercise of laboriously acquired and transmitted skills, and partly, paradoxically, because the habituation of cultural groups to a particular set of visual conventions makes them inclined to see their world through the prism of a particular visual tradition, and to be resistant to changes introduced by innovative artists. Such changes are, of course, implied invitations to visualize the world in some other way. Though the comparison is in some ways invidious, it is probably fair to say that in the period stretching roughly from the Renaissance to the Impressionists, the conventions of pictorial representation in European studio art underwent far less change than the views of philosophers as to what constitutes reality. In just the last two hundred of these five hundred years, aside from the most familiar and conventional Christian views, the natural environment—the subject of landscape painting—was variously regarded as grist for the microscope, as a decorative setting for the contemplation of moral values, as an anthropomorphic organism whose bosom heaves in sympathy with suffering humankind, as a forest of symbols or a pantheist temple, or as the formative environment of the social organism. In the same period a variety of styles may be discerned in the treatment of landscape, but technically they do not differ from each other as radically as the philosophies that underlie them.

In discussing evolutionary changes in pictorial art, we also have to distinguish between conventions of representation and conventions of composition—between changes in the acceptable ways of suggesting objects and their textures on a two-dimensional surface, and changes in what is regarded as a pleasing or meaningful organization of pictorial elements into an aesthetic whole. It is largely through compositional devices that "ideas" find expression in painting, and changes in the philosophical understanding of reality often lead to innovations in composition before any changes of representational technique occur, resulting in a perceptible tension between these two components of pictorial art. The point may be illustrated by comparing two painters who are included in every discussion of European romantic art—J. M. W. Turner and Caspar David Friedrich. Both contributed paintings of one of the favorite romantic landscapes, mountains shrouded in mist or haze; but where Friedrich's mist is overlaid on mountains depicted with careful observance of all the niceties of neoclassical landscape technique (a good example is Friedrich's best known landscape, *Der Wanderer über dem Nebelmeer* [Traveller above a sea of mist] of about 1818), in Turner's landscapes the mountain can become the mist in a swirl of line, color, and texture that is technically decades ahead of its time (his 1836 painting of the Val d'Aouste entitled *Snowstorm, Avalanche and Inundation* illustrates this point in a way that is relevant to the romantic mountain storm scenes discussed below) (figs. 1-1, 1-2). Turner's art is more "advanced" in the sense that, at its most successful, it makes both its own rules of composition and the techniques of pictorial representation that are appropriate to them, where Friedrich's art, even at its best, often communicates an awkward tension between a disturbing composition and the highly traditional representational idiom in which he chose to work.

These observations provide a framework in which to view the effect of different ways of understanding the world on the development of styles in painting. To what extent can developments in the literary landscape be viewed in the same light? Verbal art is a peculiar case: the medium in which a landscape may be verbally "painted" is the same medium in which the prevailing philosophy is expressed, so that new ways of thinking can be expected to have a more immediate effect on descriptions. The verbal medium, after all, has some properties that are not shared by visual art: both may have a suggestive, metaphorical, or symbolic relationship to the physical world, but the word is inherently abstract, and its relation-

1-1 Caspar David Friedrich. *Traveller above a Sea of Mist* [*Der Wanderer über dem Nebelmeer*], c. 1818. 74.8 × 98.4 cm. Courtesy of Hamburger Kunsthalle, Germany. Photo copyright by Elke Walford.

ship to visually perceived reality is less direct. In this situation, it is naive to simply compare the representation of landscape features and common thematic components in painting and poetry, on the assumption that what occurs in the one could as easily occur in the other, and, if it did, would occur for the same reasons. Simply by virtue of the differences between the word and the canvas as media, certain landscape features or styles of landscape depiction may in a

1-2 J. M. W. Turner. *Snowstorm, Avalanche and Inundation—A Scene in the Upper Part of the Val d'Aouste, Piedmont,* 1836. 36.25 × 48 in. (91.5 × 122.5 cm). Art Institute of Chicago. Photo copyright 1993 by the Art Institute of Chicago. All rights reserved.

given period become prevalent in one medium, for reasons that are technical rather than ideological or stylistic, and subsequently be transported with some difficulty to the other.

Verbal art, for example, has always been able to "depict" more easily than visual art a scene shrouded in mist or snow, or even in complete darkness. The ability of the word to suggest what cannot be seen became significant in the age of a philosophically inspired predilection for such scenes, which abound in sentimental and romantic literature, especially with the rise to prominence of the Gothic novel. Visual art in the same period was inevitably inspired by this predilection, but with different results, and technical accommodations had to be made when it illustrated or was directly inspired by literature. Gogol in the story "Noch' pered rozhdestvom" ("Christmas Eve," 1830), making the most of the paradoxical freedoms of the verbal picture, concludes his description of the snowstorm through which Chub and his companion ride with words that defy illustration, since their visual equivalent would be complete foreground opacity: "through the driving snow nothing could be seen." To take another preoccupation of the romantic era, it is

equally difficult to convey the idea of boundless distance by necessarily bounded pictorial means—again, the eye must be led on in
some way, as Lermontov does in one of his 1837 paintings of the
Caucasus, *Tower in Sioni.* The tower that is the ostensible subject of
this painting merely punctuates an immense mountain ravine that
leads the eye between more crags than it can quickly assimilate to a
shining white peak in the farthest distance.[4] In verbal art, on the
other hand, abstract words such as "boundless" or "immeasurable"
suggest these properties at least partly by their very abstraction,
because they do not denote a visible reality and must be mediated by
the imagination.

A similar phenomenon may manifest itself in the composition of
a landscape. The conventions of perspective place on painting a
constraint from which literary description is relatively free. In
European landscape and genre painting from the Renaissance to the
dawn of the modern period, the association of objects in pictorial
space is subject to relatively strict criteria of spatial plausibility,
whereas in verbal description objects can be combined in ways that
would appear unacceptably incongruous within the prevailing conventions of visual art. This circumstance is of the greatest importance in the case of Russia, for it separates the norms of pictorial
composition that prevailed in European landscape painting after
about the fifteenth century from the composition of the icon, in
which spatial relationships are not constrained in the same way by
considerations of optical verisimilitude. At the level at which the
composition of a painting is expressive in its own right, the icon is
composed of visual emblems, relating to religious figures or objects,
or to theological considerations, combined into a presentation that
is more than simply aesthetic and only secondarily mimetic. The
particular arrangement of these emblematic or symbolic components (including their coloration and relative scale) are construed in
their context as a narrative, a statement, or even an argument, and in
this sense the icon may be said to bridge the gap between the visual
and verbal modes of expression. It does this in ways whose sophistication is to be judged by the criteria of iconography alone. The
application to icons of the criteria by which we have come to judge
the quality of visual representation in Western European studio art
can lead to the erroneous impression that representational technique in the icon is "primitive." This point may seem insultingly
obvious, but the broadly "realist" conventions of pictorial representation are so much a part of our consciousness that even art histori-

ans are guilty from time to time of reading icons in the wrong visual language.[5] Any examination of the complex influences that shaped Europeanized Russian art in the century following Peter I's reign must include the icon, and it is important in this context not to view the legacy of the iconographic tradition—perceptible in Russian landscape art as well as in the portrait—as the survival of a less sophisticated representational technique into an age of more sophisticated European conventions.

There is by now a longstanding precedent for the use of the terms "iconography" and "iconographic" to describe the properties of almost any communicative system of visual signs or emblems. The arguments that follow require a distinction to be made between some characteristics of the tradition of Christian icon painting as such, and some more general techniques that were the accepted norms—from the viewpoint of both painter and public—in Europe of the seventeenth and eighteenth centuries. These terms will be used here in the more narrow and specific sense only when icons are discussed, and in the broader sense in other contexts. Discussion of both the relationship of romanticism to neoclassicism, and the romantic reinterpretation of the ancient Greco-Roman world, makes use of the term "classical" confusing. The word will be capitalized when it applies to the literature and art of the ancient world.

Besides confronting some fundamental distinctions between verbal and visual art, and between representation and composition, we must also face the problem of distinguishing between period styles. There is, unfortunately, no easy way to determine what is to be called "romantic" in a cultural milieu such as that of early nineteenth century Russia, in which many influences and ideologies mingled. Particularly in the world of painting, differentiating between classicism, sentimentalism, and romanticism is worse than difficult—it is an exercise that can obscure the real character of Russian art of this complex period.

The most widely accepted formulations of recent Russian art history still distinguish romanticism and classicism as separate styles or "tendencies," competing in this period and sometimes manifesting themselves simultaneously. D. V. Sarab'ianov, for example, writes, "[T]he general applicability of the term 'period style' has been destroyed once and for all: romanticism was unable to extend its dominion to every phenomenon of European artistic culture, classicism continued to develop alongside it, and by no means all forms of art could express the romantic concept—architecture, for example, could not."[6] I. Z. Serman complains that the exploration of Russian neoclassicism by Russian scholars has been obstructed by a tendency to define Classicism very narrowly as the more or less blind application of a set of abstract rules and the pursuit of "ideal" rational forms, and then to describe any phenomenon that does not fit this definition as the stirrings of stifled realism[7]—an objection that has its counterpart in the study of European neoclassicism:

> . . . [I]n the late eighteenth century, as before, antique stimuli could produce a wide range of stylistic and expressive results. The popular image of Neoclassic art too often tends to see it as inert in theme and drily imitative in style. . . . Around 1800, at the time of the most profound historical transformations of public and private experience, the classical world could be molded to meet demands as varied as French Revolutionary propaganda, romantic melancholy, and archeological erudition, and could be couched in visual vocabularies as unlike as the chaste outlines of Flaxman's classical illustrations, the icily voluptuous surfaces of Casanova's marble nudes, or the dense sculptural incrustations of Napoleon's imperial architecture.[8]

The phenomenon which Robert Rosenblum describes here—the existence of a variety of different expressions of the classical spirit, including a kind of "romantic classicism"—applies better to the Russian situation than the attempt to view the period styles as separate strands. Even so, Rosenblum's observation only partly characterizes the problem facing us in Russia, where even before the rise of romanticism an apparent commingling of styles is often to be seen within the work of a single artist. As a final complication, it should be remembered that "classicism" as a phenomenon in Russian literature was identified and named only by the generation to which the Russian romantics belonged,[9] and was defined by many of them negatively at the same time as elements of neoclassical style persisted in their work. The extent of this persistence is greatly underestimated. V. Iu. Troitsky understands clearly the nature of the creative process that is characteristic of Russian romanticism, the imaginative combination of material from various sources: "[A]s a rule, even in pre-romantic Russian prose we find a fanciful interweaving of real events, historical images, images drawn from folklore and events 'embellished' by the writer's imagination; this is equally characteristic of early romantic literature (V. Levshin, M.

Chulkov, M. Popov et al.) and of pre-romanticism." By way of illustration he cites a passage from I. Buinitsky's tale *Ermak, Conqueror of Siberia*, displaying many of the ingredients of late eighteenth-century Gothic scene-setting, which he offers however as an example of "the world of the Russian folk tale and folk epic": "[G]rey clouds, gathering on the horizon, told of a coming storm—and soon thereafter furious winds broke the fetters of the cold north, set the clouds scudding and pressed down on the torrid air. The gloom thickened, lightning flashed, rain poured. . . ."[10] The components of this scene occur in the folklore of many countries besides Russia, including, notably, the ancient Greco-Roman world—they are in fact commonplace in Classical mythology, and the diction here very strongly suggests the stereotypic storm scene of the Classical epic, which through the popularity of such late Latin authors as Statius[11] were transmitted into the imagination of medieval Europe and became eventually a part of the neoclassical tradition. Turchin writes: "The romantics had a propensity for the grandiose interpretation of natural phenomena. They perceived miniature natural catastrophes such as storms and floods with the epic sweep of the biblical flood."[12] This is true, but it is equally true of the Greek and Latin epic poets. What is described here is the process of mythologizing by which the ancients transformed the world they experienced into a language of iconic images. The romantics inherited this propensity from the Classical tradition, but gave it a new prominence for their own purposes: they, like the ancients, needed a tool to express a philosophy of life that focused on a relationship with the natural world that was close, but ambiguous rather than necessarily harmonious, as it is in the neoclassical and the sentimental canons (but not, contrary to a widespread misperception, in the ancient Classical world view). Their predilection for an "allegorical interpretation of the world" did not arise simply because they "did not find realistic means for the expression of such scales in their art."[13] Romanticism was coeval with very highly developed pictorial means for the realistic representation of virtually any subject. Paradoxically, the romantics' allegorical scenes of horror are often impressive in their pictorial realism; their allegorical subject matter and iconographic composition were a choice, not a failing.

There is in fact a need to reevaluate the debt of Russia's romantics not just to the neoclassical tradition, but to the Classical world itself, a need that goes far beyond the scope of this essay. For our more limited purposes, a detailed look at the way in which some writers and artists of the period made use of Classical material is very suggestive for the characterization of Russian romantic art, and illuminates the interaction between the verbal and the visual that played so large a role in it. Existing works on landscape painting in this period give most attention, with some justification, to the "landscape of moods" supposedly engendered by sentimentalism and inherited by the romantics.[14] This formulation is misleading in two ways. In the first place, it needs to be qualified by the reservation that sentimentalism and romanticism overlapped in Russia to such an extent that it makes sense to regard Russian sentimentalism and early romanticism as the same phenomenon. More importantly, in Europe, and in Russia even more, the label "landscape of moods" obscures two important and interconnected characteristics of the genre: one is the expression not just of emotional states but of ideas, particularly philosophical notions of the relationship of man to nature; the other is the iconographic as well as emotionally evocative role of the typical elements of the sentimental and romantic landscape.

For the romantics, in the respects that most concern us, the debt to the classics was more literary than visual. It is only in the case of sculpture and architecture that the debt of the romantics to Classical antiquity was primarily visual, and this legacy persisted throughout most of the nineteenth century, a period which saw striking departures from the Classical aesthetic in other media. In the case of landscape depiction, however, the debt was to a large extent verbal, partly because landscapes in Greek and Roman painting and mosaics were less frequent and have survived far less completely than sculptures or reliefs, partly also because in the visual art of the ancient world, landscape played a subordinate role to the portrayal of human, mythic, religious, and ritual subjects. On the other hand, Classical literature abounds with certain kinds of landscape description, and familiarity with these passages in the most popular Classical literary texts was not only a property of most artists in the period under discussion, but was something they could take for granted in a large part of their public. There could not fail to be some intrusion of Classical literary description into the perception of landscape. Broadly speaking, we are dealing with a more or less conscious revisualization of some aspects of the Classical landscape by artists of the romantic period, based on certain "verbal pictures" that were a pervasive part of their educated imaginations. Classical landscape descriptions reflect a particular view of reality (more accurately, a number of rather closely related views) and we would have to expect distortion of the original vision in the prism of late eighteenth and early nineteenth century philosophies, tastes, sensibilities, and aspirations. However, it is precisely these distortions that can tell us most about the spirit of that age, as it strove to recreate for its own purposes a world long past, and even where it overtly rejected certain elements of Classical art and the Classical aesthetic.

The sentimental and romantic filtering of the Classical landscape vision manifests itself both in the choice of subject and in the details of its treatment. In the received view, the rural idyll preponderates in the Classical tradition over wilder scenes, and the romantics, seeking a mirror in nature for disturbed inward states, reversed this order and turned to scenes of nature at her most elemental and inhospitable, which the ancients had described only as places to avoid—notoriously, the sea and the mountains. In point of fact, both sea and mountains play a considerable role in both Classical and neoclassical verbal landscape iconography, and the sentimentalists and romantics, painters as well as writers, did little more than interpret them with a new emphasis.

The sea and the mountains are only two of an array of romantic landscape stereotypes that are primarily of literary currency, including waterfalls, ravines, caves, and dark forests; any scene obscured by storm, fog, or night; ruins; and the presence of one or two travellers in any of the foregoing. An appreciation of the status of these stereotypes is important to the understanding of romantic art, European or Russian. It is of course true that poets and painters were prompted by romantic attitudes to seek out inspiring scenes of this kind, and to some extent we are looking simply at a literary influence on taste in landscapes. We should not, however, overlook the extent to which essentially verbal landscape imagery was imposed by the sentimentalists and romantics on visual experience and pictorial representation.[15] All of these landscape stereotypes were manipulated for expressive purposes in painting, poetry, and prose alike; another way of putting this is that the European romantic landscape, as it became more expressive of romantic thought, and hence more a symbolic vision, inevitably became more iconographic, in the sense that it drew on a limited number of emblematic components which were combined in ways that evoked not just moods, but ideas, even a whole philosophy of nature. As it developed in this way, the pictorial landscape of the European romantics just as inevitably drew closer to the verbal landscape, for the reasons suggested above.

In Russia, two factors made this phenomenon more pronounced. One is widely acknowledged, albeit by reference to a questionable distinction: the vitality of neoclassicism alongside romanticism in a situation in which both were cultural borrowings undergoing assimilation. The other is acknowledged little, and only with reference to portrait painting at that: a lingering predisposition of Russians, whether artists or writers or their public, to the mode of vision and expression that is characteristic of icons.[16] European romanticism already displayed a strong inclination towards emblematic imagery that makes it possible to describe at least some romantic painting as "iconographic." Such an inclination could not fail to strike a sympathetic chord with this predisposition of the Russians.

Among historians of Russian art, it is an accepted view that an interest in the portrayal of landscapes was made possible only by the process of gradual secularization of Russian life which began in the sixteenth century and achieved significant momentum only in the late seventeenth century.[17] Landscapes do appear in Russian icons, but even the most developed icon landscapes—those of Simon Ushakov, for example, painted in the late seventeenth century—are of a more restricted and conventional kind compared to what may be found in European religious art of the late Middle Ages and the Renaissance, and landscape art in the usual sense, even as a subordinate component of battle scenes or portraits, does not appear in Russia until the Europeanization of the Petrine era. What is important for our purposes is not the bare fact of this difference between Russian and European art, but its implications for landscape depiction in post-Petrine Russia. For Russian artists of the eighteenth century, the traditions and techniques of the iconographic landscape were temporally and culturally closer—present, in fact, beneath the surface of the essentially European training that Russian artists received in the St. Petersburg Academy of Art or in the studios of Europe. Much of what might be termed landscape art in Peter's time consisted in fact of battle scenes and prospects of cities, palaces, and monasteries, reflecting the historical circumstances of his reign.[18] Such pieces (often engravings) aimed at a relatively high level of accuracy as records, but were inherently celebratory in function, and it is hardly surprising that they often display a blend of neoclassical perspective drawing with echoes of the pictorial language of the icon. The appetite for battle scenes and historical records of Russian cities persisted into the late eighteenth century, becoming in fact institutionalized in the curriculum of the St. Petersburg Academy, which included a "battle class" (*batal'nyi klass*) that was distinct from the landscape, historical, and genre classes, and a perspective drawing class whose students were required "to have a perfect knowledge of the Architectural orders, and also the architecture of ships and the rules of Perspective; since the principal call is for representations of architecture. . . ."[19] The subsequent development of the romantic landscape in Russia can only be appreciated if its differentiation from this background is understood. Turchin points to the abandonment of a key element of neoclassical landscape as an identifying characteristic of the romantic landscape: "At the beginning of the nineteenth century perspective painting and landscape went separate ways. The separation of the landscape and perspective classes in the Academy of Art is itself an indication of this. Perspective drawing was associated with the notion of classicism. This is why the romantic movement began to develop in a way that bypassed this kind of principle of spatial organization."[20] However, in abandoning perspective as a principle of composition, the romantics had to find an alternative. The European romantic landscape painters based their composition at least in part on a language of pictorial imagery that is in a general sense iconographic, but does not directly derive from icon painting as such; in Russia, the tradition of the icon was sufficiently alive that what took place may well have been a reversion to principles of icon composition that were still a part of the visual lexicon of Russian culture.

This is of course not a suggestion that the entire compositional aesthetic of the icon was transferred intact to landscape painting in eighteenth and early nineteenth century Russia: this could not have been possible. The icon, after all, has its origins in an early form of portraiture,[21] and its compositional rules are a systematization of portraiture informed by theology as much as by aesthetics. However, as the icon developed it came to include a good deal more than the central figure—other figures, tokens of biblical reference, the attributes of martyrdom and sainthood, and in some cases of place, with elements of both landscape and architecture incorporated into the composition. It is in the treatment of these additional components that we find the peculiar convergence of verbal and visual expression that is only one part of the legacy of the icon tradition, but a part which came to be pervasive in Russian culture.

The interactions explored here between words and pictorial

images, native styles and borrowings, contemporary ideals and inherited traditions, may be illustrated in detail by examining the fortunes in Russia of one landscape stereotype, a typically emblematic scene, in its passage from its Classical origins to its eventual demise in a post-romantic climate.

Vasily Zhukovsky (1783–1852) proves an unusually good subject for our purposes; he was popular not only for his own poetry, but for his inspiring translations into Russian of English sentimental and romantic authors, including Thomas Gray, Walter Scott, Byron, Moore and Southey, and of such German writers as Bürger, Schiller, Goethe, La Motte Fouqué and Uhland. He also shared something of Schiller's and Goethe's ambivalent neoclassicism and of Goethe's attitude to Italy, and he translated from Virgil, Ovid, and Homer. In addition, Zhukovsky was a connoisseur of art, a moderately talented artist himself, and an admirer, friend, and benefactor of the quintessentially romantic German landscape painter Caspar David Friedrich.

Zhukovsky's 1819 translation of the story of Ceyx and Halcyon from Ovid's *Metamorphoses*[22] provides an example of a peculiarly Russian romanticization of a Classical seascape, and at the same time a warning against exaggerating the distinction between romanticism and either neoclassicism or the Classics: the scene is a storm at sea, dear to the romantics and laden with a heavy freight of romantic philosophical implications, but also an almost obligatory component of the Classical epic.

Obviously the authors of verse translations will be forced to take some liberties with the original text in order to meet the requirements of appropriate diction, metrical constraints, and rhyme in their own language, and these liberties give an interesting indication of the translator's reading of the original, and of whether the goal of faithfulness to the original was overridden by other concerns. The comparison of Zhukovsky's Russian version with Ovid's Latin reveals clearly the process by which a scene that was intended to be "horrifying," but within the canons of poetic taste to which Ovid subscribed, is made to echo both the poetical tastes and the philosophical concerns of the romantics, and at least one primarily Russian preoccupation. Halcyon's expression of foreboding (*Metamorphoses*, 11.427–28), "aequora me terrent et ponti tristis imago: / et laceras nuper tabulas in littore vidi" ("I fear the sea and the sullen countenance of the ocean deep: and lately I have seen broken ship-timbers on the shore"), is rendered with a rhetorical emphasis on the sea that is not Ovid's: *"no moria, / Moria strashus'; uzhasaet pechal'naia mrachnost' puchiny; / Volny—ia zrela vchera—korabel'ny oblomki nosili"* ("the sea, the sea I fear; the melancholy darkness of the watery abyss fills me with horror; the waves—I saw yesterday—bore the wreckage of ships"). Here Ovid's straightforward "aequora me terrent" ("the waters frighten me") becomes the repetitive *"moria, moria strashus' "* ("the sea, the sea I fear"), and where Ovid's Halcyon simply sees wreckage on the shore, Zhukovsky sees the wreckage borne by waves. "Ponti tristis imago" becomes *"pechal'naia mrachnost' puchiny,"* with the visually straightforward "imago" rendered by a noun denoting the gloom that was so dear to the romantics, and "pontus," already in Latin a poetic synonym for *mare* (sea), is transformed into another commonplace hyperbole of the romantic seascape, the "watery abyss." Ovid's one verb "me terrent" is translated twice, with the reflexive-passive *"strashus' "* and the active *"uzhasaet"* in the same line. Zhukovsky adds to Ovid's description of the storm and shipwreck a number of words that reflect typical elements of the romantic vision of human consternation before nature in turmoil. In particular, the root *uzhas* (terror, horror) appears twice more in Zhukovsky's version without any equivalent in the Latin—*"uzhasnuvshiisia kormshchik"* ("terror-struck helmsman") where Ovid's helmsman in 11.482 has no epithet, and the exclamation *"uzhasno!"* ("terrible!") is metrical ballast in Zhukovsky's rendering of 11.495.

Where the visual image is concerned, Ovid's clarity and specificity are throughout Zhukovsky's version diluted into a vague and sometimes abstract generality. Ovid observes that the sailors are unable to hear the captain's orders, and so are going about their business "sine lege" ("in confusion"); Zhukovsky presents this situation, significantly, as more general and more elemental—*"vse v besporiadke"* ("all is in disarray"). Exceptions occur when Zhukovsky has an opportunity to make the sea more active and independent. Ovid's heaving sea appears to reach the sky and sprinkle the clouds with its spray (11.497–98): "fluctibus erigitur caelumque aequare videtur / pontus et inductas aspergine tangere nubes" ("The sea rises up in waves and seems to reach up to the sky and touch the low clouds with its spray"). Zhukovsky's sea rises without the qualification of seeming, the low clouds become dark, and the neutral "caelumque aequare videtur" ("seems to reach up to the sky") is replaced by the strongly active *"do samogo neba rvetsia doprianut' "* ("strains to reach up to the very sky"). In addition, Zhukovsky's sea becomes the grammatical subject and howls, where Ovid's is merely qualified as angry: "[venti] fretaque indignantia miscent" ("[the winds] stir up the angry waves") becomes "*i more, vsdymaiasia, voet* ("and the sea howls as it rears up"). Zhukovsky introduces into his translation the romantic idea of human insignificance in the face of natural phenomena. He gratuitously qualifies the captain's call to reef the sails in 11.482–83 as "*naprasno,*" and Ovid's 11.494: "tanta mali moles tantoque potentior arte est" ("So great is the weight of disaster bearing down, so much stronger than the skill of the helmsman") becomes "*Vlastvuet buria, nichtozhnyi pred neiu iskusstvo i opyt*" ("The storm is master, and skill and experience are worthless before it"). The comparison has been reversed: the elements are "more powerful" for Ovid, whereas for Zhukovsky human powers are "insignificant in the face of the storm." In translating "Trachinia puppis" (11.502) Zhukovsky makes what for Ovid is no more than a "Trachinian ship" into an explicitly frail and helpless vessel— "*trakhinskoe legkoe sudno*" ("light Trachinian vessel") and "*igralishche buri*" ("a plaything of the storm").

If this analysis has seemed at all plausible, it is time to undermine it with a reminder that it is not always a simple matter to distinguish the style of the romantics from that of some Classical authors. Zhukovsky is certainly inflating his translation of Ovid, and with images that resemble the widely acknowledged commonplaces of romantic style, but much of the imagery he introduces, though not to be found in Ovid, could have been recalled from other Latin poets, and has been employed precisely for its Classical flavor. Horace, too, made much of the frailness of ships, and wrote at least one line that could have given Zhukovsky his "plaything of the storm" word for word.[23] Again, we are looking at a situation where the romantic artists did not always invent even the features of style that are most characteristic of romanticism, but often put to use something that was present already in the Classical or neoclassical heritage.

For the romantic reader, the most appealing of Ovid's images in the passage translated by Zhukovsky must surely have been that of the wave-tossed ship seeming by turns to gaze down from a mountaintop into the valley of hell, and up from the infernal maelstrom into the heavens (11.503–506):

> et nunc sublimis veluti de verticis montis
> despicere in valles imumque Acheronta videtur,

nunc, ubi demissam curvum circumstetit aequor,
suspicere inferno summum de gurgite caelum.

("And [the ship] seems at one moment to look down as if
from a mountaintop into a valley and the depths of Acheron,
and at another, sunk low with the water curling round it, to
gaze up from the infernal maelstrom to the highest heavens.")

Zhukovsky's version of these lines reinforces the romantic vision
of the profound and black abyss. The words "inferno . . . de gurgite"
("from the infernal maelstrom") provide a perfect opportunity to
use the matching Russian word "*puchina*," specifically defined as a
watery abyss, that occurs elsewhere in Zhukovsky's translation. He
chooses instead the more general, and more philosophically and
emotively laden, "*bezdna*" ("abyss") even though metrical constraints do not demand it. Ovid's "despicere in valles imumque
Acheronta videtur" ("seems to look down into a valley and the
depths of Acheron") becomes "*smotrit v glubokii dol, v glubokuiu mglu
Akherona*" ("looks into a deep valley, into the deep blackness of
Acheron"). "Seems" has been suppressed again, "deep" is used
twice on the strength of a single word in the original, and "dark" has
been added. It is also interesting that "sublimis . . . de vertice
montis" ("from a mountaintop") is expanded into "*s utesistoi gornoi
stremniny*" ("from a precipitous mountain cliff"), an image typical
of the Russian romantics' Caucasian mountainscapes, which themselves owe more than a little to the projection of Classical literary
commonplaces. Most interesting of all, however, is the treatment of
the glimpse of heaven from the ocean abyss. For Ovid, the ship sees
simply "summum caelum" ("the highest heavens"), but Zhukovsky's ship sees "*dalekoe nebo*" ("the distant heavens"). The
change from "highest" to "distant" is of enormous significance. For
the romantics, the image of a far-off ideal realm is most often the
distant horizon rather than the sky directly above. Both seascapes
and mountainscapes typically focused on the horizon, sometimes
allowing only a glimpse of it, so as to underscore its unattainability
or the impossibility of knowing the world beyond it. Not surprisingly, every element with which Zhukovsky enriched his translation
of this scene from Ovid can be found in his own "More" (The sea)
(1822),[24] where the sea is not only active, it is personified—it howls,
conceals a profound mystery in its "*neob"iatnoe lono*" ("unencom-

passable bosom") and is drawn up out of its land-bound prison by the *"dalekoe, svetloe nebo"* ("distant bright firmament").

The sea has a long history in literature as the most restless of the elements, beautiful but terrible, a symbol of the chaos from which the order of civilization arose, and a surface on which humans voyage at their peril. The shift in perception of the sea that is marked by romanticism was concisely described by W. H. Auden in his 1949 lectures at the University of Virginia. The Greek heroes sailed reluctantly on distant quests that were carried out on dry land, and to the Romans the "ship of state" was a metaphor only for the state in peril. Horace's third ode of Book 1 is essentially a prayer for the safety of the ship in which Virgil is sailing to Greece, and conveys well the Roman view of the time. To the early Christians (to judge from the Book of Revelation) the sea was not only the symbol of primordial chaos, but the element over which the Babylonian traders earned their wealth and spread their corruption far and wide, and with the vision of the new heaven and the new earth, the sea has vanished. But, as Auden writes: "The Christian conception of time as a divine creation, to be accepted, and not, as in Platonic and Stoic philosophy, ignored, made the journey or pilgrimage a natural symbol for the spiritual life."[25] By the romantic period, the image of the "ship of fools" gave way to that of the lone traveller over mountain and watery abyss, and the journey over both land and sea became a favorite metaphor for the individual's passage through life itself; indeed, the journey trope came to exert even more pressure than it had in Ovid's day for the inclusion of land and sea together in the same pictorial image. The sea for the romantics may also symbolize boundless space, in which context it is always associated with the sky, and the horizon, as we have seen, becomes an important element in a metaphorical composition. In Russia, the invocation of open space becomes particularly important, and the blurring of the distinction between sea and land develops a peculiar significance. No less an authority than Dmitry Likhachev, in an article entitled "Notes on the Essence of Russianness," has devoted several pages to the importance of expanses and space in the Russian character, and to their association with the idea of freedom, and he points to the role of this element in Russian poetry from the earliest times to the present.[26] K. Pigarev, in his book on the Russian national landscape of the mid-nineteenth century, discusses this trait of the Russian character in the context of Lermontov's poem "Rodina" (Mother-land) (1841), in which are celebrated the boundless expanses of steppe, forest and river.[27] He makes no comment, however, on the most interesting aspect of the poem: the floodplains of Russia's rivers, and by association the inland expanses of her steppes and forests too, are likened by Lermontov to "seas" in general.[28] Many instances can in fact be found in early nineteenth-century Russian poetry of the transference of the romantic sea metaphor to a dry-land equivalent, and of the association of the idea of freedom with either. In the opening description of M. N. Zagoskin's novel *Yury Miloslavsky* (1829) the snowy and wind-swept plain over which the two travellers are journeying is likened to "a stormy sea." The poet Baratynsky, when he wrote "Piroskaf" (The steamship; 1844), for example, had felt drawn since childhood to the "oblast' svobodnuiu vlazhnogo boga" ("free realm of the god of the waters"). Two well-known seascapes in Russian romantic poetry present voyages, and in both cases the sea evokes in the voyager's mind a vision of dry land. In his "Ten' druga" (The shade of a friend) of 1822, Ba-tyushkov's thoughts on leaving "Albion's foggy shore" are entirely consumed with "recollection of [his] native land beneath the sweet sky,"[29] and Baratynsky's thought at the conclusion of "The Steamship," despite the attraction the sea holds for his free spirit, is that "tomorrow I shall see the earthly paradise."[30]

By the 1840s, if not earlier, the sea image in Russian romantic poetry had obviously begun to seem strained to a new generation of writers, and it became increasingly the target of ridicule. The tension between sea and land is an explicit part of one of the most celebrated Russian parodies of the romantic view of nature. In the opening of Goncharov's *Oblomov's Dream* (initially published in 1849), the nest of the Oblomov family is described from the outset as uncompromisingly terrestrial. The mock-apologetic opening is followed by a humorously petulant critique of every feature of the stock-in-trade romantic seascape, and for good measure the mountainscape too, for the reason that they induce uncomfortable states of mind, but also (given that *Oblomov's Dream* is in its own way a critical definition of "Russianness") because they do not belong in the realm of that which is dear to the Russian heart and soul.[31] Goncharov's ironic use in this parodic landscape of the epithet "unencompassable" (*"neob"iatnyi"*), a favorite with Zhukovsky, recalls one of the pointedly fatuous aphorisms of the parody-poet Koz'ma Prutkov: "No one can encompass the unencompassable" (*"Nikto ne obnimet neob"iatnogo"*). The immensely popular Koz'ma Prutkov existed only to ridicule the romantics, and some of his blows are launched specifically at the romantic seascape of Baratynsky and others.[32]

A similar history can be traced for each of the essentially iconographic components of the romantic landscape in Russia, and a considerable degree of overlap will be found among them with respect to the mental states they symbolize, which perhaps partly accounts for a tendency to include several of them in one canvas or description. In Lermontov's *Ruins near the Village Karaagach in Kakhetiia*, interesting as an example not least because it is a painting by a poet, the ruins are scarcely noticeable in a scene crowded with foreground crags, distant snow-capped peaks, an expanse of water, a dense wood, a sky filled with swirling clouds, and travellers on foot, horseback and camel.[33] However, it is in poetry that the combinative tendency could manifest itself most strongly. Just as it is minor Russian landscape painters who provide the clearest examples of the iconographic assemblage of pictorial landscape elements, so it is minor romantic poets who have the least inhibition in this respect. V. I. Tumansky's "Elegy" (1824) is a contrived catalog of every inspiring or comforting feature of nature,[34] and A. I. Podolinsky's "Priroda" (Nature; 1829) presents nature as a sorceress who leads men through an assortment of natural delights to an abyss that will swallow up those who try to know her too closely.[35] The attempt to combine in one landscape elements that do not belong together in nature was perhaps the boldest experiment of romantic landscape artists of the stature of Caspar David Friedrich, but in poets of much more limited vision it seldom led to more than dreary and ill-assorted lists. In any event it came to be perceived as a violation of older norms of "truth to nature" that eventually reasserted themselves. In Russia it appears to have been more frequent than in Europe. Where elements of the Classical and romantic visions of nature are incongruously combined, this is obviously a result of simultaneous competition in the Russian imagination between the ideals of neoclassicism and romanticism. Even those who did not see the inherent contradictions clearly felt them none the less, and responded with an attempt to synthesize them. As Turchin observes, the 1830s witnessed a lively debate in Russian art circles on the rival merits of the "ideal" and the "natural" approaches to nature, and "until the mid-1830s landscape painters did not differentiate between these two notions, but rather strove towards a synthesis of them."[36] In contemporary verbal art, the competing styles and visions could be bonded, if not reconciled or synthesized, in certain kinds of nature description. The following passage of Zhukovsky, dating from 1821, is characteristic:

> What a pity it is to have to use words, letters, pen, and ink to describe the beautiful! To captivate and amaze us with its pictures, nature employs precipices, the green of trees and meadows, the sound of waterfalls and springs, the sky's shining light, storm and silence, while to express the impression that nature produces, the poor human is obliged to replace the manifold objects of nature with monotonous ink-scrawls, through which it is often far harder to arrive at an understanding than it is to arrive at a beautiful view through crags and abysses. . . . How can one depict the feeling of unexpectedness, magnificence, boundless distance, the host of mountains that has suddenly revealed itself to the gaze, like the blue waves of the sea turned to stone, the light of the sun and the sky with its myriad clouds throwing huge moving shadows on the mountains, fields, expanses of water, villages, and castles which delight and amaze the eye with their colorful variety! Every one of these may be named with a particular word; but the impression which all of them together produce on the soul, nothing can express; at this point the tongue of man is silent, and you feel that the charm of nature lies in its inexpressibility.[37]

The key phrases in this passage form a veritable mosaic of period formulae. Nature can "captivate and amaze us with its pictures" and instill "the feeling of unexpectedness [and] magnificence" in a perfectly eighteenth-century manner, but the catalog of its resources includes such typically romantic elements as "precipices," "crags and abysses," a "host of mountains," and "storm and silence," alongside more pastoral images. The sea image is brought to land with "the blue waves of the sea turned to stone," and three characteristically romantic preoccupations manifest themselves: the fascination with "boundless distance," the quest for "understanding" in the book of nature, and the barrier of "inexpressibility."

Zhukovsky's description of the Swiss scenery is a rather pedestrian synthesis of commonplaces, but where elements of quite disparate physical terrain are artificially brought together, what we are seeing may in some instances be an unconscious legacy of the aesthetics of the icon, in which the role of the artist is precisely to make figures, emblematic objects, buildings, and elements of landscape into a unified composition in which meaning arises in part from their juxtaposition. It is possible that the same legacy in the reader or viewer led for a short period to a certain degree of acceptance in Russia for works that present a dense mosaic of landscape clichés. However, the backlash, when it came, was nowhere stronger than in Russia.

Pushkin's sly assault in *Eugene Onegin* on the romantic ideal of nature in springtime is too well known to need comment, other than a reminder that he portrays very clearly the projection of landscapes of the imagination, culled from bad fiction, onto surrounding reality. His poem "My ruddy-faced critic . . ." ("Rumianyi kritik moi . . .") is a much more bitter attack on the distortion of his countrymen's vision of reality through the clichés of the European rural idyll. Three preeminent clichés (emphasized below) are scathingly contrasted with a more down-to-earth presentation of the components of the scene:

> Smotri, kakoi zdes' vid: izbushek riad ubogii,
> Za nimi chernozem, ravniny skat otlogii,
> Nad nimi serykh tuch gustaia polosa.
> Gde *nivy svetlye*? gde *temnye lesa*?
> Gde *rechka*? . . .

> (See what kind of a scene we have here: a wretched row of hovels, beyond them the black earth and the gentle slope of the plain, above them a thick stripe of grey clouds. Where are the *bright corn-fields*? Where are the *darkling woods*? And where the *brook*? . . .)

By far the most profound, dramatic, subtle, and instructive attack on the practice of superimposing visions of the imagination on the real world came from V. F. Odoevsky. In Odoevsky's story "The Painter" ("Zhivopisets," 1839) the narrator goes with a friend in the undertaking business to the apartment of a painter who has just died in poverty and madness. The painter was never able to finish a work, and had been reduced *in extremis* to accepting a commission to paint a sign for a local merchant. The sign was to portray groceries: sugar-loaves, jars of preserves, cheese, apples—"Let there be something of everything in it," the merchant had told him. He was unable to complete even this sign before fatal illness overtook him. What the narrator finds in his studio is a single canvas on which the artist had painted layer after layer of unfinished images of the most disparate kinds—a faun's head, a Gothic church, a madonna super-imposed on a "dress in the manner of Teniers," a Russian peasant beside an Egyptian pyramid, waterfalls, domestic implements, battle scenes, flowers, Greek profiles . . . the walls and windows covered with more of the same. The wretch had gone mad trying to make a picture from the mass of derivative and mainly foreign images with which his study of art had left him, while everyday Russian life took its matter-of-fact course around him. Odoevsky's story is an unsym-pathetic, even cruel indictment of the practice, all too prevalent in romantic Russia, of contriving pictures from ready-made images imported from other, more universally venerated cultures. Only the best artists could make such images come together into a coherent picture that had meaning for the world in which the Russian artist was obliged to live. Ironically, the commission which Odoevsky's artist was fatally unable to complete was for what can only be seen as an everyday icon—an annunciatory celebration of the grocer's offer-ings.[38]

With Odoevsky's indictment of the eclectic adoption of foreign images, a wheel has come full circle. Forty-two years earlier, Kar-amzin, a rather conservative sentimentalist heavily influenced by Classical sources, had issued a similar warning to poets that the "inflated description of horrifying scenes of nature" leads not to coherent works of art, but to the "strange creature" described by Horace at the opening of the *Ars Poetica*. The unfinished picture of Odoevsky's artist is sadly suggestive of Horace's celebrated aesthetic scarecrow, part woman, part fish, to which Karamzin referred. How-ever, the difference between the two is significant. Where Horace held up to ridicule lapses of poetic taste within his own cultural world, Odoevsky, like Pushkin in *Eugene Onegin* but with greater urgency, decries the tragic (as he saw it) contamination of a whole culture with the fragments of another culture's vision of both the real and the ideal worlds. Most interestingly for our purposes, Odoevsky's criterion of a healthier art is by implication the icon, with its uncontroversial celebratory relationship to the values of the world in which the artist lives.

It may seem less than probable that the iconographic tradition should blend with the highly developed artistic canons of European neoclassical painting, but we should bear in mind here two impor-tant considerations. In the first place, the European tradition did not neatly shed its roots in iconography as its emphases shifted in the

Renaissance to perspective, "illusionary" techniques of spatial and surface verisimilitude, and secular subjects. Some elements of the tradition of the icon clearly persisted in Europe, and indeed it is arguable that iconographic representation, in the sense defined above, is a fundamental impulse in the effort of human beings to capture the world around them in visual images, always present in some measure, whatever other representational conventions may predominate in a given age. Neoclassical painting was certainly never free of an element of visual iconography, and its relationship to the verbal iconography of Classical literature is manifest.

In the second place, the icon-painting tradition was not as inno-cent of perspective as has often been supposed. As early as 1907 Oskar Wulff introduced the term "reverse perspective" ("die um-gekehrte Perspektive") into the discussion of early Christian art, and Florenskii used its Russian equivalent (*"obratnaia perspektiva"*) in 1967 in a seminal article in which he demonstrated that Russian icons of the fourteenth to the sixteenth centuries made systematic use of their own rules of perspective.[39] By the seventeenth century some of the more widely disseminated images of mainstream Euro-pean painting had begun to be absorbed into the visual vocabulary of the Russian icon. A striking example of this is Simon Ushakov's icon of the *Old Testament Trinity*, painted in 1671, which includes an unusually prominent architectural background (occupying almost a quarter of the pictorial surface) that was copied from an engraving of Paolo Veronese's *Feast at the House of Simon the Pharisee*.[40] Ushakov's unexpected borrowing shows clearly that the highly stylized and formalized setting of the figures in the Russian icon had ceased to be—if indeed it had ever been—a visual world apart, having nothing in common with the highly developed conventions of perspective composition and pictorial verisimilitude characteristic of secular painting in Europe.

The situation we are examining here is in fact more complicated than it may seem at first sight. Painting, it must be repeated, is in several respects more technically conservative than verbal art, and for this reason it happens comparatively often that an ideologically new generation of artists finds itself in possession of a technique, a set of learned and practiced representational devices, developed slowly by earlier generations in response to their own theoretical and philosophical urgings. This situation does not always produce an immediate, obvious, and controversial change of technique.

More often than is realized, old techniques are revalidated, acquiring more prominence in the painting of the new generation as a result perhaps of their heightened expressivity, but remaining in a technical sense the same visual device.[41] We have seen how the figures in what was a typical and widely taught form of eighteenth century landscape, reduced to compositional insignificance for formal reasons, came to be for the romantics "dwarfed by the immensity of the grandiose natural scenery," and worked into the context of a new type of iconographic composition. Equally, the reverse may happen—images that have become part of the prevailing language of art in a given period, that are read conventionally and are not especially prominent in the context of their day, may come to stand out obtrusively when the fashions, tastes, and ideology that gave rise to them are no longer in force. What is true for verbal and visual imagery holds equally for the element of spatial composition. Turchin writes, "[I]n the heyday of romantic landscape painting a new tendency arises: the presentation of a complete pictorial view, and not just the depiction of a particular motif. Two paths led to this point. One was the construction of a whole landscape space of the 'interior' type, small, enclosed and intimately peopled, the other the use of the rules of perspective to create ordered, but not fragmented space."[42] What is described here is, in effect, the two forms of the eventual move away from iconographic space, and away from composition based on the organization of iconic elements, which by the 1810s had ceased to satisfy at least the more sophisticated appreciators of Russian art.

Understanding of the nature of Russian art of this period—an undeniably complex phase in Russia's cultural history—has always been to some extent obscured by the practice of separating out, in identification and commentary, the fundamental "isms" of intellectual history of the eighteenth and nineteenth centuries, and then seeking reasons why a given artist or writer may appear to belong to more than one of them, simultaneously and without visible discomfort. This practice is flawed on several counts. In the first place, the "isms" in question are less distinct than the mind of the scholar would have them be; in the second place, the complex of beliefs of an individual writer or artist seldom fits tidily into a category designed, quite legitimately, to clarify the broader movements of intellectual history; and third, there seems to have been a reluctance to acknowledge that, particularly in Russia from the 1790s to the 1830s, when trends that were more or less successive in Europe competed for a following, we are very often dealing with hybrid forms. The word "hybrid" should not be taken here in a pejorative sense: the successful hybrids were creative and vigorous, and organic in the sense that they were born of the talent of the Russian mind for digesting foreign intellectual and aesthetic canons as it borrows them, adopting only what it can successfully adapt for application to Russian realities. Odoevsky, at the end of the romantic period, dwelt with slightly morbid fascination on the hybrids that failed, but the Russian scholar Fedorov-Davydov in our own time offers a partial acknowledgment that only a blend of styles and inspiration could enable a Russian artist to paint convincingly in this period: "In art it was possible to have a close interaction between the heroicizing normativeness [of classicism] and the poeticizing sensibility [of sentimentalism] as a reflection of two sides of what is essentially a single problem. Such a combination may be discerned in some degree in the best artists of the period."[43] This is, however, an oversimplification with obvious debts to older formulations, and it is only in the 1980s that we encounter a willingness to abandon the tradition of schematic periodization and see romanticism as "polymorphic," characterized by "stylistic diversity, the influence of many contemporary cultures and its own past, and uncertainty as to when it began and ended," and by the quest for diversity itself, yet avoiding gratuitous eclecticism, and indeed capable at its best of synthesizing the diverse influences on which it drew.[44]

To a much greater extent than has been acknowledged, landscape presented the Russian artist, whether visual or verbal, with the challenge to make romantic art, an essentially European form, take root in Russia. Those who succeeded did so by neutralizing the rival promptings of neoclassicism, sentimentalism, and romanticism, and by invoking an older iconographic heritage which had the power to synthesize the inherent incongruities of romantic imagery, even when it was patently of foreign origin, and endow it with a Russian meaning. Those who failed were those who could neither find the synthesis nor escape the incongruities. And when finally fashions of visualization changed, the overtly romantic landscape, verbal as well as visual, ceased to be an acceptable mirror of Russian realities. However, the residual iconic vision that helped to make the romantic landscape briefly acceptable reappears in the later part of the nineteenth century, and in no period has it ever entirely lost its force in Russian art.

Notes

1. V. S. Turchin, *Epokha romantizma v Rossii* [The age of romanticism in Russia] (Moscow: Iskusstvo, 1981), 17. Though several of the arguments that follow are made by way of a disagreement with Turchin on specific points, my admiration remains undimmed for this remarkably detailed and intelligent analysis of early nineteenth century Russian art in its broader cultural context.

2. Ibid., 433. "Its development, it is important to note, was not as elemental and sudden as that of portrait-painting. It was prepared by prior evolution of the landscape genre—primarily in the form of graphic art and painting."

3. For example, V. Iu. Troitskii, "Romanticheskii peizazh v russkoi proze i zhivopisi 20–30-kh godov XIX veka" [The romantic landscape in Russian prose and painting in the 1820s and 1830s] in *Russkaia literatura i izobrazitel'noe iskusstvo XVIII–nachala XX veka* [Russian literature and pictorial art from the eighteenth to the early twentieth century] (Leningrad: Nauka, 1988), 96–118.

4. E. A. Kovalevskaia, *Lermontov: kartiny, akvareli, risunki* [Lermontov: paintings, watercolors and sketches] (Moscow: Izobrazitel'noe iskusstvo, 1980), 185.

5. To take but one instance, icons that portray patrons and founders presenting a church to the Deity are sometimes captioned on the assumption that what the saint is holding out is a model of the building. This is a gratuitously modern reading of the representational scale of the building, as well as a projection onto the Middle Ages of the architectural practices of more recent times. See for example Irmgard Hutter, *The Herbert History of Art and Architecture: Early Christian and Byzantine* (London: Herbert Press, 1988), 170, caption to illustration 172. One of the standard postwar Soviet histories of Russian art makes a similar error in captioning an icon of Prince Iaroslav Vsevolodovich.

6. D. V. Sarab'ianov, "Natsional'noe svoeobrazie russkogo romantizma i rannego realizma" ["The uniquely national character of Russian romanticism and early realism"], in *Russkaia zhivopis' XIX veka sredi evropeiskikh shkol. Opyt sravnitel'nogo issledovaniia* [Nineteenth-century Russian painting in the context of the European schools. A comparative study] (Moscow: Sovetskii khudozhnik, 1980), 56.

7. I. Z. Serman, *Russkii klassitsizm* [Russian classicism] (Leningrad: Nauka, 1973), 8–11.

8. Robert Rosenblum, *Transformations in Late Eighteenth Century Art* (Princeton: Princeton University Press, 1974), 9–10.

9. Serman, *Russkii klassitsizm*, 7.

10. I. Buinitsky. *Ermak, zavoevatel' Sibiri* [Ermak, conqueror of Siberia] (1805); quoted in Troitsky, "Romanticheskii peizazh," 99.

11. Publius Papinius Statius, who wrote in the second half of the first century A.D., enjoyed immense popularity in medieval and Renaissance Europe. His *Thebaid* is noteworthy for its abundance of descriptions, and for the

excesses of its descriptive language. The mountain storm scene of lines 346–69 of book 1, for example, is as wildly "romantic" as anything written in the age of romanticism, and indeed Buinitsky's description resembles it strikingly in both detail and tone. Statius in his turn was indebted to his contemporary Valerius Flaccus, whose *Argonautica* contains a storm at sea (book 1, lines 608–54) employing a stock vocabulary for such scenes that is shared with both Virgil and Ovid, and which through translation provided many of the characteristic epithets of romantic storm scenes.

12. Turchin, *Epokha romantizma*, 420.

13. Ibid., 421.

14. See Troitsky, "Romanticheskii peizazh," 96.

15. This phenomenon is described in detail by E. H. Gombrich in his *Art and Illusion* (London: Pantheon Books, 1960), and illustrated with an 1836 English lithograph of Chartres Cathedral in which the west facade has been disproportionately heightened and its Romanesque rounded windows pointed as if they were Gothic, to match the romantic vision of medieval cathedral architecture. I have seen an engraving of a slightly later date of Mont St. Michel in which the same transformation has been performed.

16. The evidence for the persistence of icon-painting conventions in post-Petrine Russian art is plentiful and varied, and is increasingly coming to light as interest grows in the collections of provincial Russian art museums, which often contain works by eighteenth and early nineteenth century artists who were serfs, despite their considerable skills. Such painters had almost always received their initial training in icon-painting, and had then been "noticed" by their owners and sent for further training in European-style studio art, usually within Russia. A striking example of the phenomenon is in the portraits of Grigorii Ostrovsky, who worked for the Cherevin family in Neronovo, Tula Province, in the closing years of the eighteenth century. In a number of Ostrovsky's portraits, the same noticeably stylized, elongated face is used for different subjects, both male and female, young and elderly, with the result that the sitters are differentiated almost entirely by dress and coiffure (figs. 1-4, 1-5). In the light of recent scholarship, painters of this kind now appear to have been a good deal more numerous than was generally acknowledged over the ensuing hundred and fifty years. They painted portraits of their owners and their owners' families and friends, and also genre scenes, and landscapes that can only be described as "portraits" of the landed properties of their owners. For further examples, see: S.V. Iamshchikov, *Russkii portret XVIII-XIX vekov v museiakh RSFSR* [The Russian portrait of the 18th–20th centuries in the museums of the RSFSR] (Moscow: Izobrazitel'noe iskusstvo, 1976); Ia.V. Bruk, *U istokov russkogo zhanra. XVIII vek* [The origins of Russian genre painting. The eighteenth century] (Moscow: Iskusstvo, 1990); S.F. Nechaeva, *Tul'skii oblastnoi khudozhestvennyi muzei* [The Tula Provincial Art Museum] (Leningrad: Khudozhnik RSFSR, 1983); M. D. Kurmacheva, *Krepostnaia intelligentsia v Rossii* [The serf intelligentsia in Russia] (Moscow: "Nauka," 1983);

K.V. Mikhailova et al., *Iz istorii realizma v russkoi zhivopisi* [Aspects of the history of realism in Russian painting] (Moscow: Izobrazitel'noe iskusstvo, 1982); N. M. Moleva and E. M. Beliutin, *Pedagogicheskaia sistema Akademii khudozhestv XVIII veka* [The pedagogical system of the Academy of Arts in the eighteenth century] (Moscow: Iskusstvo, 1956); S. B. Mordvinova, "Khudozhestvennye predposylki vozniknoveniia i razvitiia portreta" [Artistic factors governing the origin and development of the portrait], in T. V. Alekseeva, ed., *Ot srednevekov'ia k novomu vremeni* [From the Middle Ages to the present] (Moscow: Nauka, 1984); A. B. Sterligov, *Peizazh v russkoi zhivopisi* [Landscape in Russian painting] (Moscow: Goznak, 1972).

17. K. Pigarev, *Russkaia literatura i izobrazitel'noe iskusstvo. XVIII–pervaia chast' XIX v.* [Russian literature and pictorial art. Eighteenth and early nineteenth centuries] (Moscow: Nauka, 1966), 221.

18. Ibid., 221ff.

19. I. Urvanov, cited in N. Moleva and E. Beliutin, *Pedagogicheskaia sistema Akademii khudozhestv XVIII veka* [The pedagogical system of the Academy of Arts in the eighteenth century] (Moscow: Iskusstvo, 1956), 283.

20. Turchin, *Epokha romantizma*, 464.

21. V. D. Likhachcva and D. S. Likhachev, *Khudozhestvennoe nasledie drevnei Rusi i sovremennost'* [The artistic heritage of ancient Rus and the contemporary world] (Leningrad: Nauka, 1971), 22ff.

22. V. A. Zhukovsky, "Tseiks i Gal'tsiona. Otryvok iz ovidievykh prevrashchenii" [Ceyx and Halcyon. A fragment of Ovid's *Metamorphoses*], in *Sochineniia* [Works] (Moscow: Gos. izd vo khudozh. lit., 1954), 238–43.

23. Horace, *Odes* 1.14: "tu, nisi ventis / debes ludibrium, cave" ("Take care, lest you become the plaything of the wind").

24. V. A. Zhukovsky, "More. Elegiia" [The sea. An elegy], in *Sochineniia* [Works] (Moscow: Gos. izd-vo khudozh. lit., 1954), 94.

25. W. H. Auden, *The Enchafèd Flood, or the Romantic Iconography of the Sea* (New York: Random House, 1950), 9.

26. Dmitry Likhachev, "Notes on the Essence of Russianness," in *Soviet Literature*, 2 (1981): 129–32.

27. K. V. Pigarev, *Russkaia literatura i izobrazitel'noe iskusstvo* [Russian literature and pictorial art] (Moscow: Nauka, 1972), 27.

28. M. Iu. Lermontov, *Sobranie Sochinenii* [Collected works] (Moscow: Khudozhestvennaia literatura, 1964), 1:102.

29. K. N. Batyushkov, *Polnoe sobranie stikhotvorenii* [Complete works] (Moscow-Leningrad: Sovetskii pisatel', 1964), 170–71.

30. E. A. Baratynsky, *Polnoe sobranie stikhotvorenii* [Complete works] (Leningrad: Sovetskii pisatel', 1957), 200.

31. I. A. Goncharov, *Sobranie sochinenii* [Collected works] (Moscow: Gos. izd-vo khudozh. lit., 1959), 4:84.

32. Koz'ma Petrovich Prutkov is perhaps the only important poet in world literature who never existed. Invented by A. K. Tolstoy and the brothers A. M.

and V. M. Zhemchuzhnikov, he masqueraded as an epigone of romanticism in the pages of *The Contemporary* from 1851 until his creators unthought him in 1863. His fatuous aphorisms remain to this day a part of the proverbial speech of educated Russians.

33. Reproduced in Kovalevskaia, *Lermontov: kartiny akvareli, risunki*, 199.

34. *Poety 1820–1830–kh godov* [Poets of the 1820s and 1830s] (Leningrad: Sovetskii pisatel', 1972), 1:276.

35. *Poety 1820–1830–kh godov* 2:293.

36. Turchin, *Epokha romantizma*, 455.

37. V. A. Zhukovsky, "Puteshestvie po Saksonskoi Shveitsarii" [A journey through Saxon Switzerland] (letter from Karlsbad to the Grand Princess Aleksandra Fedorovna, June 17, 1821) in *Polnoe sobranie sochinenii* [Complete works] (St. Petersburg: Izd-vo A.F. Marksa, 1902), 12:4.

38. There is nothing strange in regarding a shop sign as a form of icon. Indeed, in Russia the tradition of commercial sign-painting has been traced from roots in icon-painting to the avant-garde of the early twentieth century, on whose work it exerted a striking influence. See Alla Povelikhina, *Russkaia zhivopisnaia vyveska i khudozhniki avangarda* [Russian painted commercial signs and the artists of the avant-garde] (Leningrad: Avrora, 1991).

39. See V. D. Likhacheva and D. S. Likhachev, *Khudozhestvennoe nasledie*, 24–25.

40. See E. S. Smirnova, *Moskovskaia ikona XIV-XVII vekov* [Moscow icons from the fourteenth to the seventeenth century] (Leningrad: Avrora, 1988), 308.

41. A striking example of this phenomenon from a later period is the expressive style which Mikhail Vrubel' derived, at least in part, from a pedagogical device of one of his teachers at the St. Petersburg Academy, Pavel Petrovich Chistiakov. Chistiakov had his students reduce figures to a series of flat planes of more or less geometrical shape. What for his teacher was an interim stage in the production of a "classical" figure drawing was perceived by Vrubel' as expressive in its own right.

42. Turchin, *Epokha romantizma*, 458–59.

43. A. A. Fedorov-Davydov, *Russkii peizazh XVIII–nachala XIX veka* [Russian landscape from the eighteenth to the early nineteenth century] (Moscow: Sovetskii khudozhnik, 1986), 19. The quotation is from an essay, reprinted in this volume, that was first published in 1974.

44. Turchin, *Epokha romantizma*, 17–18.

The Country House as Setting and Symbol in Nineteenth-Century Literature and Art

Priscilla Reynolds Roosevelt

Nineteenth-century portraits of the Russian estate both mirror the realities of life in the Russian provinces and offer a commentary on changing social and cultural patterns. Artists used the estate as a setting, a theater for action, while through its associative significance it became a dramatis persona, an alter ego for its owner. This essay seeks to trace and compare patterns of visual and verbal representation of the estate in the nineteenth century. Historians of Russian culture find literary evidence familiar terrain; Russian art is less often cited as documentation, despite its incontestable value to cultural history. As the art historian Jules Prown has argued, "Style is inescapably culturally expressive, [and] the formal data embodied in objects are therefore of value as cultural evidence."[1] The formal evidence presented in visual representations of the Russian estate, and the point of view a given artistic style suggests, add much to the literary picture of social reality. They also suggest a dynamically evolving relationship between these two types of seeing in nineteenth-century Russia.

The estate as a physical entity presented many opportunities for symbolic use. Its size, style, decoration, state of maintenance, and relationship to its surroundings instantly conveyed social, economic, and cultural information about the Russian noble who owned or inhabited it. Artists knew this world well. Most members of the nineteenth-century intelligentsia had family ties to a "gentry nest" (to use Turgenev's well-known phrase) or were frequent visitors to estates. They cherished this association chiefly for two reasons. As is evident from the lyrics of Alexander Pushkin and his generation, for the artist of the romantic period the country estate was an evocative and inspirational setting, treasured for its serenity and quiet pleasures.[2] Equal in importance was the psychological latitude the country afforded in contrast to the city. An author could fashion a more idiosyncratic milieu using a provincial setting, much as landowners sometimes used their estates to create or reflect some sort of personal identity (either by mimicking regimented and stratified "official Russia," or by ignoring it).[3]

The complex relationship between the Russian countryside and its owners, the nobility, formed the historical context for these portraits. As numerous studies have shown, throughout the imperial period the Russian nobility was an amorphous and legally evolving estate.[4] Like other European nobilities it was divided into rich and poor, to such an extent that a foreign observer of the mid-nineteenth century thought it would be an "endless task" to describe the Russian nobility's "various gradations of wealth and civilization."[5] Nobility tended to be associated with a "noble" way of life, and "true" nobility, manifested in a certain level of culture, dress, and deportment, was clearly impossible without a certain income.[6]

Thus from the eighteenth to the mid-nineteenth centuries the nobility formed three discrete groups: the poor, with less than one hundred male "souls"; the moderately to very well-off (whose upper reaches comprised the provincial elite), with between one hundred and one thousand souls; and the aristocracy, absentee owners of one or many thousands of serfs. Partially due to Peter III's decree of 1762, which freed the nobility from obligatory service to the state, a great age of suburban and country estate building began in the 1760s and continued apace up to the 1830s. Maintaining a magnificent country residence came to be considered a proper reflection of city-based power and prestige, and was used to further both. During this period also, increasing numbers of less well-to-do gentry retired early from service to take up permanent residence on their estates. One young noble of the Decembrist generation described his peers of "little means" retiring to their "secluded little rural houses" to become enlightened agriculturalists.[7]

In the reign of Nicholas I (1825–55), a property qualification of one hundred serfs or three thousand desiatins of land became mandatory for full participation in the provincial assemblies of the nobility, an indication of the continued significance of wealth for the claim to nobility. This wealth was measured exclusively in terms of the countryside (ownership of land and peasant souls, privileges restricted to the nobility), but fortunes were made and maintained elsewhere, either through high rank in state service, or as the direct result of Imperial favor, hence usually in St. Petersburg. In consequence, like the elite of *ancien régime* France, the Russian aristocracy had a highly ambivalent attitude towards the countryside. The upper stratum of the nobility continued to use suburban or country estates only as summer residences or places for occasional entertaining. Since the countryside did not provide a political base for the ambitious noble as it did in England, nor the cultural or social advantages of the city, protracted country living had overtones of exile for the elite. From this cosmopolitan viewpoint those nobles who never left the countryside were either poverty-stricken or hopeless eccentrics, and in any case, boorish.

The economic power of the nobility was already on the decline in the first half of the nineteenth century. Many family fortunes dwindled or evaporated due to the lack of a tradition of entail, patterns of conspicuous consumption in pursuit of prestige, and a disdain for commerce which made few nobles seriously interested in estate improvements to increase agricultural output.

Literary and artistic evidence confirms the social divisions and insecurity of the nobility in the pre-Emancipation period. Social ambition led many wealthy estate owners to use their estates as suburban theaters in which to parade their claims to status in Moscow, St. Petersburg, or the provincial capitals. For the same reasons, early nineteenth-century visual and verbal portraits of the manor house presented it primarily as a symbol of social position. These images also converged in tending to suffuse country living with a roseate hue. Artists and authors did so, however, in different ways and for different ends. Writers from the time of Pushkin onwards tended to adhere to the romantic fiction that simple country life was productive of natural virtue. Painters, on the other hand, while following the stylistic code of romanticism in their treatment of nature and peasants, were most concerned with stressing the status of their patrons by exaggerating the beauty and magnificence of their estates.

The cultural historian Iurii Lotman has suggested that in the early nineteenth century a "theatricalization of painting" is observable, in the similarity of many pictures to the then-popular theatrical form, the *tableau vivant*, a static presentation in which the audience is surprised by movement.[8] It is certainly the case that grandiose neoclassical mansions and their grounds were portrayed in static and iconographic fashion. In an 1810 watercolor of the estate Pekhra–

Yakovlevskoe, for instance, a typical manor house, fronted with pilasters, crowned with a belvedere, and flanked by a large wing with a columned portico and imposing neoclassical church, dominates the crest of a slope above a large lake.[9] A bridge, part of the approach to the house, spans the lake in the foreground; on either side of it we see gondolas with pleasure boaters, and on the near bank, his back to us, a man sits fishing. Scudding clouds, birds, and naturalistic vegetation soften the architectural lines of estate buildings and bridge. A lithograph of the estate of Akhtyrka presents virtually the same iconography. We are again viewing the house from the park facade across water. A semicircular, columned two-story portico with curving stairways leading to the park is at the center of the long house facade bounded by symmetrical wings. A church belvedere and bell tower are visible behind the house, while below it is a lake with an imposing landing flanked with two pylons. A gondola is approaching the landing; in the foreground a group of noble strollers heads towards the bridge leading to the estate. In this instance the plantings surrounding the house are presented as sculptural forms complementing the neoclassical house—a measure of the continued influence of eighteenth-century house portraiture—rather than in the more customary softened romantic style of the period.

Regardless of style, in such paintings the house, invariably close to or reflected in a lake or stream, was the central element, with park pavilions, pleasure boats, and people engaged in a variety of country activities as subsidiary elements.[10] Similar glimpses of estates in this period are provided by the albums of estate and park views which some owners commissioned, or which were created for an owner over time by visitors and family members.[11] These views present the estate as a series of stage sets. In all such studies the emphasis was on grandeur and entertainment, the chief features of the country pleasure grounds of the grandee.

Paintings of the more modest manor houses of the provincial nobility were less frequent. One delightfully primitive watercolor painted at the end of the 1820s (possibly by a family member) shows an unassuming one-story house with an attached brick wing and a front porch.[12] A girl with a doll is sitting on a couch on the porch; a boy on a pony, a girl with a bouquet of flowers, and a man with a walking stick occupy the drive in front of the house. Another shows Raikovo, a manor belonging to the Bakunin family.[13] Its one-storied, red-roofed house is perched on a hillside above a winding stream, the small estate garden separated from the neighboring peasant village by a low wall. In the foreground a herd of cattle tended by a reclining herdsman with a dog is drinking from the stream. Pushkin's small family estate Mikhailovskoe appears in a lithograph of 1837, similarly dominating a pastoral scene which includes peasants.[14] Here the presentation is reversed, the river and flocks in the background, while in the small courtyard a carriage approaches the house. Too insignificant to be painted, and less frequent in literature than in life were the small, square wooden houses of the impoverished nobility, with their unplastered walls and thatched roofs, barely differing in size from peasant huts.

If early nineteenth-century art, in depicting the estate, imitated the *tableau vivant*, literature likewise borrowed from theater in presenting the estate as a "set." Against this backdrop, however, literature utilized other popular theatrical genres: romantic comedy and tragedy, satire, and by midcentury, realism, in depicting life on the estate. To turn from these images to those of the estate in nineteenth-century fiction is to move from a static world to a dynamic and diversified one, in which authors used contrasting images of estates to emphasize social and economic differences between characters important to the theme and action of a story.

In keeping with the conventions of romantic fiction, the size of the estate was often inversely proportional to the virtue of its inhabitants. In Pushkin's *Eugene Onegin* the relatively modest Larin estate produces the faultlessly natural Tatyana, whereas Onegin's uncle's mansion with its huge overgrown garden is an appropriate repository for Eugene's sophisticated emptiness. In the noble rob- ber tale *Dubrovsky* Pushkin presents his readers with a wide panoply of levels of country existence. The plot begins with a feud between the rich, sybaritic, and nouveau general Troekurov and the retired, "poor but honest" lieutenant Dubrovsky of ancient lineage, whose son becomes an avenging hero. A third social level is represented by old Prince Vereisky, an absentee aristocrat and owner of three thousand souls. The social split in the countryside between rich and poor noble likewise appears in *Tales of Belkin*. The narrator of "The Shot," an impoverished noble living in the country, reflects on his position vis-à-vis those aristocrats who only occasionally visit their estates. "The arrival of a wealthy neighbor," the narrator tells us, "marks an epoch in the lives of country-dwellers. Landowners and their house servants talk about it for two months beforehand and three years afterwards."[15]

Pushkin's prose set the tone for many of the century's authors. Himself nobly born, though to a family of modest wealth, Pushkin tended democratically to favor the poorer or impoverished noble over the wealthy aristocrat, and as noted, to praise rural virtue over city sophistication. These themes outlasted the period when they might have been obligatory romantic conventions; many later writers, like Pushkin themselves members of the landowning class, utilized the theme of social differentiation he had initiated to reflect or reinforce differences in the psychology of their characters. In Herzen's *Who Is to Blame?*, published in 1846, the rich landowning Negrovs and Beltovs are contrasted with the upright Dr. Krupov and unassuming Krutsifersky. Turgenev, the supreme portraitist of the Russian countryside, endows Lavretsky, hero of *A Nest of Gentlefolk* (published in 1859, but set in 1842), with two different houses which symbolize alternative modes of existence between which he must choose. The more substantial house, Lavriky, is large, lovely, and appealing to his immoral wife; Vasilevskoe, the house in which he prefers to stay, is "a small, decrepit-looking manor house with closed shutters and an awry little porch," but solidly built of pine.[16] In *Fathers and Sons* (1861) three levels of country existence are presented through Odintsova's grand estate, the Kirsanovs' run-down property, and the small, thatched house of the elderly Bazarovs. Even Tolstoy, whose country portraits are almost exclusively of the wealthy aristocracy (his own milieu), and whose plots reflect his own abhorrence of aristocratic values, fleetingly contrasts levels of existence in *War and Peace* (written in the 1860s but set in the Napoleonic period): the Rostovs' lavish Otradnoe is contrasted to the small estate Mikhailovka of their jolly uncle; and Prince Bolkonsky's domain, Bleak Hills, is sharply delineated from the spartan atmosphere of Bogutcharovo, Prince Andrey's nearby property.

As such contrasts were meant to suggest, while all owners of country estates theoretically formed a single class in the pre-Emancipation period, their actual status was reflected in, and depended to a large extent upon, the type of country house they could afford to maintain. Pictorial architectural details, which for the contemporary reader would instantly reinforce differences in status, are plentiful in literature. Expensive building materials (brick rather than wood) and architectural styles fashionable in western Europe (most often some variant of neoclassicism, but occasionally baroque or neo-Gothic) separated the houses of the aristocracy from those of their poorer neighbors. Pushkin describes Prince Vereisky's Arbatovo as a masonry house on the Volga, neo-Gothic "in the style of an English castle," surrounded by a huge and magnificent English park. The garden's broad lake is studded with little islands, one of which has a marble statue, a second a lonely grotto, and the third a "monument with a mysterious inscription": in other words, all the icons of the romantic English garden.[17] In Turgenev's *Rudin*, Darya Mikhailovna Lasunskaia's brick mansion, which towers majestically on the crown of a hill above one of the three largest rivers of central Russia, is considered, the author tells us, the most magnificent of the province. To reinforce its image of splendour—and the local authority of Lasunskaya—Turgenev mentions that it was designed in the eighteenth century by Rastrelli, an Italian architect who designed the Winter Palace and Smolny Convent.[18] In *Fathers and Sons*, Odintsova's manor house Nikolskoe offers yet a third architectural model, the neoclassical, or Alexandrine, manor house, as Turgenev calls it; such houses typically were painted yellow, with green roofs and white columns surmounted by a pediment with the owner's coat of arms.[19] Though Tolstoy does not tell us outright that Vronsky's estate is constructed in this favorite style, Anna Karenina tells Dolly Oblonskaya that it had belonged to Vronsky's grandfather (which means that it dates from the reign of Alexander), and that it has not been altered on the outside. Our suspicions are confirmed when Dolly first sees its columned facade and her carriage draws up under a portico.[20] Prince Bolkonsky's Bleak Hills has "immense" rooms with lofty ceilings, and there are many outbuildings, including two conservatories.[21] Prince Andrey's wife Liza upon first seeing it calls it a palace,[22] and its design confirms this: it has a typical *piano nobile* with an enfilade of large reception rooms, above which are apartments for the Prince and his family.

These were the country mansions of the aristocracy, sites for lavish entertaining. In *Dead Souls* Gogol describes in an inspired passage the gap between the life of the rich landowner and that of the "petty, drab landed proprietor": "Like palaces do his white masonry houses look with their innumerable multitude of chimneys, belvederes, weather-cocks surrounded with a drove of built-on wings and all sorts of apartments for the accommodation of any and all guests who might come. What won't you find on his place? Theatricals; balls; all night his garden glows, ornamented with Chinese lanterns and lampions, and peals with the thunder of music. Half the province is attired in its best and gaily strolling under his trees."[23] Houses of the wealthy provincial nobility aped the architecture of these aristocratic palaces. Some variant of the Palladian or neoclassical style was the most common choice for the Russian manor house of the well-to-do. Pokrovskoe, for instance, Troekurov's estate, situated on a hill above a lake, is described as a huge masonry house with a belvedere and green roof, both characteristic of the neoclassical style.[24] Smaller estates, like Kistenyovka, the Dubrovsky estate, or Marino, the Kirsanov estate, tended to be wooden, painted gray, with red tin roofs, but also often imitatively columned and porticoed.[25] Sobakevich, one of Chichikov's victims, lives in a house typical of this category: it is a wooden house with mezzanine, red roof, and walls of dark gray.[26]

In many respects, writers' and artists' treatment of estate interiors differed along the same lines as their portrayal of exteriors described above. In literature, descriptions of furnishings or room arrangements highlight aspects of the characters and relationships of the protagonists, and a strong bias for country simplicity is evident well beyond the middle of the century. The old-fashioned, unsophisticated feeling of most country "nests" was for nineteenth-century authors a large part of their appeal; the response of fictional characters to such an atmosphere becomes a touchstone for their innate or instinctive morality. When Arkady Kirsanov visits the small rooms, simply furnished but clean and warm, in the wing of the manor house off the kitchen which Fenechka, his father's mistress, and her illegitimate child inhabit, he instantly understands this peasant woman's attraction for his father. In *A Nest of Gentlefolk*, Lavretsky's new bride exposes her own shallowness and superficiality when she finds the family estate Lavriky gloomy and old-fashioned. Later in the novel Lavretsky, arriving to live at his even smaller estate Vasilievskoe, is moved by the sight of the furniture, "a vivid reminder of the days of Catherine the Great."[27] Tolstoy in *Anna Karenina* (written in the 1870s) expresses, through Dolly's instinctive aversion to the lavish and fashionable redecorating Anna Karenina and Vronsky have carried out on their country estate, the moral failings of this transplanted urban couple.[28]

Interiors also figure in art, but they generally lack the psychological dimensions literature provides. The "room genre" constituted a whole movement in early nineteenth-century art.[29] Initiated by A. G. Venetsianov (1780–1847) and carried out largely by students of his school, it faithfully reproduced typical enfilades of rooms, country living rooms, or studies filled with family portraits and eclectic furniture. While these portraits were sometimes of identifiable locations or people, the emphasis is on objects and architectural perspective; the figures are, like the furnishings, treated as part of the decor. One canvas executed by an unknown artist depicts a typical provincial living room, with family members posed in routine occupations. A husband and wife are seated at a table, the wife holding a letter. Two children and an infant are behind them at the far end of the room near the window, listening to another woman play a piano.[30] N. I. Tikhobrazov's charming 1844 study of the sunroom of the Lopukhin estate, with its flowered chintz upholstery, a fringed shawl over a table, and a King Charles spaniel "begging" in an armchair near its mistress who is reading letters, conveys peace and stasis, but no information about Lopukhina's personality or character.[31]

In literature of the pre-Emancipation period, relationships between people of differing status—lord and servant, mistress and maid—were often important in revealing character or advancing the plot. In art, the occasional decorative peasant figure appears in estate portraits, but not in contact with his noble masters, and servants are absent from the type of interior just described. Two important exceptions deserve attention. One is a picture by an anonymous artist of an estate steward reading the accounts to his master.[32] The landowner, seated in a corner, is portrayed as almost twice as large as his steward, at whom he is looking with half-closed eyes, his hand thrust inside his greatcoat. The steward appears somewhat worried; another dwarflike peasant is looking on. No objects detract from the relationship of the three figures to each other. This primitive work may well have been executed by an untrained serf, for the unequal power relationship the painting expresses through the relative sizes of the figures and their expressions is clearly the perspective of a serf.

If this painting surprises by being comparable to a Gogolian or Dostoevskian psychological interior, the other exception to the rule, A. G. Venetsianov's well-known painting *A Landowner's Morning* (1823) bridges the gap in literature between the romantics' idealization of rural life and Turgenev's humanizing portraits of individual peasants. Three figures, a mistress and two servants, are posed to quite different effect than in the preceding painting. As in his other peasant studies, Venetsianov was depicting his own world on the estate of Safonkovo, which he had bought upon retiring from service in 1818. The model for the housewife arranging for the day's activities with her two servants was Venetsianov's own wife, and the classical busts on the armoire in the background, though a normal part of room decoration in this period, may have been intended to remind the viewer of Venetsianov's profession. The three figures— the seated landowner's wife and her two servants, one half-kneeling, the other standing—are intimately linked: despite the difference in status, this is a family scene. In fact, the standing maid seems to be looking quizzically at the viewer, as if asking why their usual morning routine has been interrupted by a stranger. The room is bathed in a rich golden light reminiscent both of seventeenth-century Flemish interiors and of Venetsianov's many scenes of peasants in fields. The mood this light creates and the intimacy of the scene suggest the preference of Pushkin and the Decembrist generation for the domestic solitude, the "hermit-like" existence of the quiet country over high-society salons, and their sense of the countryside as a world of equality of feeling, while the individualized faces of the servant girls recall the peasants of *A Sportsman's Sketches*.

Other interiors show us the estate as a retreat for the intelligentsia. An anonymous artist sketched the large living room of Priiutino, the estate of A. N. Olenin, around the time Olenin became president of the Academy of Arts in 1817.[33] Olenin, renowned for entertaining artists and poets, is shown with a group of friends in a room decorated with ornamental pillars, elaborate friezes, and heavy swagged curtains. Olenin's guests are amusing themselves at cards, conversation, needlework, and reading. From the 1830s an oil canvas by V. I. Shternberg (1818–45) depicts a room in Kachenovka, G. S. Tarnovsky's estate in the Ukraine. Shternberg is painting, seated in front of a Venetian window, the central portion of which opens onto a pond in the distance. The composer M. I. Glinka is working at a nearby table on his operetta "Ruslan and Liudmila," while Tarnovsky and another friend look on.[34]

By the 1840s the romantic haze veiling the countryside had given way to critical realism. Gogol's *Dead Souls* and Dostoevsky's *A Friend of the Family* revealed the squalid side of country life, while Turgenev's and Goncharov's novels abound in estates and families in decline. This change had been presaged earlier. Pushkin, who in periods of rural exile at his family estate of Mikhailovskoe had alternated between inspiration and ennui, had tempered his praise of rural virtue with undertones of irony or at least ambiguity which this later generation of writers developed. For Gogol the estate house, like all the material symbols vital to the provincial landowner's pretensions, presented opportunities for ridicule. In *Dead Souls* the fatuous Manilov, owner of two hundred serfs (close to the minimum for social respectability), advertises his specious worth by a manor house surrounded by an English garden with a gazebo pretentiously inscribed "Temple of Solitude." The miser Pliushchin's house, originally far grander than Manilov's, is depicted in an advanced state of decay. Gogol's interiors, elaborate mirrors of the psyches of the twisted types who inhabit these fussy, dusty, or moldy rooms, border on the grotesque.

Goncharov's assault on rural virtue in *Oblomov* is more subtle but no less devastating. In the famous chapter which is key to Goncharov's theme, young Ilya Oblomov, unable to deal with his responsibilities as a minor official in St. Petersburg, dreams of his idyllic childhood on the family manor Oblomovka.[35] At first glance, the apposition of the small wooden house of Oblomovka, with its fussy old-fashioned interior, to Verkhlyovo, the grand estate of a neighboring prince, seems similar to the juxtapositions of rich and poor noble found in earlier fiction. But Verkhlyovo, it is revealed, had formerly belonged to the Oblomovs; and Goncharov employs a host of telling details to transform their present cozy gentry nest into an obvious symbol of sloth and torpor. The broken step of the porch will probably never be fixed, nor will the stains on the sofa upholstery ever be removed. The inhabitants of Oblomovka are unaware that they are living on the brink. While vaguely recognizing the need to avoid spending cash (since they have no income), they do not try to make money; indeed, they fear and resist change.

The house at Oblomovka is both a personification and a searing indictment of the psychology of the ignorant country squire. It is this nobleman's psyche, incapable of grasping the nature of productive work, which accounts for young Ilya's paralysis. His dream of his childhood "nest" is a bright, almost festive celebration of the joys and rituals of country existence in pre-Emancipation Russia, a world in which only serfs and foreigners work. The macabre inertia of the gentry inhabitants of Oblomovka is clearly directly responsible for Ilya's present passive existence.

P. A. Fedotov's satirical canvases portraying the nobility, such as *An Aristocrat's Breakfast,* compare in their treatment of the landowning class to Gogol's handling of noble pretentiousness and Goncharov's portraits of sloth. But no landscape artist of the pre-Emancipation period approached the critical psychological realism of gentry authors towards estate life. This realism, while sometimes bathing country life in the warm hues of a Venetsianov canvas, also mercilessly exposed its flaws—the enormous social cleavages among the nobility, and the inability of the majority of their characters to stem the decline of family fortunes. Estate painters offered only extremely mild or veiled critiques, undoubtedly because most—in contrast to the largely highborn writers of the time—were either the paid employees, guests, or serfs of the estate owner. Sh. Rebu, for instance, was the resident art tutor at Avchurino, the Poltoratsky estate. His 1846 watercolor *The Old House on the Estate of Avchurino*[36] depicts a substantial country house with visitors standing at the colonnaded portico and seated on a balcony. The scene is a romantic one, although the unkempt dock and listing dory in the lake in the foreground suggest a declining estate economy.

Three canvases by one of Venetsianov's students, G. V. Soroka (Vasil'ev: 1823–64), executed in the late 1840s and early '50s, seem to portray the estate as a world in which the lord enjoyed himself while the serf worked. Soroka, like many other talented contemporaries, had reason to despair over the incongruities of his position as a serf artist. In view of Soroka's talent his owner N. P. Miliukov allowed him to be trained as an artist, but he refused Venetsianov's repeated requests that his student be freed. (Soroka's complaints against Miliukov ultimately resulted in the artist's suicide.) Two paintings portray Spasskoe, an estate in Tambov province belonging to a relative of Miliukov. In the first, the largest elements of the scene are two handsome white obelisks marking the entrance to the estate grounds at the end of an imposing brick dam across a serpentine stream. On the far side of the dam stands the white manor house, beyond which one can glimpse a gazebo on an island in the stream. Closest to the viewer in the left foreground is a group of three peasants. Two seated women, a rake beside them, are evidently sharing the contents of a small pot, while a young boy with a scythe stands beside them. A second painting of Spasskoe in the 1840s again places serfs—a woman washing clothes, a seated boy, and a woman with a yoke of buckets on her shoulders—in the foreground.[37] In a third painting, this time of Miliukov's estate Ostrovkii, we see an island with a neo-Gothic structure and landing, symbolic of gentry pleasures, being approached by a man on a raft with a decorative railing. Raft, landing, and island are bathed in sunlight, while in the shadowed foreground a young serf, the largest figure in the composition, is hauling a dugout canoe through the reeds which line the shore. Across the river stand the estate house and church. Although sun-filled skies and placid water establish a mood of tranquility in these paintings, the distinct space between, and variance in lighting of, the pleasure grounds of the estate and the working world of the serf, and the complete absence of gentle-folk, differentiate these paintings from typical estate portraits.

In the post-Emancipation period the manor house receded into the background, in art and literature becoming a more shadowy, im-pressionistic, and symbolic presence before which the last act of the drama of the decline of the nobility was being played out. With the loss of its "living wealth" through the emancipation of the serfs in 1861, many a Russian noble family was at a loss to make ends meet. Noble estates and lands passed into the hands of a rising merchant class eager to buy up the country mansions which had been, for the preceding century, the very symbol of nobility in Russia.

Now, artistic representations acquired motion and a critical, psychological dimension which had previously been absent. It has been suggested that the social criticism of midcentury fiction may well have stimulated a more socially outspoken art.[38] This may be so, but post-Emancipation reality—the bewilderment of many a land-owner deprived of his living wealth, the presence in the countryside of a new entrepreneurial class of merchants ready to profit from gentry ignorance, and of artists more independent in outlook than estate employees or serfs—was in itself a powerful stimulus to a more realistic approach to portraying the country house. The world of Russian art had also changed: the Itinerants, among them I. N. Kramskoi and V. M. Maksimov, broke away from the constraints of academic formalism and consciously dedicated themselves to docu-menting social reality. From the 1870s on, art and literature marched hand in hand as chroniclers of the physical decline of the Russian estate and the psychological dilemma of its owners. The inability of the landowning class to adapt to new economic realities became a major theme; the economic disaster resulting from the landowner's irresponsibility, "roistering with all the expansiveness of Russian recklessness and seigniorage, burning his candle, as they say, at both ends," as Gogol had put it in *Dead Souls*, was reproduced in multiple images of manorial decay. Artists too became narrators, the subject matter and evocative titles of their paintings reflecting gentry ruin.

The genesis of I. N. Kramskoi's *Inspection of the Old House*, a haunting painting of 1873, clearly reflects these changes. In 1867, from a village in Tula province, he wrote P. M. Tretiakov:

I am now preoccupied with a search for the old noble estate.
. . . Since I have decided to tackle this subject in a room, that
is, inside, and not from the exterior, I need such details as
could only be in a house where no one has lived for about
twenty years, but where can you find such a thing? . . . The
subject consists of the fact that the old pedigreed noble, a
bachelor, is arriving at his family estate after a long, very
long time, and finds the estate in ruins; the ceiling has fallen
in in one place, everywhere there are cobwebs and mold, on
the walls a series of portraits of ancestors. Two people of the
female sex are leading him by the hand—foreigners of
dubious appearance. Behind them is the purchaser—a fat
merchant, to whom the butler of the ruin is speaking; here,
he says, this is the grandfather of his highness, here this is
the grandmother, and this is so and so etcetera, but he
doesn't listen to him and is occupied, on the contrary, with
looking at the ceiling, a much more interesting sight. The
whole procession has halted because the village elder is
unable to open the [door to the] next room.[39]

In the actual painting (unfinished at Kramskoi's death) the women
and the noble are absent from the abandoned estate living room (fig.
2-1). An Empire side chair and round table (much like the table at
which Venetsianov's wife is sitting in *A Landowner's Morning*) frame
the merchant, whose back is to an enfilade of indistinct rooms.
Other chairs shrouded in dustcovers are pushed up against the walls.
Family portraits line the wall, but they are indistinct, as if fading;
and in fact the entire canvas is in a brownish hue which obscures
details, save for the sharply delineated face and figure of the merchant, illuminated by light from a side window. The caretaker, his
back to the viewer, is attempting to open a door out of the living
room, leaving the focus squarely on the merchant as he gazes
quizzically up at the ceiling. The way he dominates this once-
genteel milieu speaks for itself.

V. V. Maksimov's exterior portrait of a manor painted some
fifteen years later relates the same tale of gentry impoverishment. In
It's All in the Past, we see in the background a once-comfortable
gentry nest in disrepair.[40] Dying and fallen trees fill the courtyard,
weeds obscure part of the front porch, the four Corinthian columns
are discolored, and the house windows are boarded up. In the
foreground, in the shade of a lilac bush next to the front door of a

2-1 Ivan Nikolaevich Kramskoi. *Inspection of the Old House,* 1873. 93 × 119.3 cm. Courtesy of Tretiakov Gallery, Moscow.

peasant cottage, the aged owner of the estate lies propped up by pillows in an old slipcovered armchair, her feet on a tasseled pillow, undoubtedly dreaming of bygone days. Her King Charles spaniel sleeps nearby. A peasant housekeeper sits on the step of the cottage knitting, a gleaming samovar and tea-table awaiting the moment when the enfeebled mistress will awake. The double contrast between the dilapidated old house and the obviously well-kept cottage with its abundant lilacs, and the elderly, feeble gentlewoman and her servant, is striking and effective.

Surely one of the most evocative sounds in Russian literature is the thud of an axe in Anton Chekhov's last and most famous play, *The Cherry Orchard* (1904). In it, the sale of an estate orchard to a merchant who will build small summer cottages on the land symbolizes the demise of Russia's landed nobility. The purchase of land, particularly undervalued timberland, from impoverished nobles by conniving merchants was by this time not new to Russian literature: Arkady Kirsanov had reproached his father for such a sale in *Fathers and Sons,* while in *Anna Karenina,* Konstantin Levin, Tolstoy's spokesman, rails against the practice. A nobleman tells Levin of a neighboring merchant's suggestion that he cut down his lime trees and sell the wood. Levin responds, "Yes, and with that money he would buy cattle or a piece of land for a mere song . . . and he will make a fortune, while you and I must be thankful if we can keep what we have and leave it to our children. . . . We live without gaining anything, as if we were appointed, like the vestals of old, to guard some fire or other. . . . Why don't we do like the merchant?" "Why," replies the landowner, "as you have said, we guard the fire! The other is not work for the Nobility."[41]

Chekhov developed the tragedy of this attitude in greater depth in "My Life: The Story of a Provincial" (1896), a powerful story written before *Cherry Orchard*. In it he used images of decaying manors or frivolous villas as symbols for the ruin of a class and the attitudes which have brought it about. In his father's eyes the narrator, Misail Poloznev, has brought disgrace on his once-illustrious noble family by taking up the manual occupation of house painter. Using imagery which perhaps consciously recalls the dialogue in *Anna Karenina* cited above, the father shouts at his son, "Understand, you dense fellow—understand, you addlepate, that besides coarse physical strength you have the divine spirit, a spark of the holy fire, which distinguishes you in the most striking way from the ass or the reptile, and brings you nearer to the Deity! This fire is the fruit of the efforts of the best of mankind during thousands of years. . . . All the Poloznevs have guarded the sacred fire for you to put it out!"[42]

Defying his father, the narrator moves into the ruins of Dubechnya, an old manor house. "The surrounding wall, made of porous white stone, was mouldering and had fallen away in places, and the lodge, the blank wall of which looked out on the open country, had a rusty roof with patches of tin plate gleaming here and there on it. Within the gates could be seen a spacious courtyard overgrown with rough weeds, and an old manor house with sun blinds on the windows and a high roof red with rust."[43] The inhabitants of this house are paradigmatic of the reverse in social roles which has occurred. The former owner, Madam Cheprakov, is occupying a dilapidated wing of Dubechnya. In front of it, "there was washing on the line, and there were calves moving about."[44] Misail rehabilitates three small rooms in the main part of the house and moves into them with his girlfriend, daughter of the new owner (a prosperous engineer), who "in a simple woollen dress with kerchief on her head, with a modest sunshade, in expensive foreign boots" resembled, as the narrator puts it, "a talented actress playing the part of a little working girl."[45] When Misail returns home for a last attempt at reconciliation with his father, an architect, he finds him "sketching a plan of a summer villa, with Gothic windows, and with a fat turret like a fireman's watchtower—something peculiarly stiff and tasteless."[46] The father again blames him for having betrayed his ancestry, whereupon the son retorts, "How is it that in not one of these houses you have been building for the last thirty years there has been anyone from whom I might have learned how to live, so as not to be to blame?.... Our town has existed for hundreds of years, and in all that time it has not produced one man of service to our country, not one."[47]

Although the nobility, unable to adjust its viewpoint or behavior to new conditions, had clearly contributed to its own decline, such harsh condemnation was rare by the 1890s. The gentlefolk of Chekhov's plays are plaintively fatalistic. Most *fin de siècle* portraits of the estate likewise took a gentler, almost nostalgic approach to the estate as a vanishing way of life. On the one hand this nostalgia seems related to literary movements elsewhere in Europe which were reacting to the stresses of modernization either by glorifying a preindustrial world or by turning inward into a realm of private symbolism. But in Russia the nostalgia was also connected to a growing realization that the world of the estate, for all its follies and injustices, had been a distinctive element in Russian culture, and that it was dying out. Leading members of the arts establishment at the turn of the century like the collector Pavel Tretiakov, the artist and critic Igor Grabar', and members of the World of Art group like Alexander Benois felt they had rediscovered the rural world Venetsianov and his school had popularized a half-century before. They undertook a conscious campaign to recapture in art its fading beauty, as an aesthetic rebuke to their own bourgeois age so lacking in style and grace.

Two paintings by V. A. Serov (1865–1911) and V. E. Borisov-Musatov (1870-1905) from just after the turn of the century illustrate this mood. Serov, who was born into a cultivated family, sympathized with the reforming zeal of the Itinerants, but felt a sense of identity with aristocratic culture. His painting of 1904, *The Reception Room of an Old House*, shows us a corner of the main room of Belkino, the Obninsky estate in Kaluga province.[48] Sparsely furnished with a piano, a straight-backed chair, and small corner cupboard, the room is partially illuminated by light entering through a large open window in a deep wall recess and from another closed window in a niche above it.

The only occupant, a child, is shown half hidden, peeking around the French doors which lead into an adjoining room. A landscape painting above the piano, a few indistinct objects on it, and a clock on the cupboard are the room's few ornaments. Nonetheless faded glory, not starkness, is the impression conveyed by the light, the foliage visible through the open window, the thick walls and deep white arch of the doorway, the warm wood tones of cupboard, floor, and glass-paneled doors, and the suggestion of childish romping. The estate's bygone grandeur and vulnerability are highlighted by sizeable cracks in the wall and a sense of disarray.

The same feeling is amplified in a powerful canvas of 1903 by the Symbolist painter Borisov-Musatov unequivocally titled *Phantoms* (fig. 2-2). The artist, son of a former serf, after studying in Paris returned to Saratov province, where he discovered a setting he used numerous times in his work: a deserted Alexandrian country house with an overgrown garden. In a fragment of *Phantoms*, a familiar, white-columned, domed estate house, in form very similar to the central portion of Akhtyrka, looms in the background under a leaden sky. In the foreground is a spectral young woman in long dress and white shawl, drifting out of the picture as she follows another cloaked female whose face is already beyond our view. Upon closer inspection of the house, one sees more ghostly shapes on the stairs connecting the semicircular columned half-rotunda with the park. These seem to be phantoms either of neoclassical statuary, or perhaps of former occupants. Clearly both the house and all those living or nonliving relics are the "phantoms" of the title, retreating before the new century and conditions which have rendered them hollow spectres.

For literature and art throughout the nineteenth century, the country house in its myriad forms, from palace to hovel, was a symbolic protagonist acting out a part in the evolving social history of the nobility. If artists lagged behind writers in producing canvases which were outright "social documents" (as Benois termed Maksimov's *It's All in the Past*),[49] we should remember that genre painting came late to Russia, and that social conditions themselves were partially to blame, for until the Emancipation much artistic talent remained stifled or untapped. Yet early nineteenth-century portraits of the estate, however much they avoided social realities, are important evidence for cultural historians since, as has been shown, they documented not only architectural and decorative styles but also an owner's preferred image of his estate.

2-2 V. Borisov-Musatov. *Phantoms*, 1903. Tempera. Courtesy of Trotiakov Gallery, Moscow.

Midcentury realism produced the majority of artistic case studies of estate decline. But after the Emancipation, the Itinerants and even a Symbolist like Borisov-Musatov made up for the delay in artistic storytelling in their paintings depicting both the trials and the bygone glories of the world of the estate. Although stylistically distinct from the romantic realism of Venetsianov and his school, these late canvases resonate with a similar empathy for rural Russia in its entirety. In much the same way, the torments of Chekhov's provincial gentlefolk serve to remind us of their literary ancestors in happier times. On the brink of Russia's first revolution, which saw many manor houses consigned to flames, its authors and artists were producing portraits of the estate which were, appropriately, both nostalgic and full of apocalyptic presentiment.

Notes

1. Jules David Prown, "Style as Evidence," *Winterthur Portfolio* (Chicago: University of Chicago Press, 1980):197.

2. See, for instance, Pushkin's poem "The 19th of October" (1825) in his *Sochineniia* [Works] (Moscow: Gosizdat khudozh. lit., 1962), 1:211–15.

3. See Marc Raeff's discussion of the carry-over from military service into estate management in his essay "Home, School, and Service in the Life of the Russian Nobleman," in *The Structure of Russian History*, ed. Michael Cherniavsky (New York: Random House, 1970), 212–23.

4. A. Romanovich-Slavatinskii's *Dvorianstvo v Rossii ot nachala XVIII veka do otmeny kerepostnogo prava* [The nobility in Russia from the beginning of the XVIII century until the end of serfdom] (St. Peterburg, 1870) remains the classic study of the nobility up to the time of the emancipation. Terrence Emmon's *The Russian Landed Gentry and the Peasant Emancipation of 1861* (Cambridge: Cambridge University Press, 1968) describes the transition under Alexander II. Jerome Blum's essay "Russia" in *European Landed Elites in the Nineteenth Century*, ed. D. Spring (Baltimore: Johns Hopkins University Press, 1977) is the best short survey I know of. Although some families could trace their ancestry back to Riurik, founder of the Russian state, status in Russia historically had depended on personal service to the crown, not on birth or local authority. The Marquis de Custine, observing Russia in 1839, commented that it lacked a "proper" social hierarchy. Although family and titles were important, imperial favor could, in a moment, endow a parvenu with a position and wealth eclipsing that of any prince of ancient lineage.

5. J. G. Kohl, *Russia* (1844; reprint, New York: Arno Press, 1970), 43.

6. For an excellent recent comparative study of the ideals of the European nobility see "Conduct and Wealth," chap. 5 of M. L. Bush, *Rich Noble, Poor Noble* (Manchester: Manchester University Press, 1988).

7. P. Kakhonovskii, cited in *Dekabristy* [The Decembrists], ed. Vladimir N. Orlov (Moscow-Leningrad, 1951), 508.

8. Iurii Lotman, "The Stage and Painting as Code Mechanisms for Cultural Behavior in the Early 19th Century," in Iu. M. Lotman and V. A. Uspenskii, *The Semiotics of Russian Culture*, ed. Ann Shukman (Ann Arbor: Michigan Slavic Contributions, 1984), 11:165–76.

9. State Historical Museum. Watercolor. Reproduced in an unpaginated folio, *Russkii arkhitekturnyi peizazh v sobranii gosudarstvennogo istoricheskogo museia* [The Russian architectural landscape in the collection of the State Historical Museum] (Moscow: Izobratel'noe iskusstvo, 1987).

10. See, for instance, I. I. Podchaskii's 1818 painting of Vvedenskoe, O. Klodt's 1822 study of Mikhailovskoe at dusk, another depiction of Pekhra-Yakovlevskoe by Zh. E. Svebakh, and an anonymous depiction of a promenade at Ostankino, all reproduced in M. A. Anikst and V. S. Turchin, *V okrestnostiakh Moskvy* [In the outskirts of Moscow] (Moscow: Iskusstvo, 1979), pl. 86, 88, 142, 172.

11. Representative pages from such albums with views of Kuz'minki, Marfino, and Il'inskoe are reproduced in Anikst and Turchin, *V okrestnostiakh*, pl. 161–70.

12. Anonymous artist. *Nikol'skoe*, late 1820s through 1830s. State Historical Museum. Watercolor. Reproduced in Anikst and Turchin, *V okrestnostiakh*, pl. 171.

13. Anonymous artist. Raikovo estates, n. d. Watercolor. Alexander Herzen Museum, Moscow. Anikst and Turchin, *V okrestnostiakh*, pl. 67. The modest exterior is deceptive; an interior by N. Zheren of 1831 (Literature Museum, Moscow) shows the family seated in an elegant hall partitioned by Doric columns and crowned by an elaborately stuccoed and painted ceiling. Reproduced in E. Ya. Logvinskaia, *Inter'er v russkoi zhivopisi pervoi poloviny XIX veka* [The interior in Russian painting of the first half of the 19th century] (Moscow: Isskustvo, 1978), 49.

14. State Historical Museum. Lithograph by P. A. Aleksandrov from the original by I. S. Ivanov. Reproduced in *A. S. Pushkin i ego vremia v izobrazitel'nom iskusstve pervoi poloviny 19 veka* [A. S. Pushkin and his time in visual art of the first half of the 19th century] (Leningrad: Khudozhnik RSFSR, 1987), pl. 91.

15. Pushkin, *Sochineniia*, 3:222.

16. I. S. Turgenev, *Dvorianskoe gnezdo* [A nest of gentlefolk] (Moscow, 1944), 88.

17. Pushkin, *Sochineniia*, 3:286–88.

18. I. S. Turgenev, *Rudin/Nakanune* [Rudin/On the eve] (Petrozavodsk, 1971), 14.

19. I. S. Turgenev, *Sochineniia* [Works] (Moscow, 1964), 8:273.

20. L. N. Tolstoy, *Anna Karenina*, 12 vols. (Leningrad, 1968), 2: 192–93.

21. L. N. Tolstoy, *Voina i mir* [War and peace] (Minsk, 1976), 1:87–88, 102, 109.

22. Ibid., 1:97.

23. N. Gogol, *Mertvye dushi: poema* [Dead souls: An epic] (Moscow-Leningrad, 1953), 151.

24. Pushkin, *Sochineniia*, 3:300.

25. Turgenev, *Sochineniia*, 8:207.

26. Gogol, *Mertvye dushi*, 118.

27. Turgenev, *Dvorianskoe gnezdo*, 89–90.

28. Tolstoy, *Anna Karenina*, 2:195–96.

29. For a lively and provocative discussion of the phenomenon see M. N. Sokolov, *Inter'er v zerkale zhivopisi: zametki ob obrazakh i motivakh inter'era v russkom iskusstve* [The interior in the mirror of art: Notes on motifs of the interior in Russian and Soviet art] (Moscow: Iskusstvo, 1986), 27–40.

30. Literary Museum. Watercolor. Reproduced in Logvinskaia, *Inter'er*, 37. A similar living room study is shown in Anikst and Turchin, *V okrestnostiakh*, pl. 155.

31. Tretiakov Gallery. Reproduced in Sokolov, *Inter'er*, 43.

32. State Historical Museum. Reproduced in Anikst and Turchin, *V okrestnostiakh*, pl. 69.

33. Pushkin Museum. Reproduced in Logvinskaia, *Inter'er*, 30, and Sokolov, *Inter'er*, 38.

34. Russian Museum. Reproduced in Logvinskaia, *Inter'er*, 57.

35. See "Son Oblomova" [Oblomov's dream] in A. Goncharov, *Oblomov* (Leningrad, 1967), 110–61.

36. State Historical Museum. Reproduced in the folio *Russkii arkhitekturnyi peizazh*.

37. Russian Museum. Reproduced in T. V. Alekseeva, *Khudozhniki shkoly Venetsianova* [Artists of the Venetsianov school] (Moscow: Iskusstvo, 1982), 299-301.

38. Sokolov discusses the relationship between art and literature in the reform period in his *Inter'er*, 44–50.

39. Cited by S. N. Gol'dstein, *Ivan Nikolaevich Kramskoi* (Moscow: Iskusstvo, 1965), 128–30.

40. Tretiakov Gallery. Reproduced in Smithsonian exhibition catalogue *Russia: The Land, The People—Russian Painting, 1850–1910* (Seattle and London: University of Washington Press, 1986), 63.

41. Tolstoy, *Anna Karenina*, 2:239–40.

42. Chekhov, "Moia zhizn' " [My life], in *Izbrannye proizvedeniia* [Selected works], 3 vols. (Moscow, 1964) 2:256.

43. Ibid., 540.

44. Ibid.

45. Ibid., 575.

46. Ibid., 609.

47. Ibid., 610.

48. Tretiakov Gallery. Reproduced in Sokolov, *Inter'er*, 63.

49. A. N. Benois, 1902; cited in exhibition catalogue *Russia: The Land, The People*, 62.

THREE

"Montage" in Gogol's
Dead Souls

The View from the Bachelor's Carriage

Gary Cox

R ealist authors, in Russia as elsewhere, favor the model of narration underlying Stendahl's dictum that "a novel is a mirror carried down a road."[1] They wish to present reality directly, untouched by authorial tampering, often with a strong visual element. Nowadays, of course, we all understand that this goal of realism is an impossible one, for the author chooses where to point his mirror and when to begin and end the segments of reality he has selected for mirroring. He edits the reality he mirrors in much the way that a film editor edits film. In fact, since the author records his mirrorings on paper, making them infinitely repeatable, Stendahl's mirror image inevitably turns into a film image, never mind the anachronism. Realistic narrative technique anticipates the cinema, even though technology lagged behind literary theory; thus the novelist's process of selection may be profitably compared with film montage.

Gogol has been called the founder of Russian realism,[2] and although most critics quibble with this statement, one may argue that a certain visual element in his prose fiction does help lay the groundwork for realism. Of course it is the verbal character of Gogol's art that has been explicated most thoroughly.[3] The verbal level is unquestionably important, but it does not detract a bit from the brilliance of Gogol's verbal play to note that his art contains a visual element as well. Again and again, from whirling telescopes[4] and mirrors[5] to worms' eyes[6] and all-seeing eyes,[7] critics have used visual images to explain what is going on in his fiction. But Gogol's visualizations are never strictly realistic; they are almost always anomalous, ranging from the offbeat to the downright outrageous.

The visual anomalies of his prose fiction distinguish him from the realists who supposedly imitated him later in the nineteenth century, and tie him more closely to the modernists of the twentieth, many of whom acknowledged this debt. Visual elements make Gogol as much a forerunner of modernism as a founder of realism.

Several years ago, I wrote that oral performance elements in Gogol's fiction are connected with a technique I called "realistic caricature." Gogol portrays characters "atomically" through the accretion of discrete details, and a disproportionate focus on a particular detail produces a cartoonlike picture which seems real yet is exaggerated and humorous at the same time.[8] The device is rooted in oral performance, yet results in a visual effect, central both to Gogol's humor and to his "realism." It produces a complicated interplay between specific detail and generalization which is responsible for many of the visual anomalies in his works.

Elsewhere I have argued that visual elements form part of a system of contrasts underlying Gogol's earliest collection, *Evenings on a Farm Near Dikanka*. "The rural narrator is preoccupied with all types of sensuous imagery except the visual, and he conveys through this imagery a sense of repose. The urban narrator, on the other hand, relies heavily on visual imagery and uses it to convey a sense of dynamic, but fragmented and disruptive motion."[9] I pointed out that the sense of fragmentation resulting from this urban narrator's perspective presages that which characterizes Gogol's later Petersburg stories, amounting to a statement on the nature of urban, or modern, life. Pervading many of Gogol's middle and late works, including *Dead Souls*, this sense of fragmentation is often linked to a fascination with the humorous possibilities of visual anomaly, for example in "The Nose." Just what does the nose that confronts Kovalev look like? Is it a huge nose the size of an entire human being, dressed in a civil service uniform, or is it merely a person with a nose looking identical to Kovalev's; and if the latter, why is it so disturbing?

The same attitude toward visual detail is characteristic of the visualized sections of *Dead Souls*, but these passages alternate with sections devoted to authorial rhetoric, from the perspective of a self-conscious, even moralistic author figure, occasionally waxing melancholy over the passage of his youth, occasionally petulant over the ill-treatment he has received at the hands of the reading public. The narrative perspective of *Dead Souls* is unabashedly inconsistent; indeed, the inconsistency is part of the fun. In the visualized sections this author figure retires behind the scenes, much as such narrators were to do in later realistic fiction, and turns the narration over to a recording center of perceptions, a camera, presenting Chichikov's encounters visually. But Gogol's is a very odd camera, or a funhouse mirror, often notable for what it fails to see as much as for what it sees, and choosing at times the oddest perspectives.

To provide an initial frame of reference, let us contrast a visualized passage from Gogol (chapter 3 of *Dead Souls*), first with one from a standard piece of realist writing a couple of decades later (Tolstoy's *War and Peace* will do, a passage from volume 2, book 3, chapter 1), and then with some modernist prose from a period nearer our own (Bely's *Petersburg*). The Gogol and Tolstoy passages depict bachelors riding in carriages and taking in the countryside. Chichikov is visiting Korobochka; Andrey Bolkonsky is about to visit the Rostovs. The passenger in Bely's carriage, Apollon Apollonovich Ableukhov ("The Carriage Flew into the Fog," chapter 1), is not a bachelor, but might as well be one. The parallels between the texts will be more graphic if we look at them in parallel columns:

The gates were opened. A light flickered in another window. Pulling up into the courtyard, [Chichikov's] carriage stopped in front of a small house which couldn't be clearly distinguished in the darkness. Only half of it was illuminated by the light from the windows. A large puddle was visible in front of the house—the light was falling directly on it. . . . Meanwhile the hounds poured out with every possible voice: one, throwing its head in the air, carried on so ceaselessly and so intensely that he might have been getting God knows what salary. . . .[10]

Warmed by the spring sun [Andrey] sat in his carriage looking at the first sprouts of grass, the first birch leaves, and the first bunches of spring clouds hastening along the bright blue of the sky. He wasn't thinking about anything, and he looked to the roadsides unreflectively and cheerfully. They crossed the ferry where he and Pierre had spoken the year before. They passed the muddy village, the threshing floors, the foliage, the slope with a little leftover snow by the bridge. . . . At the edge of the road stood an oak. . . .[11]

Apollon Apollonovich Ableukhov cast a perplexed glance at a policeman, at the carriage, at the coachman, at the large black bridge, at the expanse of the Neva, where so dimly were drawn the foggy, many-chimneyed distances, and from which Vasilevsky Island frightfully returned the glance. . . . The carriage flew swiftly into the fog, and the passing policeman glanced over his shoulder into the dingy fog into which the carriage had swiftly flown. . . . The lackey looked at the expanse of the Neva, where so dimly were drawn the foggy, many-chimneyed distances and from which Vasilevsky Island frightfully returned the glance.[12]

Tolstoy's realist vantage point is grounded in the character's mentality; it is a "central recording consciousness"—Henry James' term works nicely for Tolstoy, even though the Russian realist typically moves his recorder from one character's mind to another. Furthermore, Tolstoy, like Gogol, builds his picture through the accretion of discrete details. The Gogol passage begins with the character and his carriage, although the character's own perspective is not used—the "camera" stays outside the character's mind. But the narrative perspective seems unable to see clearly. Constant mention is made of what cannot be seen, amounting to a visual block of sorts. And it soon veers off tangentially, looking at a puddle in the road (this, at least, is clearly visible) and then becoming fascinated by a group of barking dogs. Tolstoy's perspective also moves to the side of the road, for Andrey is about to see the gnarled oak which figures so importantly in a later epiphany. But this move is not really a tangent, for the narrative perspective never leaves the high road of Andrey's consciousness. The Bely passage is also visualized, yet indistinct, and here not only does the visualization move tangentially, but the visual perspective moves from the major character, Ableukhov, to peripheral figures, first to the policeman and then to the lackey. Likewise, Gogol's tangential moves fairly frequently result in such peripheral perspectives. In fact, tangential motion and visual block are two opposing "montage" devices that define the zigzag of Gogolian visual perspective, and peripheral perspective functions as the intersection of these devices in Gogol's prose.

Now let us follow Gogol's "camera" through the text that opens *Dead Souls* and make note of its selection of vantage points. Once again we will use parallel columns: the text from the novel will be translated on the left, while a running commentary on changes in perspective is on the right.

Into the gates of a provincial hotel in the town of N drove a fairly nice looking little spring-balanced carriage, the kind bachelors ride in. . . . In the carriage sat a gentleman who was not handsome, but not unpleasant looking either. . . . His arrival produced in the town no stir whatsoever; . . . only two Russian peasants standing in the doorway of the tavern across from the hotel

The observing perspective shows us the hotel gates, the carriage, and its occupant, who may be a bachelor and/or an officer. But from the outset our vision is blocked, as the person being described has no characteristics and his appearance is notable for its lack of effect. Even the generalization about his carriage gives no information, as it is absurd to assume that bachelors ride in made certain observations [about whether the wheel of the carriage would hold out as far as Moscow or Kazan']. . . . And then when the carriage had driven up to the hotel a young man was encountered who was wearing exceedingly tight dimity trousers that were too short for him, and a frock coat with pretensions to fashion under which was visible a shirt front fastened with a tie pin made in Tula in the shape of a bronze pistol. The young man turned around, looked at the carriage, raised his hand to grab his hat, nearly blown off by the wind, and went his way.

Once the vehicle had entered the courtyard of the inn, this gentleman was met by the servant, who was lively and fidgety to the point that it was impossible to tell what his face looked like. He ran out nimbly, serviette in hand, extremely tall and wearing a long coat of linsey-woolsey with a collar so high in the back that it almost reached beyond the nape of his neck; he gave his hair a shake and led the gentleman nimbly along the whole wooden gallery to show him the repose sent down to him by God. The repose was of a certain type, inasmuch as the hotel was also of a certain type, that is, just the sort of hotel one finds [literally, "that exists"] in provincial towns . . . with cockroaches peeking out of all the corners like prunes and with a chest of drawers always blocking off the door to the neighboring abode, where a neighbor would always be ensconsed, a taciturn and easygoing sort of fellow. . . . The external facade of the hotel corresponded to its interior: it was very long, with two floors; the lower one was not stuccoed and retained the dark red color of its bricks, which were fairly dirty in their

any other kind of carriage than those in which married men ride when they are travelling alone. The camera veers off to the periphery, looking at two peasants, and ultimately adopts their peripheral perspective, looking back at the carriage through their eyes. Their perspective includes a small detail and a point far in the distance, a zoom and a pan, if you will, neither of which contributes to the primary direction of narrative observation. We look again at the hotel and carriage, then take another right angle turn for a detailed look at a peripheral character: "a young man was encountered. . . . " The verb that makes this shift is a reflexive one, "met with," that implies mutual action involving two participants. But the carriage is not the other participant; that would be "it met with a young man," or "a young man met with it"; the other participant is the narrative "camera." Once again the narrative camera adopts the peripheral perspective, and like the peasants, the young man disappears never to be "met with" again.

The description of the hotel includes once again a detailed description of a character who will be completely peripheral, the waiter. Once again our vision is blocked, this time by the character's own motion, so that the most important detail, his face, is missed. We are shown Chichikov's room, and we are given a few very specific details about it (it has a chest of drawers, for instance), yet we are told that despite this specificity, the room represents the general case. Then once again we are led peripherally, into the room next door where we are given a glimpse of the neighbor, although we do not assume his perspective.

own right, and had gotten still darker from the changes of weather. The upper storey was painted that everlasting yellow color. Underneath were shops hung about with horse collars. . . . In the corner shop, or rather in its window, was situated an engraver with a samovar of red bronze and a face just as red as the samovar, so that from a distance one might think that there were simply two samovars placed in the window, were it not that one of the samovars had a beard black as pitch. (Gogol, 1–2)

From the neighbor's room we move back onto the street and look at the front of the hotel, this time in some detail. Finally the camera moves peripherally again and zooms in on the window in the corner shop. Then, after zooming in, it moves back and views the window "from a distance," from which vantage point it makes a visual error, then zooms in again to correct the error.

This passage is notable for the same confusion of specific detail with generalization that we have already found in earlier works. The "repose" offered Chichikov is exactly like all such provincial accommodations, we are told in a sweeping generalization, and then a very specific picture is given, including details about furniture arrangement and neighbors which are quite unneccessary. Furthermore, in an overall context which is generalized and even blurred by excessive qualification ("fairly"), there is a focus on specific details which seem to be selected randomly—the tie pin, for instance. This is a zoom effect, to use the camera image again, but the object depicted in the zoom frame is nonsensically chosen; it leads us in a direction tangential to the overall narrative direction.

The presentation of specific detail as the general case is not the only device that leads us off on tangents; tangential motion is a constant process in Gogolian montage. The move into Chichikov's neighbor's room in the hotel is a classic example.

But as the camera continually leads us away from the dominant narrative path, its lens is continually blocked in some way or other. Again and again we are told that it is impossible to distinguish the features of a phenomenon or character. In the above passage, the inability or unwillingness to visualize specific detail, the visual block, includes the refusal to name the town, "the kind of carriage bachelors ride in" (a description which tells us nothing, since bachelors ride in the same kind of carriages married men traveling alone ride in), the lack of specific characteristics for Chichikov, the lack of response to his arrival in the town, the inability to make out the features of the waiter's face, and so forth. Occasionally the visual block appears in the form of an actual mistake in perception, as in the case of the engraver who is mistaken for a second samovar by the narrative perspective, until it is noticed that he has a beard. There is no reliable perspective here, as Aleksandr Slonimskii has pointed out,[13] and that fact underlines qualities of the absurd in the work.

It is not only motion that may be tangential in Gogol; often perspective itself becomes tangential. In the peasants' commentary on the wheel, and in the examination of Chichikov by the young man with the Tula revolver tie pin, we first see the peripheral character and then adopt his perspective, the perspective of a character who has appeared suddenly, only to disappear forever, as Nabokov notes.[14]

Visual block and tangential motion are two opposing devices in Gogol. They continually check each other, and thus they define by their opposition the zigzag motion of the narrative visualization. Peripheral perspective brings the tension between them together in one device, for there the tangential motion reaches a dead end tantamount to visual block.

The opening chapter's description continues:

While the gentleman who had just arrived was examining his room, his belongings were being carried in.

It was the coachman, Selifan, who brought them. . . .

While the servants were taking their time arranging things, the gentleman set off for the lobby. What these lobbies are like—every traveller knows perfectly well: the very same walls, painted with oil paint, darkened from above by smoke from the chimney and polished from beneath by the backs of various travellers and even more by out-of-town merchants . . . ; the very same soot covered ceilings, the very same sooty chandelier with an abundance of pendant crystals, . . . the very same paintings all over the walls, done in oils—in a word, everything was exactly like every place else, with the single difference that on one painting was depicted a nymph with breasts so large that the reader has certainly never seen the like. (Gogol, 3)

The perspective we would expect to be central (the hero's examination of his room) becomes peripheral as the narrator's point of view veers off to a description of his servant. Eventually, the narrative viewpoint follows the hero downstairs and examines with him the lobby and its artwork. And in this highly visualized scene, a collection of very specific details is once again said to be a generalization. An appeal is made to the readers' general knowledge and experience, but visual experiences are attributed to us as readers that we very likely have never had, that even Gogol's contemporary readers had very likely never had. The moment ends with another kind of visual block: the description is based on what the reader does not see, and indeed has never seen.

Visual block is also present in the "description" of Manilov in chapter 3, as is the same peculiar attitude toward visual detail, but these devices are realized in a very different way.

Although the time during which they will go through the porch, the foyer, and the dining room is a bit shortish, still we will try whether we mightn't somehow manage to utilize it and say something or other about the master of the house. But here the author must confess that an enterprise of this sort is very difficult. It is much easier to depict characters of a grand scale; there you just throw the paints at the canvas with all your might: blazing black eyes, overhanging brows, a forehead intersected by a large crease, and slung over the shoulder, a black cloak, or one crimson as fire—and the portrait is ready. But then there are all these individuals, the world is full of them, who at first glance are very similar to one another, but then when you look a bit closer, you see lots of the most elusive peculiarities—these persons are frightfully difficult to depict in a portrait. Here you've got to concentrate your attention to the utmost as you force all these tiny, almost invisible features to step out and parade before you. And in general you've got to go a long way to intensify your vision, already quite refined in the science of coaxing out details.

. . . [To] all appearances [Manilov] was a fine figure of a man. The features of his face were not devoid of pleasantness. . . . He smiled alluringly, and he was blond, with light blue eyes. In the first minute of conversation with him, you can't help saying, "What a nice, pleasant person!" In the minute just after that you won't say anything, and

It begins with the narrator's claim that he is taking the reader aside while the characters are otherwise preoccupied. This is a stroke emphasizing the narrator's relationship with the reader, at the same time as it underlines the manufactured, artificial quality of the piece. Then the narrator laments to the reader that people like Manilov are very difficult to describe, when they are contrasted with vivid characters "of a large size." He outlines the portrayal of such a person with vivid visual images completely lacking in detail (again a sort of visual block)—instead, simply a few splashes of color.

People like Manilov, on the other hand, are identical and composed of slender, almost invisible characteristics. We are told that he is "visible" (*vidnyi*), and although this figurative expression should be rendered in English as something like "he was a fine figure of a man," still the use of this word in the same passage in which we are told that his features are "almost invisible" (*nevidimye*) can be seen as an ironic commentary on the subject of visualization in descriptive prose. His description then proceeds from the perspective of a hypothetical observer, but again almost completely omitting visual details: we know only that Manilov is smiling, blond and blue-eyed. A recital of types follows, but without much of a visual component, and concluding with a repetition of the assertion that Manilov has no particular interests. So in a descriptive passage strewn with remarks about the impossibility of describing, we end then in the third you'll say, "What the devil!"—and back off a bit; if you don't back off, you'll experience the most deathly boredom. Everyone has his "hobby horse" . . . but Manilov had none. (Gogol 20–21)

up knowing essentially nothing about what this character looks like.

This impossibility is explicitly linked with the difficulty of relating specific visual details. But the narrator has no trouble with visual detail in describing Mrs. Manilov:

Chichikov, to be precise, saw a lady whom he nearly missed altogether as he was exchanging bows with Manilov in the doorway. She wasn't bad looking; her clothing complemented her face. She wore a house coat of pale-colored silken cloth which fit her well. Her small delicate hand threw something hurriedly on the table and grasped a cambric handkerchief with embroidered corners. (Gogol, 24)

Still, it is very interesting that he has us visualize her from Chichikov's peripheral perspective. Furthermore, that peripheral perspective is very nearly blocked, as Chichikov stands in the doorway bowing to Manilov. Finally, the view from this perspective is partially blocked—it sees the handkerchief clearly, but seems unable to discern what she threw on the table.

In chapter 8, however, the difficulty of description is expressly linked with female characters (Gogol, 167). The distinction between visualized characters and blurred ones seems to be based on the narrator's momentary whim. The extended similes may be viewed as instances of a peripheral perspective that takes over the narration. This simile in chapter 9, for instance, briefly dominates our field of vision:

Their situation during the first moment was similar to the situation of a sleeping schoolboy whose early-rising comrades have shoved into his nose a "hussar," that is, a bit of paper filled with snuff. In his drowsiness drawing all the tobacco in with all the vigor of a sound sleeper, he awakens, leaps up, looks around, like a goggle-eyed idiot, in all directions, and can't understand where he is or what has happened to him. And only later does he discern the walls of the room, illuminated by the

This may be the most spectacular example of such a simile, visually speaking. It describes the stupefaction of the townspeople of N as they come to terms with the nature of Chichikov's enterprise. Here the central character of the interpolated simile becomes a vantage point for a dynamic and vividly visualized scene. In fact, the scene that is described is much more richly visualized than we could expect if the perspective were still the boy's. How, for instance, can he see the "illuminated slanting rays of the sun, the laughter of his comrades hiding in the corners, and the morning, just begun, peeking into his window: the awakened forest resounding with the voices of thousands of birds, the stream, catching the early rays, here and there disappearing in little flashes of gurgling ripples between slender reeds, with scattered groups of naked boys calling him to swim—and only later does he realize that he's got a hussar up his nose. (Gogol, 202)

stream," with all the details included in that vista, from his bed? The perspective has become peripheral to the already peripheral perspective of the boy. But in doing so it has become a fairly standard third-person omniscient narrative vantage point, a rare phenomenon in Gogol. Yet even as it becomes standard, it illuminates a scene absolutely alien to the primary direction of the narrative. It is a complete dead end.

The generalizing tendency of the prose of *Dead Souls* is related to the visual block that we have noted from the outset of the text. Instead of visualizing a scene or character, the narrator will make the offhand remark that similar scenes are well known to the reader and may easily be imagined: "The repose was of a well-known type . . . " (Gogol, 2). Thus he leaves the visualization up to the reader. Of course this device is complicated by the occasional insistence that a visually particular scene (the painting in the hotel lobby, above) is a generalization and that the reader ought to fill in the particulars.

These visual peculiarities may be illuminated by a look at the author's lyrical digressions at the beginnings of chapters 6 and 7, which are commentaries on the visualization of detail in prose. At the outset of chapter 6, he connects the visualization of detail with youth and freshness, and links the ignoring of detail with jaded middle age:

Earlier, long ago, in the years of my youth, in the years of childhood that have flashed past irretrievably, I was always glad when I drove up to an unfamiliar spot. No matter whether it was some little four corners, a poor provincial burg, a village, or the other side of the tracks, my curious childish gaze would always discover something curious. Every building, everything as long as it bore the stamp of some sort of noticeable particularity—everything was arresting, was striking. . . . [N]othing slipped past my fresh sensitive attentiveness. . . . From a distance, through the leafy green foliage, would flicker to me alluringly the red roof and white chimneys of a homestead, and I would wait impatiently, while on both sides the gardens standing guard would part and the house would show its own facade, alas, then it would not be a bit dreary, and I would try to guess from the house what sort of person the homesteader might be.

Now I drive up to an unfamiliar village indifferently and gape at its dreary exterior with indifference. My gaze, grown chill, finds no haven; nothing amuses me; and what in earlier years would have aroused a lively expression, laughter, and irrepressible blather now slips past and my motionless lips preserve torpid silence. Oh my youth! Oh my freshness! (Gogol, 114–15)

But in the introduction to chapter 7, generalization, or the ignoring of visual detail, is connected with the happy, middle-aged, married, traveller, and with a superficial, romanticizing, authorial stance:

Happy is the traveller, who after a long, tedious journey . . . sees at last a familiar roof, lights rushing to meet him, and familiar rooms rising up to meet him. . . . Happy is the family man who has such a corner, but woe to the bachelor!

Happy is the writer who may pass by characters who are dull, repulsive, impressive only through their pathetic reality, and approach characters exhibiting the highest worth of humanity; the writer who can select, out of the great maelstrom of images that whirl around us daily, just a few exceptions, who has not once betrayed the lofty mandate of his lyre, has never lowered himself from his height to his poor insignificant brethren, and who, never touching earth, is plunged completely in the distant magnified images he has torn from [the earth]. . . . But not such is the lot, different is the fate of the writer who has dared to summon to the surface everything that is constantly before our eyes, but which our indifferent eyes do not observe, all the horrible shocking slime of trifles, which has enmeshed our lives. . . . For the judgement of our contemporaries does not acknowledge that equally marvellous are telescopes observing suns and microscopes transmitting to us the motion of unnoticed insects. . . . (Gogol, 139–40)

If the visualization of detail is connected with a childlike honesty, and the generalizing mentality that ignores detail and imposes visual blocks is connected with an adult authorial stance, it is easy to see that these issues are related to Gogol's own ambivalence toward his role as an author and, indeed, as an adult. The tension between these opposing attitudes, and the tendency to deflect visualization to a peripheral perspective, relate to fundamental polarities in Gogol's work. But Gogol himself exhibits some confusion about these polarities. At times he sees himself as a frivolous humorist, preoccupied with risible descriptions of the particular. Occasionally (as in chapter 7) he realizes (as Belinsky did) that such lampoons can be profoundly serious in the moral effect of their critique. But most often he derogates this aspect of his art and aspires to be a writer of grander scale and less detail. It is just such grandeur that he associates in chapter 7 with superficiality, and it is just such ignoring of detail that he associates in chapter 6 with jaded middle age. This confusion is never resolved, and the tension between visualization and generalization in *Dead Souls* is a monument to his ambivalence.

The dichotomy between visible and invisible, between surface and interior, is important here. At some points, detail is said to be "invisible" (*nevidimyi*), as in the numerous instances of "visual block," including Manilov's description quoted above, and the reference to all those "elusive peculiarities" that the narrator noted in Manilov's character. We are told that Gogol's skill is for catching the elusive detail, but the details he actually presents are rather strikingly peculiar than elusive. Further, they are said to represent the general case despite their peculiarity. If they are the general case, in what sense are they invisible or elusive? As far as that goes, if they are strikingly peculiar, in what sense are they invisible or elusive? Is Gogol deliberately misstating the nature of his art for a literary effect? It is hard to imagine what that effect might be. Or does he simply misunderstand his art? This critic suspects, alas, the latter.

Note also the formulation: "Laughter visible (*vidnyi*) to the world and unobserved (*nezrimye*) tears, unknown (*nevedomye*) to it" in chapter 7 (Gogol, 141). Pleasant details are visible; unpleasant ones are invisible (besides being elusive). But at the same spot, it is stated that the critical humorist, poor fellow, "summons to the surface" unpleasant details. So although these unpleasant details are beneath the surface and hence invisible, the author makes them visible (when he wants to, apparently). Once again, the dichotomy is inconsistently developed, since we are told that these "invisible" details are "before our eyes every minute," but our "indifferent eyes do not see them." This is a very Belinskian model indeed; the function of art is the exposition of negative aspects of human life which must then be corrected. But the fact that the ignoring of detail is connected with indifference is ominous, since in chapter 6 the author had lamented his own indifference upon reaching middle age.

Escape is what is called for, and the image of escape is embodied in a visual technique we may call "fast forward" (again, with apologies for the anachronism). The image is hinted at in chapter 7, with the exclamation "To the road! To the road!" (Gogol, 141). And it takes over in the troika passage that closes the book:

> The miles fly, and flying to meet us are merchants on the seats of their covered wagons, the forest flies past on both sides with its formations of firs and pines, with the sound of the axe and the raven's cry, the whole road flies past, no telling where, into the distant abyss. There is something frightful contained in that stream of objects flashing past so rapidly it is difficult to make sense of them [literally, where the disappearing object "does not succeed in having a meaning" ("*ne uspevaet oznachit'sya*")]—there is only the sky over one's head and light clouds, and the moon penetrating through them, and they seem to be motionless. (Gogol, 269)

Notice that the physical motion described is the same as that posited for the imaginative, curious child in the lyrical introduction to chapter 6 and for the returning family man in 7: the visualizing perspective (the camera) is moving through trees toward a spot in the distance, in 6 and 7 identified as a "roof." In 6, the roof belongs to the homesteader whose particulars the child imagines; in 7 the imagined homesteader is the self for the family man, but not for the bachelor, who has become distracted by peripheral details "flickering" or "flashing" before his eyes. The verb "to flicker" or "flash" (*mel'kat'*, *mel'knut'*) occurs in just about every passage in which Gogol talks about visualization. Both Chichikov and the narrator are bachelors, and this pattern describes exactly their motion at the beginning of each of the chapters of the first half of the novel. In each case the homesteader they find is repulsive. But in the troika passage above, which closes the novel, it is not the repulsiveness of the landowner that makes the "flickering" so frightening; it is his absence. Here there is no "roof" as the primary destination for the moving perspective. The result is tangential motion, continually checked by visual block, producing the zigzag characteristic of Gogol's narrative perspective.

This narrator is right: there is something frightening in a panorama that flashes so rapidly before our eyes. And in Gogol's prose, despite the diverting elements, one does often feel the disquieting sense that objects flashing before our eyes are falling into an abyss where it is difficult to make sense of them, where "the object does not succeed in having a meaning." This is one reason why the anomalies of Gogolian visualization tend as much toward the absurdist elements of modernist prose as toward the realism of his immediate successors.

Notes

1. Stendahl, *The Red and the Black* (New York: New American Library, 1970), bk. 2, 359.

2. See Vissarion Belinsky, "O russkoi povesti i povestiakh g. Gogolia" [Concerning the Russian short story and the short stories of Mr. Gogol] in *Polnoe sobranie sochinenii* [The complete collection of works] (Moscow: Izdatel'stvo Akademii nauk S. S. S. R., 1953), 1:267; in English, see also "Chichikov's Adventures, or Dead Souls: Gogol's Epic Poem," in George Gibian, ed., *Dead Souls: The Reavey Translation, Backgrounds and Sources, Essays in Criticism* (New York: Norton, 1985).

3. See, for example, B. Eikhenbaum, "Kak sdelana shinel' Gogolia" [How the overcoat was done] in *Skvoz' literaturu* [Through literature] (The Hague: Mouton, 1962), 171–95.

4. See Hugh McLean, "Gogol and the Whirling Telescope," in *Russia: Essays in History and Literature*, ed. L. H. Legters. (Seattle: University of Washington Press, 1972), 79–99.

5. See Donald Fanger, "The Mirror and the Road," in Gibian, 489–492.

6. See Dmitrii Chizhevskii, "O shineli Gogolia" [About Gogol's overcoat] in *Sovremennye zapiski* [Contemporary notes] (Paris) 67 (1938): 172–95; translated in *Gogol from the Twentieth Century: Eleven Essays*, ed. and trans. R. A. Maguire (Princeton: Princeton University Press, 1974), 293–322.

7. See Leon Stilman, " 'Vsevidiashchee oko' u Gogolia" [The all-seeing eye in Gogol] in *Vozdushnye puti* [Aerial ways] (1967): 279–92; translated in Maguire, 375–87.

8. Gary Cox, "The Writer as a Stand-Up Comic: A Note on Gogol and Dickens," *Ulbandus Review* 2, no. 1 (Fall 1979): 45–61.

9. Gary Cox, "Geographic, Sociological, and Sexual Tensions in Gogol's Dikan'ka Stories," in *Slavic and East European Journal* 24 (1980): 219–32.

10. N. V. Gogol, *Mertvye dushi* [Dead souls] in *Sobranie sochinenii* [Collected works], ed. S. I. Mashinskii et al. (Moscow: Gosudarstvennoe izdatel'stvo khudozhestvennoi literatury, 1959), 45–46. In English, see Gibian, ed., *Dead Souls*, 42. Further page numbers will refer to this translation.

11. L. N. Tolstoy, *Voina i mir* [War and peace], in *Polnoe sobranie sochinenii* [Complete collected works] (Moscow: Gosudarstvennoe izdatel'stvo khudozhestvennoi literatury, 1959), 5:171; in English, see L. Tolstoy, *War and Peace*, trans. Rosemary Edmonds (Baltimore: Penguin, 1957), 491.

12. A. Bely, *Petersburg* (Munich: Wilhelm Fink Verlag, 1967), 28; in English, see A. Bely, *Petersburg*, trans. John Malmstad and Robert Maguire (Bloomington: Indiana University Press, 1978), 9.

13. Aleksandr Slonimskii, *Tekhnika komicheskogo u Gogolia* [The technique of the comic in Gogol] (Providence: Brown University Press, 1963); translated in Maguire, 323–74; see also Carl Proffer, *The Simile and Gogol's "Dead Souls"* (The Hague: Mouton, 1967).

14. Vladimir Nabokov, *Nikolai Gogol* (New York: New Directions, 1944).

FOUR

The Optics of Narration

Visual Composition in *Crime and Punishment*

Roger Anderson

In Russia, as in Europe generally, the nineteenth-century novel aspired to what E. M. Forster has called the portrayal of life by time.[1] Like history, time's flow in the realist novel was considered to run in straight lines—past conditions determining options in the narrated present, which in turn produce conditions out of which the future inevitably emerges. With theme and character bound to a linear chronology, narrative technique favored the kind of synoptic exposition of event and motive which Norman Friedman defines as "neutral omniscience."[2] Like the historian, the omniscient narrator of Dickens, Balzac, or Goncharov rendered fictive life as evolutionary change whose progress can be seen clearly from above and outside.

Towards the end of the century, however, the assumption that novels replicate history was clearly breaking down. The postrealist world was fast coming to the conclusion that, as José Ortega y Gasset has it, "all knowledge is knowledge from a definite point of view,"[3] not the decrees of some privileged, external seat of judgment. Both Proust and Joyce, for example, broke the illusion that objective time was the supreme regulator of human affairs as recorded by a dispassionate author. This is the point of Roger Shattuck's observation that, while the realist novel progresses by a sequence of "and then" statements, modern fiction grows by a series of jarring "and" declarations whose connectives lie outside sequential time. "Without causal progression," he continues, "everything is middle."[4] The result is a disjointed narrative line that subordinates event to discrete scenes in which a character's subjectivity first detaches from and then exceeds authorial explanation.

As fiction lost confidence in history's ability to make synoptic sense of human affairs it gravitated toward alternative compositional models, often based on spatial forms rather than the illusion of real time. Joseph Frank is still the foremost explicator of this shift in textual ordering from time to space. He uses the term "space-logic"[5] to indicate something of a conversation between visual images, quite independent of narrative time, in much postrealist fiction. Bypassing the notion of time's illusion, spatial forms (e.g., objects, details, colors, architectural space) are introduced, then juxtaposed at unpredictable moments in the narrative to create compositional relationships independent of chronology. As such spatial images accumulate they establish patterns of "reflexive references" between themselves which the reader retains eidetically in memory.[6] The process of reading thus becomes more like filling in a mosaic than unrolling a scroll. Instead of a history of sequential events, we confront a montage of related images which must be taken in as a whole. The resulting canvas of visual forms has a primary compositional value in the narrative; its meaning must be "read" as an optical ordering rather than narrated sequence. As Frank suggests: "To be properly understood, these word-groups must be juxtaposed with one another and perceived simultaneously. Only when this is done can they be adequately grasped; for while they follow one another in time, their meaning does not depend on this temporal relationship."[7]

In Russia, too, the established notion that fiction reflects history's evolutionary process was growing thin. With the concurrent disruptions of serf emancipation, a rapid transition from feudal to capitalist economy, and the rise of philosophical empiricism, the present was increasingly seen in terms of rupture and disjunction instead of continuity and transition.

Dostoevsky especially captures modernity's fascination with sudden change in a world where starkly opposed forces—of class, wealth, and personality—arise suddenly to defy history's trust in explanations. His explorations of the unconscious, with all its private associations and logical leaps, anticipate Freud by speculating on psychological forces which defy the logic of causality. It can be argued that these unexpected junctures between private experience and dream images are primary forces behind modernism as a general movement. Dostoevsky and Freud together reflect the advent of an age that contemplates familiar environments which can turn suddenly into *terra incognita;* for both, logic floats free of real time.

In this modern world in which narrative is infiltrated by the private mind of characters the omniscient narrator's privileged knowledge of motive and event (what M. M. Bakhtin calls the monologic author) is severely limited or even rendered unreliable. Biography and social causality fade as we confront a character's sudden confrontation with unpredictable events and objects which intrude suddenly into his field of vision.

This entanglement of the subconscious with the ordinary world, with its eccentric results, is basic to Bakhtin's understanding of Dostoevsky's fiction. It is also basic to what Sharon Spencer considers to be modern fiction's general insistence that "readers observe and acknowledge that reality is polymorphous, illogical, fragmented, chaotic, and above all, myriad faceted."[8] The questions Dostoevsky asks have more to do with how a character sees his world and himself at a particular moment than with how history brought him to that moment.

In a novel like *Crime and Punishment* this substitution of lived-space for time-as-biography provides an especially good example of Frank's theory about spatial forms in postrealist fiction. Dostoevsky's several distortions of real time, perceptual fields, and narrative causation join to create a world which Raskolnikov takes in as flux and discontinuity. His movement through the novel is recorded in a composition of unpredictable, brilliantly marked scenic episodes, each of which he experiences as an independent psychological event with its own duration. Intervening time, often whole days, is either telescoped or ignored. In a fundamental way, narrative is made up of scenes perceived and lived from the inside out rather than events explained from the outside in.

Such scenes are marked by the presence of unpredictable objects and details which hold a special significance for Raskolnikov. Their seemingly unrelated spatial images accumulate into patterns of repetition and juxtaposition which carry the secrets of his compulsion to explore his own disjointed interiority. He recognizes such objects and details as highly important even while he cannot quite understand why they are. He is constantly on the verge of intuiting some mysterious connection between unpredictable visual stimuli and his own subconscious preoccupations.[9] Ordinary things—the shape of a room, the style of a hat, a familiar view from a bridge, all manner of thresholds[10]—fuse directly with parts of that inner self he desperately seeks to define and declare.

It is just these flashes between Raskolnikov's ontological search and suddenly revealed patterns of his jumbled urban environment that are most open to us as readers. Such moments join the Hay Market's dirty crossroads to the disturbing shapes and colors of an apartment, a bridge, or a police station. Although no logic of causation unites them, these disparate scenes hang together by what they share visually. They are of the order of those "spots of time" which Murray Krieger describes, a mosaic of hauntingly connected spatial forms which direct theme and give psychological definition to character beyond the limits of biography.[11] Those flashes have duration in the Bergsonian sense; they speak to each other and must be considered as external to the very notion of progressive time.

An example here will illustrate my point. Early in the novel we see Raskolnikov standing on a bridge thinking of suicide by drowning. When a kindly passerby gives him a few coins he is unaccountably stunned by the objects he holds in his hand. He stares at them so intently that time stands still for him. The coins draw together a complex of competing needs in his subconscious. He has sought some measure of control over life by killing another, ostensibly for money. The act of suicide—killing himself—would be the ultimate control over the secret motive these stolen valuables imply for him. At the same time he desperately seeks the sort of emotional linkage to others which the coins also suggest (the woman's kindness in giving them to him, and its echo in his gift of money to protect a young girl on the street, or his future use of money to help Mrs. Marmeladov after her husband's death).

When Raskolnikov throws these coins instead of himself into the water, his competing, even contradictory needs for independence and contact become momentarily inseparable from the physical coins themselves. At that moment on the bridge we as readers cannot separate coin from emotion—or emotion from action—any better than the hero can, and the narrator does nothing to explain such a compositional knot for us. We must finish the whole novel, then recollect the several instances of Raskolnikov's complex response to money, in order to interpret the coins' meaning in this one scene. Sequence thus loses its explanatory value. Memory, prophecy, and immediate experience become compressed into an unexplained physical form. That form reverberates independently through the novel; it influences our definition of its hero and how meaning is established in the novel generally. Contemplated coins serve as unmediated contact with the hero's subjectivity, which is itself bound to an ever-expanding network of interrelated visual imagery. Psychological struggle and physical form are fused and must be taken in together—quite apart from narrated sequence—in order to place this scene within the work's order as a whole. We thus "read" *Crime and Punishment* by "seeing" its spatial properties, storing away their hidden impact on the hero's mind, waiting until money reappears in other scenes to add needed parts to a more general pattern of the novel's meaning for us.

It is important to note that in this bridge scene narrative point of view is subordinated to the interplay of Raskolnikov's restless eye and subconscious mind. There is no authorial distance from the hero's fascination with the coins. Indeed, as John Jones points out, Dostoevsky's authorial language so takes on Raskolnikov's own stylistic features that, at times, there occurs something of a merger between first and third-person narration. The result is what Jones calls a "deflected stream of consciousness"[12] which binds our perception to Rodion's own unpredictable response to the coins.

The range of potential linkage between spatial detail and Raskolnikov's active unconscious is essentially unlimited. It associates revered cultural symbols with everyday things in idiosyncratic ways—anything can hold an unexpected significance for him as he moves about the city. Be it a bulging piece of old wallpaper or a crucifix, any object is potentially significant, its value determined only by its unpredictable role within a particular scenic moment and by how it might be juxtaposed to related spatial forms at other odd points in the novel. Dirt, a color, some striking architectural angle—or money—are all subject to detachment from their usual sign value, if any. They are all incipient symbols, raw material to be reassembled by Raskolnikov's own radical eye and psyche. As such, spatial images accumulate into the kind of self-reflexive patterns within a closed visual system which Frank has in mind. The novel gains compositional cohesion as a web of such intersections between Raskolnikov's subconscious and a kaleidoscope of unpredictable objects and forms. As that web gradually fills out it supersedes the realist's traditional reliance on chronology, causation, descriptive verisimilitude, and a reliable narrator. Here visual images assume a compositional value by the sheer density of their accumulation and juxtaposition.

With Raskolnikov's definition largely bound to the *bricolage* of unexpected object meeting unconscious process, we come to the broader question of how that visual ordering of psyche helps shape the novel's overall ideology. The question has two somewhat involved answers which, together, go to the heart of Dostoevsky's divided world view in the 1860s.

In one sense the very randomness of the spatial fields unfolding around Raskolnikov anticipates the more general denial of history and cultural traditions common to the West's modernist aesthetic. That is, his rejection of his society and family is of a piece with the modern Western hero's conclusion that life is a pastiche of disconnected experiences, none of which has meaning beyond the transient utility he happens to take from it. At odds with the urban world he inherits, Raskolnikov finds enticing hints of a new self scattered among the broken fragments of the new cityscape. With his sense of reality bound to what strikes his eye and unconscious mind, Raskolnikov journeys into the kind of relativism and epistemological doubt common to much modern fiction. His alienated consciousness drifts toward the same kind of "reality . . . possessed of an infinite number of perspectives, all equally veracious and authentic,"[13] which Ortega y Gasset sees as typifying the emerging twentieth century.

Like later examples of the alienated hero, Raskolnikov is eager to subordinate the world to his own, at times capricious, will, to "be a Napoleon," to "say his own word." What Bakhtin calls the "unfinalizedness"[14] of Dostoevsky's art is itself consonant with the modernist conception of life as so many moments which are freed of sequence or synthesis. With time stopped and his inner self engrossed in the odd visual forms he seizes upon, Raskolnikov has the sensation that life is malleable, supremely open to his private manufacture. Yet the multiple potentials of an unlimited self neither cohere nor satisfy him. The prospect he faces is an early example of the modern antihero's flight from culture into the alienation of multiple, value-neutral experiences. The price Raskolnikov comes close to paying is giving up forever the hope of finding what life might mean as a whole. As Svidrigailov suspects, Raskolnikov is capable of committing suicide.

In this respect Raskolnikov seems trapped in a condition which the contemporary Dutch critic Douwe W. Fokkema calls "metalingual scepsis."[15] It is a mistrust of language's capacity to convey past values into present experience in any meaningful or usable form. It is for Fokkema a basic premise of postrealist fiction generally.[16] The term's reference to broken continuity and an embrace of unresolved doubt applies well to Raskolnikov's sense of estrangement from his culture's core historical beliefs. His attraction to a world filled with physical images which carry the unjoined parts of himself carries considerable existential danger for him, as when he is tempted by suicide on the bridge. The value of Svidrigailov is largely that of illustrating the ultimate fate awaiting one who fully accepts such scepsis.

Dostoevsky's potent modernist use of a visual composition is only part of the story, as his prescient vision of private experience is only part of his greater divided vision of modern life. Dostoevsky's stick always has two ends, and the alienated Raskolnikov also serves clearly recognizable Orthodox and Slavophile beliefs, beliefs held by the author himself. Of particular interest to the present discussion is the suggestion that the spatial properties resonating through the novel's important scenic moments also serve those religious and cultural tenets.

After all, Raskolnikov does, finally, discover and experience his own authenticity—not in the solipsism of private will, but in communion with the same religious and national values he denies. He is one of Dostoevsky's great intellectual sinners whose egocentrism brings him to an existential crisis which, paradoxically, spurs his spiritual reformation. The nature of that reformation has an allegorical quality which, as Michael Holquist suggests, advances a timeless spiritual vision of *kairos*[17] in the novel, a time-less alternative to realism's general attention to a character's dependence on social and biographical history.

Crime and Punishment is an important Christian document, and the term "Medieval morality play," which Konstantin Mochulsky uses[18] to describe Raskolnikov's experience of crime and confession, is central to the work's final metaphysical statement. The coincidence of self-imposed isolation from and reunion with the Russian community localized in Raskolnikov has a clearly homiletic value. It is an old Christian repetition of man's free will coinciding with his discovery of divine grace. Of particular interest is Mochulsky's suggestion that the novel's religious world view itself is realized as a "unity of place,"[19] subject to a visual and spatial organization.

As will be suggested here, this second visual organization in the novel shares certain principles common to the icon. First, the novel replicates verbally some of the icon's optical properties to present man's encounter with experience outside the ordinary limits of everyday reality. And, second, this encounter with a higher realm carries a message of religious grace, Raskolnikov's discovery of personal inclusion within that Neoplatonic ideal. Here Raskolnikov's visual progress through the novel has a richly allegorical potential in its repetition of one of Russia's most popular parables and icons, the story of Lazarus. In this second spatialized organization of narrated scenes, Dostoevsky develops the timeless Lazarus story within the modern city, joining narrated and visual text in ways that draw on the distinguished Russian religious traditions of iconography.

Raskolnikov's passage from isolation to reunion with the collective of his *narod*, his community, reflects Dostoevsky's own answer to the skeptical relativism and materialism then gaining strength in modern Russia. As early as 1858 Dostoevsky wrote his brother Mikhail about the same problem in Russia of that new, Westernized generation of whom he complained to Mikhail Katkov in September 1865.[20] In both cases Dostoevsky clearly indicates that the new generation's obsession with an amoral intellect is one of those badly thought-out ideas which seem to hang in the air. Edward Wasiolek, in his commentary on the letter to Katkov, points out how Dostoevsky saw Christianity's moral force as the only viable answer to Raskolnikov's—and his generation's—dangerous aggrandizement of the private ego.[21] Raskolnikov represents not only Russia's modern need to confront its legacy of communal spirituality, but also a potential reintegration back into the origins of that legacy.

To a considerable degree this Christian value of Raskolnikov as a religious metaphor develops out of the same interplay of the hero's unconscious with spatial forms discussed above. Indeed, it is the union between what arrests his eye and guides his psychological movement from isolation to regeneration that underlies the novel's liturgic value. Dostoevsky's joining of spatially ordered scenes to his hero's roiled subjectivity advances a highly traditional, essentially medieval, answer to the amoral individualism of Russia of the 1860's.

This second visual ordering of images in and between important scenes invokes a thoroughly Orthodox conception of man's place in a God-centered cosmology. More particularly I would suggest that key scenes in the novel are organized in ways which replicate certain optical principles and themes common to the medieval Russian icon. In turn, the narrative value which guides the icon's formal organization is itself fundamental to the allegorical potential of Raskolnikov's movement through solipsism towards an epiphany of reconciliation with Russia's communal religious legacy.

It is perhaps not all that surprising that Dostoevsky should adapt some visual and homiletic properties of the icon to the composition of *Crime and Punishment*. As Joseph Frank points out at different points in his multivolume biography of the author, Dostoevsky was perhaps the most traditional believer among his Russian novelist-contemporaries.[22] The value of the icon as a focus for his artistic imagination is in keeping with the central value of the image (*obraz*) within popular Russian culture generally. The icon has, after all, traditionally been considered the homiletic equal of the word in Russia.[23] The icon's unique importance for the Orthodox—as the precise point at which human limitation in nature intersects with divine grace—translates well into the novel's meditation on a modern hero's search for some higher meaning to his life amidst the devitalized routines of his temporal world. Dostoevsky was a sensitive participant in his visually oriented, religious culture. It should not be surprising, then, that the semiosis involved with seeing the icon's organization of space, and the allegory it advances, can serve as a model for the semiosis of reading his written text.

A few remarks outlining the icon might be helpful at this point in our discussion of the novel. The icon contemplates scenes from the Bible or the lives of saints which declare the mystery of man's access to divine grace outside history and nature. That mystery is central to the technique of painting and determines all visual relationships depicted. As a result, events, objects, colors, and architecture, as well as human forms and gestures, are not represented "realistically" in the icon, at least not in the ordinary sense of the word, but as manifestations of that mystery. Purposeful visual distortion is prominent, and its range of detail is strictly subordinated to religious expressiveness. The result is a Neoplatonic vision of what Leonid Ouspensky calls the "essential" meaning behind all being.[24]

Centering on the mystery of grace which elevates individuals beyond their own natural limits, the icon depicts scene and topic with distinctive optical effects. For example, there is no illusion of depth in the icon because the miracles it depicts are meant to fill the entire scope of the painting. Therefore, naturalistic details, converging lines, volume, and size relative to the viewer's external position are all eliminated. In the icon's world, all things and people radiate from the center, from God; nothing is independent of that center. This is also why shadows are impossible, for the icon is illuminated from within by divine light which suffuses the entire depicted scene. As Ouspensky describes it, "there are no shadows in the Kingdom of God."[25] By eliminating the independence of naturalistic detail, perspective, and light within a realistic volume of space, the icon denies the viewer's penetration into or behind those images: "In the icon space and volume are limited to the surface of the panel and must not create an artificial impression of going beyond it."[26] Thus the work's visual symbolism must be taken in as a whole, as expressing a reality beyond optical rules of the temporal world. By removing the image from ordinary realistic perception and interpretation, the picture states the primacy of a religious message.

To pursue the specific proposal advanced here—that the allegorical union in Raskolnikov of human isolation and religious epiphany accords with basic optical properties of Medieval Russian art—we can focus on a limited number of the icon's characteristics which have particular compositional value in *Crime and Punishment*. These center about the structural value of inverse perspective and the specific religious allegory which this perspectival system serves in the icon.

The icon's inverse perspective gives a unique order to what we see, how we interpret the whole of a visual field, and how that field reveals the Neoplatonic religious view. Dostoevsky's spatial organization of key scenes in the novel presents us with striking parallels to characteristics of inverse perspective as we contemplate a visual order which relates Raskolnikov to what he sees in ways which move him towards Dostoevsky's celebrated phrase "reality in a higher sense."

The optical organization of Raskolnikov's psychological perception of urban environments celebrates a recognizable body of narrated Christian belief. The specific allegorical "story" visually ordered for us in *Crime and Punishment* is that of Lazarus, one of Russian Orthodoxy's most revered homiletic mysteries. Like Lazarus, Raskolnikov is shut away within a fearful isolation—not literal death, but the condition of solipsism within a modern secular city. By grace he, like Lazarus, is transfigured by a restoration to the loving community from which that isolation has excluded him.

The technical implications of what we know about inverse perspective are important to Dostoevsky's spatial organization of scenic moments in *Crime and Punishment*. Inverted perspective shifts the viewer out of temporal experience into the center of a divine mystery. When our point of view is located within the icon's pictorial center, inside the space occupied by the icon's central figures, we are surrounded by the depicted world as it radiates outward, towards the icon's farthest edges. The effect of our being put visually inside the picture—as if looking out instead of looking in—distorts the posture of human figures, imparts an unnatural torsion to architecture, and reverses our usual sense of distance as denoted by converging lines.

In short, we are called on to give up our ordinary optical sense of reality, just as we are called on conceptually to move from our daily routines into the traditional Orthodox world view. Perhaps the most famous example of this spatial distortion is Rublev's *The Holy Trinity* (fig. 4-1). The lines of the platform which the angels occupy spread out, rather than converge as we would expect in direct perspective. By manipulating the optics of our perception, as if we were located within the icon—looking out from its center, connected to its visual elements—the artist keeps his central figures, and us, firmly located within the depicted mystery.

Inverse perspective is perhaps the icon's most basic feature and stands in clear contrast to the direct (realistic) perspective which became the artistic norm during the Renaissance.[27] While the viewer of an icon is made a participant within the whole of a religious cosmology, from the Renaissance on the viewer perceives a naturalistic world which he looks in upon, as would an observer intellectually situated outside the depicted subject.

Both Boris Uspensky and Iurii Lotman suggest a most interesting parallel between certain narrative points of view and inverse perspective.[28] The realist novelist's illusion was that of an external vantage point from which the narrator, and the reader, could look in on character and event, as through an imaginary window or other aperture. The result repeats the direct perspective common to painting since the Renaissance, in which the viewer contemplates a scene or event from a spot beyond its frame. The presence of a doorway or window in the Renaissance work reinforced this separation of viewer from subject and proclaimed that the work's subject was to be considered from an emotional and conceptual distance.

Dostoevsky, however, locates his narrative voice within the scenic event, tying his reader to the visual and emotional specifics of Raskolnikov's own perception *as it occurs*. Without realism's privileged, external narration, we find ourselves inside the scene with the hero, looking out upon the unpredictable things which catch his eye. We are subject to his compulsive curiosity and associative memory because there is no external narrative place for us to stand. We lose independent perspective and judgment as we gain an intensified perceptual sense of unpredictable object and event. Therein lies one reason for *Crime and Punishment*'s uneven narrative line, the hectic

4-1 Andrei Rublev. *The Holy Trinity* [*Sviataia troitsa*]. 15th century. 44 × 55.5 in. Courtesy of Tretiakov Gallery, Moscow.

style of its narrative language, and our immersion into the multiple, independent narrative sources Bakhtin describes so well. In strictly formal terms, then, our sense of being put inside a scene approximates the inverse visual perspective of the icon and carries significant compositional implications for narrative. As Uspensky suggests, the icon painter makes the viewer "part of the world being depicted."[29] In Dostoevsky's novel, our sense of physical environment is that it radiates out from the central point of Raskolnikov's, and our own, subjectivity.

Appropriately, when Sergei Eisenstein proposed adapting Dostoevsky to the screen, he wanted to create the impression of inverse perspective by using special lenses and camera angle within key scenes.[30] The selectivity of highlighted spatial forms, which Eisenstein sought in this borrowing from the icon, is necessarily connected with the visual effect of locating the camera at the subjective center of the scene. The effect distorts the physical world, as with a wide-angle lens, to enhance our perceptual identification with Raskolnikov as he looks out onto his surroundings. This wide-angle distortion is itself a corollary to what Uspensky calls the convex quality of inverse perspective at the icon's center.[31] As a director, Eisenstein was especially attuned to Dostoevsky's visual potential as it applies to the larger issue of how the human mind takes in the world, responds to it, and tries to organize visual stimuli into a coherent field.

The convex quality of such visual fields in the icon thus has potential value for our sense of Raskolnikov's physical perception. In holy image and novel alike, what arrests the eye obliterates normal distance and ignores intervening objects. The result is a two-dimensional or flat visual and narrative plane on which all objects in the scene become available to the central figure. This largely accounts for the difficulty we have in keeping an objective sense of how detail is arranged within spatial volume in many of the novel's scenes (something less the case, for example, in Turgenev).

To share Raskolnikov's perspective of the scene we must give up our own external position, adjusting ourselves to a very different visual orientation within which all objects represented derive their importance from the scene's focal point, which is itself aligned with the character's subjectivity. Here we remember Raskolnikov's fixation on such things as his hat, a door bell, or the shreds of his bloodstained sock. We have no sense of any objective context for such details, only those disjointed bits of the world which stand out from a generalized background to frighten or otherwise excite him. This results in a highly stylized ordering of detail determined by the extreme subjectivity flowing out of the scene's center (Raskolnikov's subjectivity). That subjectivity floods his surroundings like a lamp, highlighting now one, now another detail which stands out sharply from an otherwise nondescript backdrop. Relative distance between him and the thing that rivets his eye loses its usual meaning; objects are arranged and given meaning according to optical rules governed by the pressing needs of the figure looking at them, not by the illusion of realistic spatial volume. As in the icon, there is no shadow here, for gradations of light, like objects themselves, are determined by their symbolic value.

There are some interesting secondary results attached to this inverted perspective which clarify Dostoevsky's handling of scenic moments. Of particular significance here is that the details which arrest Raskolnikov's attention in one scene gain potency from their resonance in scenes we will witness or have already witnessed. That juxtaposition orients him, and us, towards related moments which collapse or eliminate elapsed time, exchanging its objective flow for a network of spatial references.

For example, Raskolnikov faints during his first visit to the police station, thereby attracting Porfiry Petrovich's attention. The reason for his behavior lies in the physical configuration of the police station (where he is questioned about the murder) and its striking visual similarities to the pawnbroker's apartment house (where he has committed the murder). The police office, like Alena Ivanovna's apartment, is on the fourth floor of a grubby, sprawling and noisy building. The motif of yellow colors that so characterizes the murder scene, including the gold Raskolnikov steals there, is repeated in the yellowish water he is given at the police station, in a glass which is itself yellow, and in the flashy gold jewelry worn by the German madam he sees there.

To continue this visual interfolding of shared details between scenes we note that the room in which Raskolnikov hides from Koch and the others has been freshly painted, exactly as have the rooms in the police office. Raskolnikov gets paint on his shoes in both places, a detail which adds to his sensation of bridging time and enhances his chronic anxiety about what exactly he must do next. Also, the fear of being seen, which he experiences while trapped in the apartment building, comes true in the crowded station. His fear both times is that he will be noticed, stared at, recognized for what he knows he has done.

This replication of spatialized scene, joining clearly marked visual images to the same order of fear about his discovery, erases ordinary time boundaries for Raskolnikov. The two places gain a physical, and psychological, equivalency. As spatial forms unite within his subconscious he becomes disoriented, unsure of exactly where he is. In each case he is out of control, prone to rash decisions, and drawn to the same desire to "get it over with" as a way of relieving the pressure he feels in himself and sees in surrounding details. Motive and behavior, then, are primarily available to us through the shared visual fields Dostoevsky creates. The narrative point of view in each is technically akin to the convex properties of inverse perspective.

As a central principle of medieval religious art, inverse perspective extends to the secondary technique of summation in the icon. Again, we find here a visual device which has a corollary in Dostoevsky's optics of narration. Uspensky explains the term as a "multilateral embrace," a central figure in space presented from multiple angles of vision simultaneously.[32] We must form a composite of these visual planes, thereby exerting considerable energy to form our own mental mosaic of what we see. The result is a feeling of remarkable roundness and simultaneity. These suffuse the icon with a complex of juxtaposed facts which far exceeds the realist's illusion of a singular, normative (external) perspective.

Picasso did much the same in this century with a montage of visual planes typical of his cubist works. As observers, our sense of involvement rises as we are drawn into the picture's simultaneous multiple angles. With no external place to locate ourselves "outside" the picture, we must confront a wholeness based on a composite of intersecting and contradictory visual senses of the subject. The result is an internal dynamism which removes a psychology expressed over time in favor of a single, tensive spatial gestalt.

Uspensky's chosen example for such spatial summation is the sixteenth-century *The Annunciation* (fig. 4-2).[33] It is a particularly good choice for our purposes, for the variety of visual planes involved correspond to a compacted, collapsed set of emotions in the Holy Mother at the appearance, and then the message, of Gabriel.

Compare this purely visual phenomenon with how Dostoevsky compresses Raskolnikov's typical mixture of moods—arrogance and humility, cold analysis and quick generosity—which distinguish him at particular moments when conversing with others (e.g., Sonya, Porfiry, Svidrigailov, or those at the Marmeladovs'). In conversation Raskolnikov does not so much exchange one mood for another as he expresses a morphology of constantly coexisting moods. What we read about his shifting thoughts is the function of sustained but contradictory potentials within himself, all going on at the same time. For much of the novel he is for us a complex of mental states which coexist at the same moment. When considered as all available

4-2 Moscow School. *The Annunciation* [*Blagoveshchenie*], 15th century. 17 × 21 in. Ikonen Museum, Recklinghausen, Inv. Norway.

at the same time, his ambivalence and sudden jumps to emotional extremes form the same sort of pattern of intersecting planes which the viewer must take in as a mosaic, as is the case in "summation."

Raskolnikov's ambivalence is made all the more pronounced by the presence of this internal simultaneity, a version of the inner dialogue in which, as Bakhtin has shown, multiple voices are in constant competition, quite beyond the scope of narrated sequence. Indeed, we miss the dynamic between those intersecting planes of mind if we apply to them the sense of intervening causes and change, of historical sequence, which typically cause mental shifts and changes in the realist novel.

The matter of the icon's frame also helps us grasp the importance of inverse perspective and its value to Dostoevsky in defining his hero. Uspensky makes the point that the icon lacks the formal border-frame typical of most secular painting. The reason is that any such formal separation of viewer from holy subject defeats the icon's ideological imperative—to include the viewer within the depicted mystery[34]—the goal served by inverse perspective generally.

Instead of the usual physical frame, icons tend to demarcate the center from the outer edges of a depicted scene by the arrangement and portrayal of objects and figures. This entails two visual events: putting relatively unimportant figures and objects (what Uspensky calls "extras," as in a movie) [35] at the outer edges, and rendering these conventionalized figures in direct perspective.[36] Thus the lesser semiotic value of incidental personae and details in an icon is what forms the frame. This is a condition stated by the affinity such figures and details have for the temporal world (the world the marginalized viewer is used to seeing), and by their more naturalistic status of being presented in direct perspective (again, a condition which the viewer leaves behind while contemplating the *obraz*).

The novel has numerous secondary characters who represent this normal workaday world. As in an icon, they inhabit the periphery of Raskolnikov's attention and our own. They mark off temporal routines from the hero's more vital spiritual drama. Here we find people like the kind charwoman Natasha, the explosive police lieutenant, the painters, Zametov, and many others. These characters inhabit a world whose surface exhausts its depth, what Georg Lukács calls a "biological and sociological life [which] has a profound tendency to remain within its own immanence."[37] Their concern with job and routine, like the spatial treatment that orders their description, refers to the kind of third-person omniscience which Goncharov or Turgenev employed. Money is present or absent, a room is comfortable or not, large or small. As on the periphery of an icon, such characters have reduced semiotic value. They are oriented outward, toward the secular and temporal periphery, not inward toward the work's symbolic center.

For example, when Natasha comes into Raskolnikov's room to give him his summons we first share her visual sense of the room as she passes through the doorway. She brings with her the realist's objective sense of scene. She sees Raskolnikov exhausted, holding the cut-off threads of his trouser cuff. When she laughs it is simply out of good humor at seeing a half-asleep man clutching trifles "like a treasure." His hysteria at being seen holding incriminating evidence, however, is the shock of a mind fixated on the single detail of those threads.

The scene thus contains two separate visual organizations. Subjected to the psychological equivalent of inverse perspective, we feel ourselves inside Raskolnikov's visual field, seeing a world distorted by his fear and dominated by a small number of highly selective details (the trouser cuttings). The general disorder of jumbled objects in the room has no objective value within his pressured mind. The other visual field, devoted to Natasha, is in direct perspective. Entering the scene from outside, she takes in the whole visual ground in a dispassionate, utilitarian way, seeing cluttered trifles which make her laugh, and concentrating on the tea she has brought a sick tenant. Thus Raskolnikov and Natasha inhabit different realities, psychologically as well as visually, which we as readers must hold in our mind at the same time, much as the initiated can appreciate an icon in which two perspectives coexist in space.

The allegorical and homiletic value of the icon's visual organization is served by the technique of perspective, summation, and frame. There are two scenes in *Crime and Punishment* which, when considered together, present an especially good example of how technical optics facilitate the allegory of Lazarus (long considered the organizing theme behind the novel's religious ideology)[38] to organize the novel's central theme.

The first scene is that in which Raskolnikov hides his paltry loot under a stone in an out-of-the-way Petersburg courtyard. The second is the decisive second interview he has with Sonya in her room. It is here that he agrees to go to the symbolic crossroads and confess before the multitude. The rigorously flat, two-dimensional plane of the icon's panel is especially prominent in the architecture of each scene. The small number of details which Dostoevsky emphasizes in both lends them that uncluttered "monumental" quality whose highest expression marks the classic icons of Rublev in the fifteenth century. The courtyard is "enclosed on two sides by blank walls. On the right, directly by the entryway, the blank unwhitewashed wall of a neighboring four-story house jutted into the yard."[39] Note the distortion of architectural angles, so common in inverse perspective: "On the left, parallel to the blank wall, also starting directly by the entryway, ran a wooden fence—about twenty paces into the yard, with a sharp turn then to the left. It was a vacant, secluded spot" (114). From behind the fence Raskolnikov can see "the corner of a low, sunken stone shed."

Dostoevsky directs our eye as if we were reading a schematic plan. It is a strikingly sparse scene emphasizing improbable angles and flat, empty spaces, with none of the visual depth common to realistic painting or narrative description. It is an abstract place, undefined by ordinary human activity, ready to accept an overlay of symbolism. The only details we are given come in the phrase "various odds and ends were lying about" (114), as if these were incidental, the conventionalized decorative objects one sees at the periphery of an icon.

The central focus in this visual field is, of course, Raskolnikov hiding his sin-laden booty under the rock. An allegorical value is paramount here; the blank flatness of the background keeps our attention on the moral question of the hero entombing his soul along with the money and gold. Framing this visual center we read that, on the other side of the wall from where Rodion stands, there are people going about their daily business on the sidewalk. The thin line of the wall closes his essential drama off from the peripheral world of history and nature. The visual scheme is presented as of the sort, seen from above, as in many medieval paintings.

We see both sets of activity simultaneously, clearly receiving the message of their different value. This separation of focal from incidental descriptive planes, which exist simultaneously in space, replicates what Uspensky sees as a fundamental schematization of space in the icon generally: "[T]he central figures (the figures in the foreground) are opposed to the secondary figures by the fact that there is a lesser degree of semiotic quality or of conventionality in their description. A lesser degree of semiotic quality is naturally associated with a greater degree of realism (verisimilitude) in the description; the central figures, as opposed to the secondary ones, are less semiotic (conventional) and, accordingly, more lifelike."[40] Hanging exactly over Raskolnikov's head as he struggles with the stone is a piece of illiterate graffiti, "No hangin' 'round allowed." As readers we are struck by this modern, urban variant of the abbreviated emblemata found in so many icons based on stories from the Gospels.

This visually rich symbolism of entombment is carried to its allegorical end in Raskolnikov's second visit to Sonya's room. This is one of the novel's most famous moments. It is also here that we find a striking reproduction of the same architectural plan and specific images which distinguish Raskolnikov's burial of self along with the stolen money. The scene with Sonya is a symbolic complement, the second member of a diptych, in which the hero is called forth from his tomb. Sonya's room is described as large with low ceilings: "It had a highly irregular rectangular shape, which gave it a grotesque aspect. A wall with three windows facing the canal embankment cut across the room at an angle, so that there was one terribly sharp corner that plunged into depths one could not even make out in the weak light. . . . The other corner was disproportionately wide" (327).

As in the earlier "burial" scene we note here distorted and improbable angularity of architectural lines and corners, sharply delineated shadows, and scanty detail scattered randomly about a flat, open, and abstract surface. These combine to deny the reader access to the illusion of objectivity in what we see. We must give up that privilege and put ourselves, instead, inside the description in order to "see" the scene and take in its thematic message.

The two-dimensionality of the scene is prominent here, as in its earlier complement; in both cases it enhances an unambiguous lesson. Likewise, there is a semiotically weak periphery which is extraneous to the scene's visual center. This again reproduces in words the optical character of inverse perspective, where distance fans out from the center towards the semiotically less important, rather than narrowing into converging lines, as occurs in direct perspective. The icon-like value of the place is completed by dedication to a sense of spatial abstraction, a plane without temporal orientation: "In the whole large room there was almost no furniture. . . . By the opposite wall, close to the sharp corner, stood a small chest of drawers, made of plain wood, which seemed lost in the void" (327–28).

Dominating this flat, abstract space we find Sonya reading aloud the story of Lazarus being called forth from tomb to new life. As an eidetic spatial detail to make its diptych parallel with Raskolnikov's burial the more clear we note Dostoevsky's remark that the room suggests a tool shed, a visual rhyme with the stone shed included in the courtyard's description. The stone, of course, is a central symbol in "The Raising of Lazarus" within Russian iconography, for it is the reminder of Lazarus' being sealed away and the grace of his release from the limits of that isolation.

We need not dwell on the relevance of Lazarus' resurrection to Raskolnikov. It is, however, worthwhile to mark the degree to which Dostoevsky endows these two scenes, the beginning and conclusion of the work's central allegory, with a specific rhyming of architectural and visual properties. These paired moments are morphologically joined to state a profound difference, optically and metaphysically, from the ordinary world. They stand side by side, not in real time, but visually, like two joined panels which, together, proclaim a Christian miracle—the intersection of human will and divine grace.

Given Dostoevsky's Orthodox biography, within which icons were synonymous with Gospel narratives, it is perhaps not unexpected that he moves our mind by organizing our eye within his narrative composition. Dostoevsky lifts Raskolnikov out of history into contact with religious essence. The spatial order of scene, and connections between scenes, portray a mind desperately seeking meaningful permanence in the midst of modernity's confusion and impermanence. When we admit the possibility of a distinctly visual-spatial ordering to Dostoevsky's art, then such intersections are enriched by the extraordinary wealth of spirituality which has so long moved within the icon.

Notes

1. E. M. Forster, *Aspects of the Novel* (New York: Harcourt Brace & Co., 1927), 86.

2. See Norman Friedman, "Point of View in Fiction: The Development of a Critical Concept," in *Approaches to the Novel*, ed. Robert E. Scholes, rev. ed. (San Francisco: Chandler, 1961), 113–42.

3. José Ortega y Gasset, *The Modern Theme* (New York: Norton & Co., 1933), 90.

4. Roger Shattuck, *The Banquet Years: the Origins of the Avant Garde in France, 1885 to World War I*, rev. ed. (New York: Vintage Books, 1968), 347.

5. See Joseph Frank, "Spatial Form in Modern Literature," in *The Widening Gyre* (New Brunswick, N.J.: Rutgers University Press, 1963), 13.

6. Ibid., 14.

7. Ibid., 12–13.

8. Sharon Spencer, *Space, Time and Structure in the Modern Novel* (New York: New York University Press, 1971), 98–99.

9. Frank's concept of spatialized fiction has on occasion been applied to *Crime and Punishment*. Most notably, James M. Curtis has convincingly described Dostoevsky's emphasis on particular details (e.g., hats and dresses) which, by their repetition at widely different points in the novel, create

common linkages between the lives of those who wear them (see Curtis, "Spatial Form as the Intrinsic Genre of Dostoevsky's Novels," *Modern Fiction Studies* 2 [1972]: 147). Then, too, Curtis sees Dostoevsky as mapping St. Petersburg, much as Joyce would Dublin, to orient Raskolnikov towards one or another landmark important to his subconscious struggles with his divided inner potentials (e.g., when he stands on the Voznesensky Bridge and sees what Curtis is sure is Sonya's apartment window (ibid., 153).

10. The whole issue of thresholds—doorways, windows, bridges and the like—has been actively discussed in Dostoevsky criticism for some time. One of the best general analyses of the symbolic importance of such liminality is found in V.N. Toporov's "O strukture romana Dostoevskogo v sviazi s archaichnymi skhemami mifologicheskogo myshlenia" [Concerning the structure of Dostoevsky's novel relative to archaic schemes of mythological thinking], in *Structure of Texts and Semiotics of Culture*, ed. Jan Van Der Eng and Mojmir Grygar (The Hague and Paris: Mouton & Co., 1972), 225-302.

11. Murray Krieger, "Ekphrasis and the Still Movement of Poetry: or, *Laokoön* Revisited," in *Perspectives on Poetry*, ed. J.L. Calderwood and H.I. Toliver (New York: Oxford University Press, 1968), 338.

12. John Jones, *Dostoevsky* (New York: Oxford University Press, 1983), 213.

13. Ortega y Gasset, *The Modern Theme*, 91–92.

14. Mikhail Bakhtin, *Problems of Dostoevsky's Poetics* (Berkeley: University of California Press, 1986), 144.

15. Douwe W. Fokkema, *Literary History, Modernism, and Postmodernism* (Amsterdam: John Benjamins, 1984), 19.

16. Ibid., 28.

17. See Michael Holquist, *Dostoevsky and the Novel* (Princeton: Princeton University Press, 1977), 93.

18. Konstantin Mochulsky, *Dostoevsky: His Life and Work*, trans. M A Minihan (Princeton: Princeton University Press, 1967), 296.

19. Ibid.

20. See Dostoevsky's letter to his brother Mikhail of 1858 in *Letters of Fyodor Dostoevsky*, ed. Avram Yarmolinsky (New York: Horizon Press, 1961), 100.

21. Edward Wasiolek, *The Notebooks for "Crime and Punishment"* (Chicago, University of Chicago Press, 1978), 170.

22. See Joseph Frank, *Dostoevsky: The Seeds of Revolt, 1821–1849* (Princeton: Princeton University Press, 1976), 43, and Joseph Frank, *Dostoevsky: The Stir of Liberation 1860–1865* (Princeton: Princeton University Press, 1986), 307.

23. See Leonid Ouspensky and Vladimir Lossky, *The Meaning of Icons*, trans. G. E. H. Palmer and E. Kadloubovsky (Cristwood, NY: St. Vladimir's Seminary Press, 1983), 30, 42, and Boris Uspensky, *The Semiotics of the Russian Icon*, ed. Stephen Rudy (Lisse: Peter De Ridder Press, 1976), 11.

24. Ouspensky, *The Meaning of Icons*, 26.

25. Ibid., 40.

26. Ibid., 41.

27. See Rudolf Arnheim, *New Essays on the Psychology of Art* (Berkeley: University of California Press, 1986), 159–78, for a detailed discussion of the historical shift from inverse to direct perspective.

28. See Uspensky, *Semiotics of the Russian Icon*, esp. 57, and Iurii Lotman, "Point of View In a Text," *New Literary History* 6 (1975): 339–52 (esp. 339).

29. Uspensky, *Semiotics of the Russian Icon*, 35.

30. See N. M. Lary, *Dostoevsky and Soviet Film: Visions of Demonic Realism* (Ithaca: Cornell University Press, 1986), 99.

31. See Boris Uspensky, *A Poetics Of Composition* (Berkeley: University of California Press, 1973), 144.

32. Uspensky, *Semiotics of the Russian Icon*, 49.

33. Ouspensky gives a detailed assessment of these compound responses, and the intersecting visual angles of the Virgin's posture which carry them, in his *The Meaning of Icons*, 172.

34. See Boris Uspensky, *Poetics of Composition*, 143.

35. Ibid., 156.

36. Ibid., 158–59.

37. Georg Lukács, *The Theory of the Novel*, trans. Anna Bostrock (Cambridge: MIT Press, 1971), 90.

38. The Lazarus reference for Raskolnikov is one that has often been raised. In his *Dostoevsky and the Novel*, 93, 98, Holquist suggests the story as a clue to Raskolnikov's creation of a meaningful identity for himself. In a rather fuller assessment of this parallel Konstantin Mochulsky, in his *Dostoevsky*, 274, points out that the intellectual isolation Raskolnikov endures is a necessary prelude to his life's broader possibilities, which coincide with Sonya reading the Lazarus story. Mochulsky considers this second interview with Sonya "the most mystical scene" (277) of the novel. The claustrophobic imagery of Raskolnikov's room and the mental tension he feels there are, of course, well served by the "entombment" of Lazarus when applied to his own isolation during much of the novel.

39. F. M. Dostoevsky, *F. M. Dostoevskii: sobranie sochinenii v desiati tomakh* [F. M. Dostoevsky: Collected works in ten volumes], ed. L. P. Grossman et al. (Moscow: Gos. Izd., 1956–58), 5:114. Further parenthetical references in the text are to this edition.

40. Uspensky, *Poetics of Composition*, 163.

Chekhov's Use of Impressionism in "The House with the Mansard"

Paul Debreczeny

The subtitle "An Artist's Story" which Anton Chekhov gave to his "House with the Mansard" (1896) alerts the reader to the role of the visual arts in the shaping of the narrative. It scarcely needs more than the introductory page of the text to reveal that the first-person narrator sees the world as contrasting structures of artistic space. The ancient mansion he rents has "a huge pillared hall, with no furniture but a wide sofa on which I slept, and a table on which I played patience. All the time, even in still weather, the old ceramic stoves hummed, and during thunderstorms the whole house shook as though about to crack into pieces; it was somewhat frightening, especially on stormy nights when the ten large windows were all illuminated by lightning."[1] The house on the neighboring estate, Shelkovka, which the narrator soon comes to view, offers a contrast with its wide terrace, conducive to social intercourse, and its mansard whose low-ceilinged rooms imply old-fashioned domesticity and comfort. (Nikolai Gogol mentions that in the provincial city of NN, around which the action of *Dead Souls* [1841] takes place, "there were houses of one story, of two stories and of a story and a half with the inevitable mansard, which the provincial architects considered exceedingly handsome.")[2] As soon as the painter sees this cozy house he feels as though he had "fallen under the spell of something like home, something very familiar" (*Sochineniia* [Collected works] 9:175); "after the huge, empty pillared hall," he comments, "I felt at ease in this comfortable little house" (177); and even after his quarrel with Lida, when his break with the Volchaninovs is imminent, he still views it as a "dear, naive old building whose dormer windows seemed to look at me as if they were eyes" (189).

What is Chekhov's purpose in so clear an introduction of the visual arts into his narrative? Has he simply chosen a painter for his hero? Is he making a comment on the particular trend in painting which his hero represents? Or else, is he transposing the devices of one kind of art to another, providing a verbal equivalent to visual representation? Finally, how does his story fit within the development of the arts at the end of the nineteenth century?

Let me begin with his hero. His painterly perception of the world suggests that Chekhov is once more restricting the point of view to a subjective consciousness, as he had done before, especially in the "physiological sketches" of the late 1880s, such as "The Name Day Party" (1888), "A Nervous Breakdown" (1889), and "A Tedious Story" (1889). The reader familiar with the earlier stories may assume that this time the subjective distortions will arise, not from the perceptions of a woman about to have a miscarriage, a student about to see his moral world collapse, or an old professor about to die, but from those of an artist to whom the world means a composition of lines and colors. There is a touch of the "clinical study" in the passage where the narrator describes being a painter as almost a malaise: "My life is dull, burdensome, monotonous, because I am an artist, an eccentric; from my early days I've been torn apart by envy, dissatisfaction with myself, and disbelief in my profession" (*Sochineniia* 9:182).

The vision of the world we are presented with depends, of course, on what kind of an artist he is. The most readily available definition, attributed by the narrator to his antagonist, Lida, is a negative one. "She disliked me," he surmises, "for being a landscape painter, for not trying to depict the needs of the people in my pictures" (178). Lida might have read Vsevolod Garshin's story "Artists" (1879), which suggests that only mediocrities can be content with landscape painting. In Lida's thinking a truly gifted artist would be compelled to choose for his subject, as did Garshin's Riabinin, an industrial worker exposed to health hazards. Such a preference reveals Lida to be an adherent of the ideas of the "revolutionary democrats" of the 1860s, whose main representative in art criticism was Vladimir Stasov. She was no doubt brought up on realistic works by Ilya Repin and the *peredvizhniki* ("Itinerants," so called because of their traveling exhibitions).

Lida would have admired something like Repin's famous *They Hadn't Been Expecting Him* (fig. 5-1), which captures a dramatic moment—a prisoner, presumably political, arriving home unannounced. In addition to presenting a political "narrative," this

5-1 I.E. Repin. *They Hadn't Been Expecting Him* [*Ne zhdali*], 1884. Oil on canvas, 63.10 × 66 in. (160.5 × 167.5 cm). Courtesy of Tretiakov Gallery, Moscow.

painting displays all the attributes of the realistic school: it shows a perfect balance of line and color and, putting perspective to full use, achieves an illusion of three-dimensionality. Another Repin work that might have shaped Lida's taste in art is the well-known *Barge-men On the Volga* (1873), which is devoted to the suffering of the people and utilizes nature, beautifully rendered as it may be, only as a background to the human figures. The landscape is subordinate to humanity also in Grigorii Miasoedov's *Mowers* (1887), which shows a peasant family at work in a field. It might not have pleased Lida with its attempt to foreground the male head of the family, reducing women, younger men, and children in size, but it would have appealed to her by its glorification of the working people, making them look beautiful despite their toil, against a backdrop of radiant nature. Incidentally, it might have been this kind of idealization of labor that prompted the narrator to describe the peasants' work as "coarse animal toil," which keeps people "by the stove, at the washtub, and in the fields" (185) all the time, depriving them of a spiritual life.

The narrator's choice of landscape painting as his *métier* and the opinions he expresses mark him as an artist of Chekhov's own generation, to whom the movement of the *peredvizhniki* had already lost its freshness.[3] Chekhov's hero appears to be under the sway either of a Russian plein air group—forerunners of Impressionism, influenced by the French Barbizon School—or, very probably, of the Impressionists themselves.

Because of the pervasive presence of realism in the 1860s and 1870s, Impressionism had not at first won much following in Russia.[4] It is interesting that Repin, during a visit to France in the middle of the 1870s, was much taken with the new movement's techniques and himself painted a few Impressionist pictures. This, however, drew censure from his fellow *peredvizhniki*,[5] and he eventually reverted to realism with a social message—indeed it was in the late 1870s that he began work on *They Hadn't Been Expecting Him*.[6] Under these circumstances, the only kind of landscape painting that could survive in Russia was that which made accommodation with realism. Although it might have shifted its emphasis from people to nature, from line to color, and from narrative to atmosphere, it essentially remained a branch of realism until a new generation of artists emerged in the 1890s.

Chekhov had visited France twice—in 1891 and 1894—prior to writing "The House with the Mansard," but both visits were short, and the only exhibition he reported seeing was one at the *Salon* in 1891, representing academic traditionalists, who, Chekhov commented, were inferior to Russian painters of the day (*Pis'ma* [Letters] 4:220).[7] It is true that his guide through Paris during that first visit was Ivan Iakovlev-Pavlovskii, correspondent for the St. Petersburg *New Time*, who must have at least described a great deal of Parisian cultural life to Chekhov even if he did not have time to take him to more than a handful of places. This, however, merely confirms that Chekhov was familiar with contemporary cultural trends, without proving that he had a significant exposure to French Impressionists. Even the exhibition of French painters held in St. Petersburg in November 1895 was dominated by representatives of the *Salon* and the Academy, and contained only a few canvases by Claude Monet, Auguste Renoir, and Alfred Sisley.[8] By contrast,

Chekhov personally knew many Russian painters of his generation, since his brother Nikolai had studied at the Moscow School of Painting, Sculpture, and Architecture. It will therefore be best to look among Russian landscape painters if we want to discover what manner of art the narrator of "The House with the Mansard" pursues.

The man most likely to be revealing in this regard is Chekhov's friend Isaak Levitan, who had painted a landscape personally for Chekhov (*Istra Creek*, 1885–86), who was described by the writer as a "king" in comparison with the French landscape painters of the *Salon* (*Pis'ma* 4:220), and who served as a prototype (not appreciating the role) for the artist Riabovskii in the short story "The Grasshopper" (1892).[9] He has even been mentioned as the actual prototype for the hero of "The House with the Mansard," though the evidence to that effect is not conclusive.[10] He was one of those landscape painters who had actually gained acceptance by the realists even though he was Chekhov's contemporary, and continued exhibiting with the *peredvizhniki*.

Levitan's *Autumnal Day. Sokol'niki* (fig. 5-2) is close, except for the season, to the scene observed by Chekhov's narrator as he enters the park at Shelkovka: "The sun was already setting and long evening shadows lay over the flowering rye. Two rows of ancient, closely planted, towering fir trees stood against each other like two solid walls, forming an avenue of somber beauty. . . . It was quiet and dark . . . " (*Sochineniia* 9:171). The painting and the verbal depiction share an emphasis on the play of light on objects, and they both highlight atmosphere. What is more, Levitan's treatment of the human figure as just another item in the landscape is emulated by the narrator as he comes up against the house with the mansard: he describes the Volchaninov sisters against the backdrop of a sturdy white gateway adorned with lions, and remarks that the girls' charming faces seemed as familiar to him as the house itself. Even though he is a stranger intruding into their yard, he makes no apology, establishes no contact, and perceives them merely as figures contributing to an overall image.

In some other paintings, notably in *After the Rain. Reach of River* (fig. 5-3), Levitan comes close to the Impressionists' rendering of a shimmering quality of ephemeral light. This feature, too, appears in several of the narrator's verbal paintings. "Only high in the treetops could one see a brilliant, gold, glimmering light, iridescent like rainbows on the spiders' webs" (*Sochineniia* 9:174), he says of the

5-2 I. I. Levitan. *Autumnal Day. Sokol'niki* [*Osennii den'. Sokol'niki*], 1879. 24.9 × 19.7 in. (63.5 × 50 cm). Courtesy of Tretiakov Gallery, Moscow.

approach to the park; the village behind the house draws the narrator's attention chiefly by a "high, narrow belfry with its cross blazing as it reflected the last rays of the setting sun" (175); and the most notable features in the nocturnal landscape are "the pale reflections of the stars shimmering almost imperceptibly on the surface of the pond" (187).

5-3 I. I. Levitan. *After the Rain. Reach of River [Posle dozhdia. Ples]*, 1889. Oil on canvas, 31.5 × 49.2 in. (80 × 125 cm). Courtesy of Tretiakov Gallery, Moscow.

Most of Levitan's paintings are not fully impressionistic since they preserve realistic perspective. Also, he is noted for the careful finish to his work—a feature most French Impressionists would have concealed even if a lot of work had gone into the casual look of their sketches. Chekhov's narrator, habitually drawing sketches [*etiudy*] (179, 181), appears to be more of an Impressionist than his reputed prototype. Moreover, his observation that in the moonlight "the dahlias and roses in the bed before the house were distinctly visible and looked the same color" (189) sounds like an Impressionist manifesto. Indeed, during the first half of the 1890s, when realism was losing its grip on the artistic scene and Repin published a series of letters from abroad arguing against utilitarianism in Russian art,[11] Impressionism did exert some influence on younger Russian artists. Superseded as it was by that time in the West, it did not gain dedicated adherents in Russia; yet several Russian painters went through a brief impressionistic phase before moving on to Symbolism, Expressionism, Constructivism, or other trends.[12]

The Russian painter whose impressionistic phase lasted perhaps the longest was Konstantin Korovin—also acquainted with Chekhov through Levitan.[13] His sketch [*etiud*] *In the Summer* (fig. 5-4), painted the same year Chekhov wrote his story, strikes the viewer as a work of pure Impressionism, and comes very close to Chekhov's representations of his female characters in their colorful dresses blending in with the surrounding trees and shrubs. ("On weekdays she [Zhenia] usually wore a bright blouse and a dark blue skirt. She and I would stroll about, pick cherries for jam, or go rowing . . . " [*Sochineniia* 9:179].)

Using Impressionism to characterize his narrator does not, of course, make Chekhov an Impressionist. He could have disliked Impressionism and still made it an attribute of his hero. On closer examination, however, one may well conclude that an impressionistic vision informs not only the perceptions of the character but also the literary structure of the story. As H. Peter Stowell has observed, the Impressionist painter's subjects—"snow, blossoms, clouds, sailboats, crowds, steam, speed, and mist"—are not appropriate for the impressionistic writer, for the subjects of fiction are "the myriad intrigues of changing human relationships." The question is whether a writer renders "love, jealousy, growing up and growing old, daydreams, sleeplessness," and so forth, in an impressionistic way, that is, whether he presents these human actions or states of being as "impalpable surfaces of sensory data."[14]

5-4 K. A. Korovin. *In the Summer* [*Letom*], 1895. Courtesy of Tretiakov Gallery, Moscow.

Ever since Lev Tolstoy and Dmitry Merezhkovsky called Chekhov an Impressionist,[15] there have been attempts to use that designation for characterizing his mode of writing in general. As the literature on this question has been surveyed recently both by R. G. Kulieva in Russian and by Thomas Eekman in English,[16] there is no need to go into detail here, but it should be stated that Eekman is right to be skeptical about the correctness of the term when it refers to Chekhov in general. On the one hand Kulieva, in order to salvage the term for Marxist users, dilutes Impressionism to such a degree that it becomes a subcategory of "Realism" and loses meaning as a critical concept. Stowell, on the other hand, considers a host of modern writers from Gustave Flaubert to Alain Robbe-Grillet Impressionists, and, despite some valuable insights and formulations, ends up force-marching Chekhov into future trends all the way to Existentialism and the *nouveau roman*. It seems more justified to define literary Impressionism within the strict chronological limits of Impressionism in painting, and to view its techniques as equally limited. The most convincing analyses to date of Chekhov's impressionistic methods have used individual stories, notably "Sleepy" and "On the Road," as illustrations to general points.[17] I will also limit myself to drawing conclusions from one story only, even though I am ready to admit that some generalizations based on groups of stories could be valid.

A look at some impressionistic canvases by two more Russian painters of Chekhov's time will reveal something about the techniques of painting which he may have been employing to create literary form. Arkhip Kuindzhi's *Patches of Sunlight on Rime* (fig. 5-5) (like several of Mikhail Vrubel's paintings, *Bouquet in Blue Vase* [1887], for example), shows a precedence of color over line. Chekhov creates a similar effect of blurred outlines by a distance of years: his narrator is hard put to remember every detail, and concentrates his attention on recreating the mood of that memorable summer six or seven years ago. The narrator reports, for example, that "the moment she [Zhenia] got up of a morning she buried herself in a book and read, either seating herself in a deep armchair on the terrace, with her feet scarcely reaching the floor, or secluding herself with her book in an avenue of lime-trees, or else carrying it through the gates into the fields. She read all day, with her eyes riveted to the book; and only an occasional look of weariness, pallor, and perplexity revealed that her reading had caused a mental strain" (*Sochineniia* 9:179). Not telling the reader what the heroine read is a

5-5 A. I. Kuindzhi. *Patches of Sunlight on Rime* [*Solnechnye piatna na inee*], 1876–90. Oil on oilcloth, 9.6 × 10.7 in. (24.4 × 27.2 cm). Russian Museum, St. Petersburg.

particularly glaring omission for a Russian writer, brought up on Pushkin, whose heroine in *Eugene Onegin* is characterized by a full list of her readings. The allusion to Tatiana is unmistakable, since Pushkin's heroine, too, "Wanders alone among the stillness of the woods / With a dangerous book in hand" (chapter 3, stanza 10). The implication in Zhenia's case is that the exact detail is unimportant; the narrator cannot recall it; what matters is the atmosphere that surrounded the heroine's reading. "Write about something cheerful and bright green," Chekhov advised Elena Shavrova on 28 February 1895, "a picnic, for example" (*Pis'ma* 6:30). Chekhov might not have actually had Edouard Manet's *Le Déjeuner sur l'herbe* (1863) in mind, but his wish to see a literary work composed of mood and color is quite explicit.

In the kind of fiction Chekhov's reader was used to it was expected that the characters' emotions would be highlighted and clarified. The narrator of "The House with the Mansard," by contrast, leaves his motivations unexplained. "I loved Zhenia," he recollects; "I must have fallen in love with her because of the way she met me and saw me off, and because she looked at me tenderly, with admiration" (*Sochineniia* 9:188). Why he did fall in love, it seems, is a puzzle to himself; perhaps he wouldn't have if Zhenia had lived in a drab, dreary house. After a summer of walking and talking with her he is only able to "suspect that she had an unusual mind" (188). The changing moods of the park, the cozy atmosphere of the house, the play of light on the belfry are just as important as the characters' relationships; and all of these are seen on a two-dimensional picture plane, with no foregrounding of essentials. Chekhov, as Boris Pasternak has observed, "inscribed man in a landscape on equal terms with trees and clouds."[18]

The Vrubel painting I have referred to is a good example of the Impressionists' use of a "rainbow palette."[19] Vrubel's celebration of color for its own sake has its literary equivalent in Chekhov's lyrical passages. In chapter 2, for example, there is a description of how the narrator and Zhenia, returning from their walk, met Lida by the porch, after which the older sister distractedly rummaged through the house and wouldn't come to dinner until the rest of the family had finished their soup. She was cross about something, one would naturally conclude; but instead of responding to Lida's behavior in appropriate terms, the narrator joyously remarks: "For some reason I remember and love all these trivial details; I have a vivid recollection of all that day, even though nothing particular happened in it" (180–81). His insistence on joy even within the wrong context is also evident in his description of a Sunday morning: "When the garden, green and sparkling with dew, lies radiant and happy in the rays of the sun, when the oleanders and the mignonette smell sweet by the house, when the young people, just back from church, drink tea in the garden, when everyone is so cheerful and so charmingly dressed, and when you know that all these healthy, well-fed, attractive people will do nothing all the livelong day, I wish for life to be always like this. These were my thoughts that particular morning, too, and I went walking about the garden, ready to stroll about aimlessly, with nothing to do, all summer" (179). A celebration of idleness in the impoverished Russian countryside, which had recently suffered through famine and a cholera epidemic, seems to lack the proper perspective.

Most critics of "The House with the Mansard," after its appearance in the April 1896 issue of *Russian Thought*, were upset by its social and political implications.[20] Raised on the large ideological novels of Tolstoy and Dostoevsky, they wanted to know where Chekhov stood on the social issues he had raised in the story. In a letter to the editor a certain A. A. Andreeva wrote that some of the women she knew who had read the story had complained about Chekhov's lack of appreciation for Lida's useful work.[21] A reporter on the cultural scene, writing in *Russian News* under the pseudonym I-t, joined Lida in condemning the artist's "lack of a social instinct."[22] In general, the critics found it incomprehensible that the discussions between Lida and the narrator concerning burning issues of the day should be treated as so many patches of color on the canvas, along with trees and houses and a budding love relationship; that these weighty discussions should appear reduced in size and out of focus from the vantage point of the artist's bittersweet recollections. One is reminded of another painting by Vrubel, *Portrait of a Man in Traditional Costume* (fig. 5-6), which foregrounds the man's dress and shows a clear lack of interest in his person. Similarly, Zhenia as a person seems to be lost among the ample folds of the narrator's nostalgic remembrances. "She spoke to me of God, of life everlasting, of miracles. And I, unwilling to admit that I myself and my imagination would perish in death forever, would answer: 'Yes, human beings are immortal'; 'Yes, life everlasting awaits us.' And she would listen, believing me without demanding proofs" (180). The tilted perspective of the artist's memory makes philosophical questions less important than Zhenia's charming way of running ahead of him in order to look him straight in the eye when asking questions. As P. V. Sobolev has observed, the artist's emotional perspective also creates "artistic time": although, chronologically, the beginning of chapter 4 directly follows the end of chapter 3, the narrator breaks the flow of the narrative in order to introduce a different mood.[23]

The curious feature of the frame cutting across the man's eyes in Vrubel's *Portrait*—reminding one of Edgar Degas' *Ballet Seen From an Opera Box* (1885)—also has a literary equivalent in "The House with the Mansard." Up to the second half of chapter 4 we have been treated to a full account of the narrator's emotional state through a summer, but at this point the narrative breaks off abruptly.[24] How could a young woman like Lida become such a tyrant not only over her younger sister, but even over her mother? Why did those two submit to her will? Why did the painter give up so easily, not even attempting to find Zhenia? These questions perplexed Chekhov's readers so much that the critic A. M. Skabichevskii even suggested that the artist should have gone after Zhenia to the Penza Province: "After all, Penza Province is not beyond the seven seas, and once

5-6 M. A. Vrubel. *Portrait of a Man in Traditional Costume* [*Portret muzhchiny v starinnom kostiume*], 1886. Watercolor on paper, 10.9 × 10.6 in. (27.8 × 27 cm). Museum of Russian Art, Kiev.

there, far away from Lida, he could have tied the nuptial knot with Zhenia."[25] But the questions arising at the end of the narrative remain unanswered, and a sense of warped perspective is enhanced by gratuitous information given about irrelevant matters, such as Lida beating Balagin in the local elections and Belokurov marrying his obese mistress. The upper half of Zhenia's fate is cut off, so to speak.

As a formal feature, such a truncated structure is within the tradition of Impressionism, yet there is a difference. The Impressionist painters wished simply to establish an idiosyncratic angle of vision, suggesting that life could look like a broken surface at a given moment but it would continue beyond the cutoff point into ever-changing new shapes. Such an arrangement did not interfere with the generally cheerful mood of an impressionistic painting. The unabashed lyricism of several passages in "The House with the Mansard"—the narrator's focus on the "radiant and happy" garden, his joyous contemplation of the dear house even in the evening after his quarrel with Lida—suggests that Chekhov wished to create the general atmosphere of an impressionistic painting. It is true that a certain wistfulness hovers over the narrative from the beginning— the chronological distance intimating something irretrievable—but that wistfulness might not amount to more than "a sad recognition that everything, however long it may seem, comes to an end in this world" (182). Recollecting his temporary association with a lovely young woman, the narrator seems to be celebrating along with the Impressionists the many colors of life. But the ending is less than idyllic.

Lida's crass act of wilfulness, Zhenia's meek submission ("If only you knew how bitterly Mamma and I are weeping!" [190]), and the artist's passive acceptance induce the disturbing feeling that something has gone wrong. Instead of bringing a bittersweet experience to an acceptable though possibly melancholy conclusion, the denouement creates a jarring effect of bewilderment, which forces the reader to reexamine the text once more. Like Fedor Dostoevsky's novels, "The House with the Mansard" can only be understood when reread, when its component parts are arranged as though in a spatial configuration. (For a more detailed discussion of spatial form, see the essay by Roger Anderson in this volume.)

Several features of the text that are unsuspected at first sight emerge from a rereading. First of all, the artist may not have spent his summer simply loafing. More likely, he was a *flaneur* of Manet's type: keenly observing while affecting laziness.[26] Despite his claim that he is "a carefree individual, always seeking an excuse for constant idleness" (179), we see him at his easel with an admiring Zhenia behind his shoulder (179); he shows his sketches (not just one) to an equally appreciative Mrs. Volchaninova (181); and after the memorable Sunday he had spent at Shelkovka he reports that he "felt like painting for the first time that summer" (182). The context leads to the conclusion that a freewheeling, footloose existence is a precondition for artistic inspiration. "Idleness" acquires the Push-kinian connotation of "unfettered indolence, friend of contem-plation," which invites the Muse ("The Countryside," 1819). As far as his own profession was concerned, the artist had every right to defend himself from the kind of *vie engagée* that Lida would have

forced on him. In that case the contrast between him and Belokurov—one taking it easy yet accomplishing much, the other
bustling around with no result—falls neatly into place.

If, however, it turns out that he in fact had a productive summer
roaming the grounds of the house with the mansard, this puts a
different complexion on his relationship with Zhenia. It is telling
that on his way home after the Sunday at Shelkovka, just after he has
reported that he feels like painting, he advises Belokurov to fall in
love with one of the Volchaninov girls, either Lida or Zhenia—as
though his own interest did not extend beyond finding artistic
inspiration. Perhaps he just exploited Zhenia for his art, drawing out
her emotions in order to titillate his imagination; and even though
he claimed by the end of the summer that he was in love, he did not
find it hard to part with her because he had had what he had
sought—a productive summer. This makes him rather a self-cen-
tered man, stuck in a dull recoil from involvement, in which case the
words he addresses to Belokurov apply even more to himself: "Why
do you live in such an uninteresting way, why do you take so little
from life?" (182).

The ambiguities of the text, however, allow other interpretations.
One can take Zhenia as a Turgenevian heroine—like Elena of *On the
Eve* (1860)—who passively observes yet profoundly judges the clash
of social ideas around her and finally gives her hand, as a prize
awarded the winner, to the person who represents the "correct"
attitude.[27] Zhenia, it can be argued, listened to the debates between
the artist and her sister all summer and decided he was wrong when
he came to his final hysterical outburst: "The life of the artist is
meaningless, and the more talented he is, the more absurd and
incomprehensible becomes his role. . . . I don't want to work and will
not work. I don't want anything: let the earth swallow up the whole
damn thing" (187). As B. F. Egorov has observed, by the time the
narrator goes outside at the beginning of chapter 4 the relationship
between him and Zhenia has been reversed.[28] Now it is he who seeks
her glance, trying to clarify what she is thinking. And as soon as he
voices his despair once more—"Humanity will degenerate and there
will not be a trace of genius left" (188)—she decides to return to the
house, wishing him good night and using an imperative, her sister's
verbal mood, for the first time in the story: "Come tomorrow"
(188). He entreats her twice to stay with him a little longer and
mentally pictures her as his future "queen" (189); but to all intents
and purposes she has already rejected him, as expressed by her

gesture of throwing off his coat when he tries to protect her from the evening chill.[29] Her statement, after he kisses her, that "we have no secrets from one another, and I shall right now have to tell my mother and sister everything" (189) is a clear indication that she has given preference to her sister over him. Having understood her rejection to its full extent, he is of course not about to go after her to Penza.

Still another possibility, which Egorov has persuasively argued, is that the story is about the artist's potential emotional entanglement with Lida. A careful reading will reveal that the older sister does take interest in her new neighbor: when they first meet she counts herself among his admirers; she issues an invitation, saying "mother and I would be very glad to see you" (175), which conspicuously omits any mention of her younger sister; and when she so crossly bustles through the house, having just seen the artist and Zhenia return from their walk, she is probably jealous.[30] Even their final showdown is provoked by her, for it is she who turns to him, saying, "Excuse me, I keep forgetting that this sort of thing [local politics] doesn't interest you" (183). And in the course of the ensuing discussion she does give him the benefit of the doubt, listening and asking questions, rather than just laying down the law. The denouement, as Egorov sees it, has to do with his failure to come up to her expectations; and he only takes an interest in Zhenia as a consolation.[31]

One can go even a step further. There is no doubt that the artist finds Lida very attractive from the moment he first sets eyes on her, describing her as "slender, pale, very beautiful, with a great shock of auburn hair and a small, obstinate mouth" (175). The painter in him is especially pleased by her mouth, which is not only obstinate but also "finely drawn" (178). Egorov may well be right in suggesting[32] that it is the painter's sudden view of himself in comparison with the active, efficient Lida that brings on the depression reported at the beginning of chapter 2: "I was tormented by dissatisfaction with myself; my life, which was passing so rapidly and trivially, filled me with a sense of regret; and I kept thinking how good it would be to tear out my heart, which was becoming such a heavy burden" (178). One cannot help noticing the suicidal impulse that surfaces among his feelings just at a moment when he might be falling in love. If Lida likes to provoke him, the feeling is mutual: seated inactive at the bottom of the stairs, hearing her bustling about, he grumbles that in trying to cure people without proper medical training she might be doing more harm than good. Fair enough: this seems to be a valid argument, and if he really wanted to he could also argue his case as an artist. He could question what kind of a future Lida was building for her beloved mankind if she was to exclude beauty and joy. But he does not wish to win, it seems. In the final confrontation he comes out in favor of some kind of transcendental philosophy (totally alien to Chekhov himself) which, he says, should replace science. He also advances the absurd idea, perhaps in mockery of Tolstoy,[33] that if all the propertied classes (five percent of the population?) started to work the people would be liberated from backbreaking labor; everyone would have to toil only three hours a day and would be able to devote the rest of his or her time to matters spiritual. The crowning folly of his argument is that "it is not schools we need, but universities" (186). True, Chekhov is reported to have said just that, in a moment of exasperation when his school-building projects around Melikhovo seemed to be bringing painfully slow results,[34] but put in the context of the artist's discussion with Lida, the exclamation becomes absurd.

It is as though the artist had a compulsion to put himself in the wrong, in order to be punished by a figure at once seductive and authoritative—a teacher and an "admiral" (181), who, "slender, beautiful, lit up by the rays of the sun," holds a horsewhip in her hand (180). The portrait of Lida with a horsewhip is followed by the scene of her cross fluttering through the house which I have already mentioned; and Egorov's suggestion that her bad temper is precisely what puts him in a lyrical mood rings true.[35] He gloats over her face "aflame with anger" (187) after their final quarrel, too. She herself is no more accommodating, of course; and one has to conclude, without attempting deep analysis, that their tug of war is at best neurotic and holds no hope for a future. Zhenia is accidentally caught in the middle, which may be the reason why her fate is not followed up at the end of the tale.

The story's denouement, reverberating back through the text, produces, then, a mood incompatible with the lyrical tonality of the surface. If the Impressionists generally chose cheerful subject matter, celebrating life in a burst of color,[36] Chekhov is not one of them. Nor did the Impressionists, descendants as they were of Naturalism, wish to make their representations obscure: although they discarded perspective and clear outline, they claimed to be showing nature as it appeared to the accidental viewer, at a given moment, more distinctly than even the traditional realists had been able to do.[37] "The House with the Mansard," by contrast, presents a complex structure, open to different interpretations, with meanings not readily accessible to the reader. I would like to suggest that in this story Chekhov uses an impressionistic mode only to lure his readers into believing that they are being treated to bittersweet reminiscences with a melancholy but serene mood; and when their senses are lulled into lyrical receptiveness, he assaults them with a jarring, disconcerting conclusion.

Is Chekhov, subverting Impressionism as he does, alluding to some subsequent trend in the visual arts? Various post-Impressionist trends were already represented, if not yet prevalent, on the Russian artistic scene by 1895 and Chekhov was aware of them: he refers, for instance, to expressionism in "The Grasshopper" (*Sochineniia* 8:14).

Several of Kuindzhi's paintings, such as *Winter Sunset. Seashore* (1876–1890) could be considered examples of the latter trend. Although these paintings are still close to Impressionism, their somewhat arbitrary colors do not exclusively represent nature as perceived by the viewer: they are just as much projections of the painter's feelings on his subject. They convey dramatic emotion rather than a serene mood. One could say that the ultimate failure of Chekhov's characters to live up to their humanity produces as forceful an emotional effect as these dramatic colors.

Even further from Impressionism, Vrubel's *Seated Demon* (fig. 5-7), which is an illustration to Mikhail Lermontov's verse tale *The Demon* (1829-39), makes no pretense about representing earthly reality; its concern is to create a symbol of an imagined higher world that is also expressive of the inner workings of the painter's mind. By their formalistic arrangement of visual components and by their conspicuous thick masses of color, both Kuindzhi's *Winter Sunset* and Vrubel's *Seated Demon* draw attention to technique, baring their devices. Demanding emotional participation as well as mental work on the part of the viewer, they are not as readily comprehensible as Impressionistic paintings. Similarly, by manipulating his readers, making them reconsider and reconstruct their understanding of his story, Chekhov draws attention to artistic method.

These features of Chekhov's writing, parallel to post-Impressionism in the visual arts, demonstrate that he participated in a search for radical forms of modernism characteristic of fin-de-siècle culture in

5-7 M. A. Vrubel. *Seated Demon. A Sketch. [Demon sidaiashchii. Eskiz]*, 1890. Watercolor on paper, 5.2 × 10.6 in. (13.2 × 27 cm). Courtesy of Tretiakov Gallery, Moscow.

general. "The House with the Mansard," with its teasing use of Impressionism and with its deliberate ambiguities, represents a complex structure aimed at weaning the reader away from the easy comfort of accustomed aesthetic norms.

Notes

1. A. P. Chekhov, *Polnoe sobranie sochinenii i pisem* [Complete collected works and letters], 30 vols. (Moscow: Nauka, 1974–83), series *Sochineniia* 9:174. All subsequent citations from Chekhov will refer to this edition, with the series (*Sochineniia* or *Pis'ma*), the volume, and the page number indicated in parentheses within the text.

2. N. V. Gogol, *Polnoe sobranie sochinenii* [Complete collected works], 14 vols. (Moscow: Akademiia Nauk SSSR, 1937–52), 6:11.

3. For a discussion of the role of the *peredvizhniki* [Itinerants] in Russian culture, see Elizabeth Valkenier, *Russian Realist Art: The State and Society: The Peredvizhniki and Their Tradition* (Ann Arbor, Mich.: Ardis, 1977), 115–34.

4. See D. V. Sarab'ianov, *Russkaia zhivopis' XIX veka sredi evropeiskikh shkol* [Russian art of the nineteenth century among European schools] (Moscow: Sovetskii khudozhnik, 1980), 166–81.

5. Valkenier, *Russian Realist Art*, 117–18.

6. Sarab'ianov, *Russkaia zhivopis'*, 170–71.

7. The identity of the exhibition is argued in Simon Karlinsky and Michael Henry Heim, trans. and ed., *Anton Chekhov's Life and Thought: Selected Letters and Commentary* (Berkeley: University of California Press, 1973), 200, n. 7.

8. G. Iu. Sternin, *Khudozhestvennaia zhizn' Rossii na rubezhe XIX XX vekov* [The artistic life of Russia between the nineteenth and twentieth centuries] (Moscow: Iskusstvo, 1970), 262.

9. For a discussion of Levitan as a prototype for Riabovskii, see Chekhov, *PSSP, Sochineniia*, 8:431–35.

10. See S. Prorokova, *Levitan* (Moscow: Molodaia Gvardiia, 1960), 175; and L. P. Grossman, "Roman Niny Zarechnoi" [The novel of Nina Zarechnaia], *Prometei* 2 (1967): 255.

11. I. E. Repin, "Pis'ma ob iskusstve k redaktoru *Teatral'noi gazety*" [Letters about art to the editor of *Theatre Gazette*], *Teatral'naia gazeta* [Theatre Gazette] 31 October; 5, 7, 12, 17, 19 November 1893; rpt. Repin, *Vospominaniia, stat'i i pis'ma iz zagranitsy* [Remembrances, articles and letters from abroad], ed. N. B. Severova (St. Petersburg: E. Tile, 1901), 76–108; also Repin, "Zametki khudozhnika" [Notes of an artist], *Knizhki "Nedeli"* [Books of "The Week"] 1, 2, 6 (1894); rpt. *Vospominaniia*, 109–59.

12. Sarab'ianov, *Russkaia zhivopis'*, 171–81.

13. Konstantin Korovin, "My Encounters with Chekhov," trans. Tatiana Kusubova, *Russian Literature Tri-Quarterly* 28 (1973): 561–67.

14. H. Peter Stowell, *Literary Impressionism, James and Chekhov* (Athens: University of Georgia Press, 1980), 49.

15. A. B. Gol'denveizer, *Vblizi Tolstogo* [In the presence of Tolstoy] (Moscow: Goslitizdat, 1959), 68–69; and D. Merezhkovsky, *O prichinakh upadka i novykh techeniiakh sovremennoi russkoi literatury* [Concerning the reasons for the decline and new directions of contemporary Russian literature] (St. Petersburg: M. O. Vol'f, 1893), 83–84.

16. R. G. Kulieva, *Realizm A. P. Chekhova i problema impressionizma* [The realism of A. P. Chekhov and the problem of Impressionism] (Baku: Akademiia Nauk Azerbaidzhanskoi SSR, 1988), 8–33; and Thomas Eekman, "Chekhov—An Impressionist?" *Russian Literature* 15 (1984): 203–4.

17. On "Sleepy," see Charanne Carroll Clarke, "Aspects of Impressionism in Chekhov's Prose," in *Chekhov's Art of Writing: A Collection of Critical Essays*, ed. Paul Debreczeny and Thomas Eekman (Columbus, Ohio: Slavica, 1977), 123–33; for "On the Road," see Savely Senderovich, "Chekhov and Impressionism: An Attempt at a Systematic Approach to the Problem," in *Chekhov's Art of Writing*, 134–52.

18. Boris Pasternak, "Three Letters," *Encounter* 15, no. 2 (1960): 4.

19. For a discussion of the concept, see R. H. Wilenski, *Modern French Painters* (New York: Vintage Books, 1960), 1:11.

20. See a summary of critical reviews in Chekhov, *PSSP, Sochineniia*, 9:494–96.

21. Quoted from a manuscript; Chekhov, *PSSP, Sochineniia*, 9:494.

22. I-t [I. N. Ignatov], "Zhurnal'nye novosti" [Journalistic news], *Russkie vedomosti* [Russian Gazette] 117 (29 April 1896): 2.

23. P. V. Sobolev, "Iz nabliudenii nad kompozitsiei rasskaza A. P. Chekhova 'Dom s mezoninom' " [Notes on the composition of A. P. Chekhov's short story "The House With a Mansard"], *Uchenye zapiski Leningradskogo Gos. Pedagogicheskogo Instituta im. A. I. Gertsena* [Transactions of the Leningrad A. I. Hertzen Pedagogical Institute] 170 (1958): 237.

24. The aesthetic effect of this abrupt change of pace has been discussed by Senderovich, "Chekhov and Impressionism," 147.

25. A. M. Skabichevskii, "Bol'nye geroi bol'noi literatury" [Sick heroes of sick literature], *Novoe slovo* [New word] 4 (January 1897); rpt. Skabichevskii, *Sochineniia*, 3d ed., ed. F. Pavlenkov, 2 vols. (St. Petersburg: Iu. N. Erlikh, 1903), 2:593.

26. See Robert L. Herbert, *Impressionism: Art, Leisure, and Parisian Society* (New Haven: Yale University Press, 1988), 34.

27. For a discussion of Turgenevian elements in the story, see Joseph L. Conrad, "Chekhov's 'House with an Attic': Echoes of Turgenev," *Russian Literature* 26 (1989): 373–96.

28. B. F. Egorov, "Struktura rasskaza 'Dom s mezoninom' " [The structure of the short story "House With a Mansard,"] *V tvorcheskoi laboratorii Chekhova*

[In Chekhov's creative laboratory], ed. L. D. Opul'skaia et al. (Moscow: Nauka, 1974), 265.

29. Pointed out by Egorov, *V tvorcheskoi*, 266.

30. Ibid., 260.

31. Ibid., 263–64.

32. Ibid., 258.

33. Suggested by V. B. Kataev, *Proza Chekhova: Problemy interpretatsii* [Chekhov's prose: Problems of interpretation] (Moscow: Izdatel'stvo Moskovskogo Universiteta, 1979), 232–33.

34. See V. N. Ladyzhenskii, "Pamiati A. P. Chekhova" ["Memories of A. P. Chekhov,"] *Sovremennyi mir* [Contemporary world] 6 (1914): 114.

35. Egorov, *V tvorcheskoi*, 261.

36. H. H. Arnason, *History of Modern Art: Painting, Sculpture, Architecture*, rev. ed. (New York: Harry N. Abrams, 1977), 31.

37. See Arnason, *History of Modern Art*, 29, and Wilenski, *Modern French Painters*, 1:6.

The Composed Vision
of Valentin Serov

Alison Hilton

Coloristic harmonies do not, any more than musical ones, yield themselves to description and definition," wrote Aleksandr Benua in his *History of Russian Painting in the Nineteenth Century* (1902).[1] Thinking of Valentin Serov and other members of the Moscow school, whose works of the 1890s offered alternatives to the critical realism of the 1870s and 1880s, Benua continued: "The impressions from Serov's paintings are purely painterly, and perhaps indeed of a musical nature."[2] Like other artists and critics of the period, especially those in the World of Art (*Mir iskusstva*) group, Benua was searching for a new vocabulary appropriate to the visual effects—nuances and suggestions rather than descriptions—achieved by contemporary artists. The musical analogy is not surprising. Charles Baudelaire's phrase, "melody is unity within color" and G.-Albert Aurier's reference to painting as a "symphony determined by colors" were familiar to the World of Art group.[3] Moreover, the analogy was appropriate to Serov, the child of two composers, knowledgeable about music and at home in musical circles. Among his friends were writers, actors, and musicians, and he painted or drew memorable portraits of Rimsky-Korsakov, Glazunov, Shaliapin, Diaghilev, Karsavina, Pavlova, Ermolova, Stanislavsky and Gorky, among others.

Benua might well have extended his search for verbal equivalents to Serov's visual style into the realm of theatrical spectacle: both artists were involved in Sergei Diaghilev's ballet productions. The concept of the total work of art, or *Gesamtkunstwerk*, which Russians eagerly adapted from Wagner,[4] might be a key to understanding the nature of Serov's stylistic innovations, and the reasons why they were so important for artists of his own and a slightly younger generation. The idea implies not only the unification of diverse art forms but also a determination to achieve a heightened spiritual awareness through art. Benua credited Serov with bringing together the disciplines of portraiture, landscape, and genre painting, and with discovering the value of striking decorative effects unknown to the "sober realists" of the previous generation.[5]

Paraphrasing Benua's caution that nothing is more difficult than to describe Serov's paintings in words,[6] I would add that nothing is more tricky than to draw parallels between stylistic features in visual and musical or verbal art forms. Serov was certainly attuned to the literature, music, and theater of his time, though not so directly or continuously involved in literary illustration and theatrical production as were Benua, Konstantin Somov, and other members of the World of Art group. Unlike many contemporaries, Serov was not given to making pronouncements about art in general or about his own work. Only in a few cases is there evidence to relate Serov's use of a particular technique or style to the stylistic qualities of specific literary or theatrical forms. Focusing on such relationships means neglecting other important aspects of Serov's work, and I do not want to oversimplify and falsify his art by ascribing its style to any single factor. But I think that some innovations—essentially ways of going beyond the limits of realistic representation—were stimulated by his involvement in allied arts. Serov's illustrations, stage designs, and portraits of creative artists give indications of the ways in which he drew upon aspects of each genre, as Benua has suggested, in order to create new sensory effects and to convey subjective feeling on several levels. Considering these works as a group, together with his contact with men and women working in other fields of art, helps to explain how Serov's art, once seen as "pure, spontaneous realism,"[7] became a paradigm for the psychological subtlety and visual refinement characteristic of art at the turn of the century.

Born in St. Petersburg on 7 January 1865, Valentin Serov was introduced early to a cosmopolitan intellectual and musical circle. His father, Aleksandr Serov, was a composer and music critic, who advocated a Wagnerian or European-oriented school of music; his mother, Valentina Serova (née Bergman), was a pianist who later earned a reputation as a composer, social activist, and pioneer in musical education for peasants. They took four-year-old Valentin to Munich and to Bayreuth, to visit their friend Richard Wagner, but of this potentially formative experience Serov later remembered only how he used to ride on Wagner's huge St. Bernard dog.[8] (As an adult, he returned to Bayreuth for the operas.) When Aleksandr

Serov died, Serova continued her musical studies in Munich and later in Paris. In Paris in 1874, young Valentin began studying seriously with Ilia Repin, then becoming known as a realist painter. The following summer, they returned to Russia and lived at Abramtsevo, a country estate owned by Savva Mamontov, a railway tycoon and amateur singer and sculptor who would shortly become the founder of an important private theater and a major patron of contemporary Russian art. Serov was practically a member of the Mamontov family, living with them during the summers, and in autumn going to school at the Mai gymnasium in St. Petersburg, sometimes joining his mother in Kiev, or living with the Repins in Moscow. In 1880, Serov entered the St. Petersburg Academy of Arts. He became close friends with Mikhail Vrubel, and later with Konstantin Korovin and Isaak Levitan; together the four represented the most significant new voices in the art of the late 1880s and '90s. During his student years, Serov travelled widely in Russia and Europe, and often returned to Abramtsevo. It was in the sun-filled dining room of the Mamontov house that Serov painted the twelve-year-old Verusha Mamontova.

Girl with Peaches (fig. 6-1) immediately captivated other artists, and won first prize at the 1887 Exhibition of the Moscow Society of Lovers of Art. Serov later told his friend and biographer Igor Grabar': "All I achieved was freshness, that special freshness which you always feel in nature and do not see in painting. I worked on it more than a month and wore her out, poor girl. But still I wanted to preserve that freshness of touch along with complete finish, just as the old masters did."[9] The way Verusha leans forward so that her pose balances the oblique edge of the table and the irregular verticals of door and window-frames, the way the yellow of the peaches picks up the yellow-on-white of the majolica plate on the wall and the leaves glimpsed through the window, and the striking effect of light from behind the figure, edging the contours of the girl, chairs, and peaches, and bringing out the deeper rosy and chestnut tones, were prophetic of the balance Serov achieved in later paintings.

Serov insisted that *Girl with Peaches* was not a traditional portrait but a complete picture.[10] This idea became even more important for his later portraits. Without neglecting the personality of a model, often a friend, Serov rejected detailed description in favor of a gesture, pose, or special coloration that pervaded both figure and setting. His portrait of Nikolai Rimsky-Korsakov (fig. 6-2) is based on a composition of interlocking triangles and rectangles and a color

6-1 Valentin Serov. *Girl with Peaches,* 1887. Portrait of Verusha Mamontova. Oil on canvas, 98 × 58 cm. Courtesy of Tretiakov Gallery, Moscow.

harmony of charcoal grey, warm brown, and white, with a brilliant pink album cover framing and accenting the composer's outstretched hand. Later, in portraits of the actress Mariia Ermolova and of the writer Maxim Gorky, Serov reduces detail and visual variety still further, to emphasize not the mere physical appearance but the artistic personality of the sitter.

Serov was one of the artists responsible for developing an Impressionist style in Russian painting. Influenced by Repin and Vasilii Polenov (a member of the Abramtsevo circle and teacher of Korovin and Levitan), as well as by French Impressionism, Serov and his

6-2 Valentin Serov. *Portrait of Nikolai Rimsky-Korsakov,* 1898. Oil on canvas, 94 × 111 cm. Courtesy of Tretiakov Gallery, Moscow.

friends rejected the ideological realism of the 1870s and instead sought "freshness" and "joy" in painting.[11] More than any of his colleagues, Serov extended an Impressionist approach into the realm of portraiture, but this was not a matter of dissolving the features of his subjects into the color patches associated with French Impressionism. Serov used large areas of pure, smoothly applied color, often black, and kept faces and gestures distinct. His alliance with Impressionism was more conceptual than technical. He did not imitate nature, but instead sought graphic or painterly equivalents for faces, scenes, moods evoked by scenes, and above all the "inner life" of his models.[12]

"One must be able to work for a long time on one thing," Serov said, "but in such a way that the labor is not visible."[13] He always took a long time, was rarely satisfied, and once said, "for me each portrait is an illness."[14] By the mid-1890s, Serov was the best-known portraitist of his generation; he was called upon to paint royalty, aristocrats, and leading figures of the intelligentsia, and he continued to portray his friends and colleagues in the art world. He maintained the distinction between a traditional portrait and a picture, achieving characterization not through accessories and details but through placement, color, and the rhythmic patterns of contours and brush strokes, aspects of style that owed much to his extraordinary graphic technique.

Serov developed a distinctive type of inhabited landscape which showed not only effects of light, atmosphere and season, but conveyed a mood and a sense of human presence. In *October. Domotkanovo* (1895, Tretiakov Gallery), and other rural scenes, the horizontal, monochromatic landscapes envelop the forms of humans and horses, but the slightly off-center figures focus the attention and make the landscape, in contrast, seem changeable, as if glimpsed obliquely by a mobile observer. Serov applied the same effect in two imagined portraits of Pushkin (both 1899, All-Union Pushkin Museum, St. Petersburg), in which sketchy marks of grasses, hills, road, and sky act as foils to the dark, angular, and asymmetrically placed figures. His most original blending of illustration, portraiture, landscape, genre, and history painting appeared in a group of works done between 1900 and 1910, featuring historical figures (Peter I, Elizabeth, and Catherine II) and characters from Greek myth. The interaction between figures and distinctive backgrounds was also crucial in his work for the theater.

Following his debut in 1887, Serov exhibited regularly in Moscow and St. Petersburg and abroad; in 1896 he had his first showing at the Munich Secession; in 1898 he took part in the Exhibition of Russian and Finnish Painters organized by Diaghilev in St. Petersburg; and the following year, he contributed works to Diaghilev's first International Exhibition of Paintings, held under the auspices of the journal *Mir iskusstva* (World of art). Meanwhile, in 1897, Serov began another sphere of professional activity, teaching at the Moscow School of Painting, Sculpture, and Architecture, where his colleagues were Polenov, Korovin, Levitan and Leonid Pasternak, and his students included some of the leading artists of the next generation.[15] In 1903, the Imperial Academy of Arts elected Serov a full member.

While working in St. Petersburg in January 1905, Serov witnessed the massacre of a group of peacefully demonstrating workers by a troop of cavalry under the command of Grand Duke Vladimir, who was also president of the Academy. Serov wrote a letter of protest and resigned from the Academy.[16] He followed up his gesture by drawing political caricatures for the new satirical magazine *Zhupel* (Bugbear), including the stunning, poster-like *Soldiers, Brave Fellows, Heroes Every One!* (1905, Russian Museum). This work once belonged to Maxim Gorky, whose portrait Serov painted in 1905.[17] During the next few years, Serov was active with portrait commissions and projects connected with the theater. He also travelled: to Greece, with Bakst in 1907; to Germany, Austria, Italy, and France; and he spent several intervals working in Paris in 1909, 1910, and 1911. In the fall of 1911, Serov returned to Moscow, and on 22 November, he suddenly died of a heart attack. This summary leaves out important aspects of Serov's work, but indicates key points at which his literary, musical and theatrical interests merged with and contributed to his developing artistic goals.

Theatrical Design

Serov's participation in the Abramtsevo circle and the World of Art group gave him opportunities to work with musicians, writers, and directors, as well as artists like Polenov, Levitan, Korovin, Vrubel, Benua, and Bakst, all of whom were engaged in designing and painting scenery. Korovin once said that the experience of painting sets for Mamontov's theater alongside Polenov and Levitan helped him to understand the difference between copying nature and creating a natural effect using "incomplete drawing" and "vanishing patches" of colors.[18] Although Serov did not design stage sets until several years later, he had taken part as a child in amateur theatricals, including Mamontov's biblical drama *Joseph*, and for his 1884 operetta *The Black Turban*, Serov not only acted but produced sound effects and sketches of group scenes.[19] He was also in contact with theatrical activity through the portraits Mamontov commissioned him to paint of leading foreign singers, including the Swedish coloratura soprano Marie van Sandt (1886, Samara Art Museum), and tenors Antonio d'Andrade (1885, Sumy Art Museum), Angelo Massini (1890, Tretiakov Gallery) and Francesco Tamagno (1891, Tretiakov Gallery). Even these early portraits immediately reveal Serov's fascination with artistic personalities, and with models accustomed to presenting themselves to the public.

Because the Private Opera failed to attract a large enough audience, Mamontov curtailed productions in 1887; but he continued to hold amateur performances at his house, in which Konstantin Stanislavsky, a relative of Mamontov, participated. Serov worked with

Vrubel on the sets for one of these plays in 1889. In 1896, Mamontov was able to revive his opera, partly thanks to the effectiveness of the stage sets by artists in the Abramtsevo group. Even more important was Mamontov's discovery of the young Fedor Shaliapin, who had been working regularly, but without much encouragement, at the Mariinskii Theater in St. Petersburg. Mamontov undertook Shaliapin's aesthetic education and introduced him to his circle of artists. For two remarkable seasons, 1897/88 and 1898/99, Shaliapin performed as Ivan the Terrible in *Pskovitanka*, as Boris Godunov, and in numerous other roles.

Mamontov's 1898 production of Aleksandr Serov's opera *Judith* brought Shaliapin and Serov together as collaborators: Serov designed the sets and costumes, and Shaliapin sang the role of Holofernes. For Serov, this opera had special importance. He had tried unsuccessfully, some ten years earlier, to arrange a production at the Mariinskii Theater to mark the twentieth anniversary of its first performance. At the same time, he was working on a portrait of his father (1889, Russian Museum), based on photographs. For several months he did research in books on the ancient Near East, making sketches to show the theater administrators, and this preparation was helpful when Serov undertook the responsibility of artistic director for the Mamontov production.[20]

The artist and the singer spent hours studying photographs of Assyrian reliefs; one source indicates that during the early rehearsals Serov helped Shaliapin to visualize Holofernes as a "bas-relief come to life," by making a series of drawings, all in profile, of various gestures and movements.[21] The two worked well together, and remained close friends throughout Serov's life; Serov did more than twenty portraits of the singer.[22] They both felt that it was worth sacrificing naturalism in order to underscore the stylized formality of the setting, and the almost ritual character of the story. Serov himself painted the sets, worked on costumes, and even put the makeup on Shaliapin's face and hands, emphasizing the monumental, sculptural effects, and beyond this, the "evil drunkenness" in the second act.[23] The production was quite successful, and when the opera was revived in 1907, finally at the Mariinskii Theater, Serov again designed and executed the decor, basing the costume and makeup designs on his earlier ones. The set designs show the combination of massive, obliquely placed forms, like the cliffs at Bethul, or the canopies of Holofernes' tent (fig. 6-3), and strong contrast of light and dark, which Korovin, Bakst, Golovin, and

6-3 Valentin Serov. *Holofernes' Tent,* set design for *Judith,* act 3, 1907. Tempera on paper, mounted on cardboard, 55 × 71.5 cm. Russian Museum, St. Petersburg.

others used so effectively in Diaghilev's ballets. The sets and costumes also show results of the Abramtsevo group's keen interest in history and archaeology. Serov's drawing of Shaliapin in costume as Holofernes (1907, Russian Museum), in strict profile, and with beard and garments rendered as small, repeated patterns, like those on Assyrian reliefs, is probably much like his earlier costume drawings.

Ironically, during the same season in which he produced *Judith,* Mamontov also staged Valentina Serova's opera *Ilia Muromets,* but without success. Although Shaliapin sang the role of Ilia, Serov was not involved, and there is no record of the sets or costumes. Serova herself admitted that she must have neglected national coloration and even musical concerns for the sake of social ideals.[24]

The only stage designs Serov did for Diaghilev's Ballets Russes were for *Scheherazade,* presented at the Théâtre du Châtelet in Paris in 1911. The idea for the ballet was primarily Diaghilev's, who brought Bakst in as designer at an early stage and credited him on the posters. Originally Benua was to serve as artistic director, but he withdrew over a disagreement, and Serov, whose sets for *Judith* had impressed Diaghilev, was asked to take his place.[25]

Rimsky-Korsakov's symphonic suite based on themes from the *Arabian Nights* suggested decorations in a "Persian" style, so Serov studied Persian miniatures and decorative arts at the Hermitage, the Louvre and in other museums during the course of planning the sets, making numerous studies. While he worked on the designs for the curtains in his Moscow studio, he had his daughter play Rimsky-Korsakov's music on the piano.[26] Several watercolor and gouache sketches survive (1910, 1911, Russian Museum, Bakhrushin Theatrical Museum, Tretiakov Gallery, and private collections), in varying degrees of finish, showing the overall compositional scheme as well as details of parts of the curtain. One design (1910, Serov family collection, Moscow) has the coloration of manuscript illustrations of hunting scenes (dark green sea, lavender hillocks, and dark, almost purple foliage) as well as the elegant, sinuous lines, especially in the contours of the hills, the waves and the racing cheetahs and horses. Other sketches convey the effect of intense color contrasts and emphatic contours of hillside, sea, and palm trees with only minimal indication of landscape features, figures, or animals, and no exotic details.

Serov painted the curtain itself in Paris, with the help of his cousin Nina Simonovich-Efimova and her husband Ivan Efimov, a sculptor. The task of translating the elegance of miniatures onto a canvas some twenty meters wide was daunting, but the artists, though working to the point of exhaustion, seem to have conquered the technical problems while keeping the excitement, the "atmosphere of the fantastic."[27] The overall effect was strong and even monumental, a foil to the graceful finery of Bakst's costumes. Serov, rarely satisfied with any of his work, found this project one of his most enjoyable, both in progress and on its completion; he was especially touched when the audience applauded the curtain at the first performance.[28]

Literary Motifs

Serov's works on literary or historical themes sometimes began as commissions, but grew beyond the framework of the initial projects. Among these were illustrations commissioned from several artists by the publisher Petr Konchalovskii for a memorial edition of Lermontov, published in 1891, and a centennial edition of Pushkin, published by I. N. Kushnerev in 1899. Serov's watercolor illustrations for *The Demon* and *A Hero of Our Time* (1891, Tretiakov Gallery) followed the powerful images created for the same publication by Vrubel, as did the works of most of the other collaborators. For the Pushkin volume, Serov did two imagined portraits, one showing Pushkin riding down a country road and another with him seated at the corner of a garden bench, and a related landscape called *Winter Road* (1899, All-Union Pushkin Museum).

In the mid-1890s, Serov also illustrated tales by Pushkin and Mamin-Sibiriak, such as "The Tale of the She-Bear" (1895, Russian Museum) and "The Crow and the Canary" (1896, Tretiakov Gallery) in readers for school children. He began a series of more than twenty illustrations for Krylov's fables, only some of which were ever published.[29] They range from accurate portrayals of animals, based on studies of wolves made in the northern woods and of lions made in zoos, such as *The Wolf and the Shepherds* (1898, Russian Museum), to virtual caricatures, such as *The Daw in Peacock Feathers* (1895–1911, Russian Museum) or *The Monkey and the Eyeglasses* (1895–1911, Tretiakov Gallery), which remind one of the humorous drawings Serov often made of his friends (he did Benua as an orangutan).[30] Serov's continual fascination with the fables was part of his lifelong absorption in the problem of rendering a subject so that its meaning is made clear with the most economical means: line, minimal shading, and placement of figures on a page. Serov managed to turn apparently simple tales into marvellous probings of character and of human foibles and qualities. His work in this sphere was of great value for his later portraits.

Technically more adventurous, and closer in spirit to his theatrical work, were pastel and tempera paintings for publications on Russian life and history; not illustrations to literature in a traditional sense, but rather thematic series. The first, a prelude to more extensive projects, was *In the Tundra, Reindeer Ride* (1896, Tretiakov Gallery) for a book called *Pictures of Russian Nature and Daily Life* published by Mamontov's brother Anatolii in 1898.[31] Serov's picture, in which the reindeer and sleigh are surrounded by a large, horizontal expanse of blank paper accented with white, is similar to several paintings he and Korovin had done of the Russian north in 1894, on commission from Mamontov. In style and technique, it looks forward to Serov's two major graphic series done after the turn of the century.

Serov accepted a commission from N. Kutepov to do illustrations for his book, *Royal Hunting in Russia*.[32] The first one completed, *Peter II and Princess Elizabeth Riding to Hounds* (fig. 6-4) was the most

6-4 Valentin Serov. *Peter II and Princess Elizabeth Riding to Hounds*, 1900. Tempera on cardboard, 41 × 39 cm. Russian Museum, St. Petersburg.

detailed, with a church and village and a stream of huntsmen and borzois in the background, in the lower left corner a humble old peasant couple apparently thrust aside as the royal pair on horseback and their hound race past. Though the dominant colors are gray and a rosy brown, evoking mud and an overcast fall sky, the flecks of white and red on the horse-trappings and riding costumes, the pert smile on Elizabeth's face and the visual parallels of her fan, Peter's pigtail and the horses' and dogs' tails make the picture very lively. *Peter the Great Riding to Hounds* (1902, Russian Museum) is at first sight more static. Peter has stopped his cavalcade to roar with laughter at a clumsy old boyar who has fallen in the snow. But Serov achieves a remarkable effect of potential movement with the sharp disjunctions of scale and the assymetry of the composition: the left half is almost completely filled with large figures of Peter, four companions and horses, while the right half, with only one hound in the foreground, and much smaller human figures and dogs in the middle distance, seems empty. The snow, indicated by roughly brushed white tempera, both emphasizes the emptiness and silhouettes the forms of dogs, horses and boyars, making them grotesquely misproportioned. Indeed, the key to the expressiveness of the scene is in gesture conveyed by contour and spacing. *Catherine II Setting Out to Hunt with Falcons* (1902, Russian Museum), in contrast, is central in its compositional focus: the bright red carriage in which a soberly clad Catherine rides. But the Empress's glance over her shoulder at the young huntsman riding up behind her directs attention to the brief psychological interchange between the two. The falconers and their poised hunting birds in the background offer a decorative counterpoint to the understated action on the front plane. These three paintings might be categorized as book illustration or as historical genre. But they clearly demonstrate Benua's contention that Serov found novel ways of combining the disparate techniques and genres of visual arts. They share many characteristics of theatrical design, as developed in Mamontov's and Diaghilev's productions, with their attention to overall compositional structure and the interaction of "actors" and setting.

After completing this project, Serov turned to a similar historical subject in *Catherine the Great Driving Out* (1906, Russian Museum), treating the motif of the Empress in her sleigh in a much more decorative manner. Using pastels as well as tempera, he made no attempt to suggest continual space but instead placed the silhouetted outriders, sleigh, and postillion (in sepia with flecks of white and gold) between bluish-white forms of ice-laden fir trees along the front edge of the composition, and the golden facade of the palace, which extends almost from one edge to the other. The layered effect of a stage set and the unnatural colors accent the feeling of artifice, appropriate both to the era of Catherine II and to the stage. In this work Serov comes closest to the character of the World of Art, especially the eighteenth-century imagery and rococo style of Benua and Somov.

Serov's most significant works on Russian historical subjects were those focusing on Peter I. In 1907, he received a commission from the publisher Knebel for illustrations to a *Pictorial History of Russia* to be used in schools.[33] *Peter the Great* (1907, Tretiakov Gallery) shows the Tsar overseeing the construction of St. Petersburg, a theme that fascinated Serov, as it did his friends in the World of Art group. This composition, too, employs the theatrical device of silhouetting dark figures against a bright background; and here, the angular forms of the briskly striding Peter and the almost doubled-over bodies of his servants contrast with the softly billowing clouds behind them. Though the picture is small, the viewpoint from slightly below the ground-line (as if from the orchestra of a theater) and the extreme diminution in scale of the boats and buildings in the background render Peter monumental. There is grandeur, but also an element of irony or even caricature in the sharp contrasts within the image; Serov's acute use of line owes much to his royal hunting series and to the drawings for Krylov's fables.

Serov continued to explore the image of Peter the Great in a group of paintings and sketches showing Peter in differing aspects or moods: hearty celebration, *The Great Eagle Cup* (1910, Picture Gallery, Erevan); lonely contemplation, *Peter the Great at Monplaisir* (1910, Picture Gallery, Odessa); and the practical energy of building a city, *Peter the Great at a Construction Site* (fig. 6-5).[34] In these works, especially the last, Serov not only probes aspects of Peter I's character, but he visually juxtaposes the forms of power and dependency. Peter's figure always dominates the flat landscape and low horizon; the workers, their huts, and the wooden crosses marking their graves are small and marginal. Undoubtedly both style and message grew out of Serov's political convictions and his experience in expressing outrage at the killing of civilians by imperial troops in January 1905. It is no accident that he worked in tempera and emphasized a graphic, poster-like character in his portrayals of Peter.[35] After 1905, Serov turned often to the themes of political power and psychological extremes, and he continually found new vehicles for treating these themes. An important aspect of Serov's character, often mentioned by his friends, was his reticence and apparent lack of passion. He did not identify with the subjects he painted but kept some distance, maintaining a methodical, concentrated approach to his work. Even *Soldiers, Brave Fellows*, his most politically engaged work, done quickly and under stress, shows Serov's purposeful exploitation of such compositional means as abrupt change of scale, an empty central area, light and dark contrasts and graphic contours—techniques studied earlier in his Royal Hunting series.

6-5 Valentin Serov. *Peter the Great at a Construction Site*, 1910–11. Tempera on cardboard, 63 × 92 cm. Russian Museum, St. Petersburg.

Serov's deliberation about style led him to a study of classical art and mythological subjects, and in May 1907 he traveled to Greece with Bakst.[36] Even as a student Serov admired classical sculpture, and was especially delighted by the "small Greek figurines" in the Hermitage.[37] Among his early commissions were decorative murals on mythological themes for the Seleznev estate in Tula province, such as *Phoebus Effulgent* (1887, Art Museum, Tula). During a trip to the Crimea, he made a series of studies of a figure gazing out to sea for *Iphigenia in Tauris* (1893, Tretiakov Gallery, and variants), and by 1903 he was beginning to think about the story of Nausicaa and Odysseus. Although most of his works on mythological themes were rather small, there was definitely a connection between antique subjects and decorative projects. In 1904, Serov and Polenov discussed plans to paint the walls of the Museum of Fine Arts in Moscow with antique images; Polenov's idea was to involve several artists, including Korovin, Golovin, and other experienced painters of stage scenery, and let each artist choose a subject. Unfortunately the plan was never realized.[38] In any event, Serov had definite expectations of the trip to Greece.

Serov filled two albums with sketches, topographical views, pictures of architectural and sculptural landmarks of Athens, Olympia, Delphi and Crete, and several studies of models. He used these a few years later, when he turned to the subjects from Homer and Ovid. There is a spaciousness and serenity in the compositions of *Odysseus and Nausicaa* (1910, Tretiakov Gallery), and in *The Rape of Europa* (1910, Serov Family Collection) that contrasts with the scenes of *Royal Hunting in Russia* and the Peter the Great series, although some of the same pictorial devices are used. In all the versions of *Nausicaa*, the composition is strongly horizontal, frieze-like, focusing on the train of the princess with her mules, chariot, and laundresses proceeding from right to left along the shoreline, followed by the swathed figure of Odysseus. Colors are light blue, a warm tan, grays, white, and black, the tonality cool but luminous. The low horizon and small figures increase the sensation of boundless space.

In *Europa*, the spatial effect is quite different, not boundless but unmeasurable, because there is no shoreline or horizon; sea and sky are undistinguishable and flattened out. The viewpoint is slightly elevated and very close to the centrally placed, diagonal form of the bull carrying the kneeling woman on its back. The viewer might almost confront Europa directly, but for the fact that her eyes are blank, her face turned slightly away and smiling calmly, like an archaic *kore*. There is no illusion of motion, either; the white foam churned up by the bull, the reflections, the splashing of the dolphins, and the waves on the sea are abstract signs, as conventionalized as the bull and the woman, thick white wedges, reddish slivers, and dark blue patches against the lightly painted blue ground. For *Europa*, as he did for many of his late works, Serov used tempera on canvas rather than oil (though he used oil along with other media for studies). Serov also turned Europa and the Bull into sculptural form, first in plaster, and then in terra-cotta, porcelain, and bronze versions (1910, Novosibirsk Picture Gallery, Tretiakov Gallery, Russian Museum and private collection), another indication of his interest in the technical and expressive possibilities of different media.

Serov's last work based on mythology was for a commission to decorate the dining room of the Nosov house in Moscow with scenes from Ovid's *Metamorphoses*. He did not complete the project, but left several sketches in pencil, charcoal and watercolor, including *Diana and Actaeon* (1911, Tretiakov Gallery) and *Apollo and Diana Killing the Niobids* (1911, Tretiakov Gallery). The stylization, emphasis on contours, and decorative elements such as deer antlers

6-6 Valentin Serov. *Portrait of Henrietta Girshman,* 1907. Tempera on canvas, 140 × 140 cm. Courtesy of Tretiakov Gallery, Moscow.

are even more apparent than in the independent mythological works, in part because of the decorative intent of the project. The experience of working on the curtain for *Scheherazade* in 1910, and translating sources which were intricate in detail into large-scale forms which could still communicate the essence of the "Persian" style, would have aided Serov in adapting classical, sculptural forms to interior decoration.

Synthesis in Portraiture

Serov was working in all these areas—theatrical decoration, commissioned illustrations, sketches for the Krylov series, studies of Greek motifs, at the same time that he was producing his most outstanding portraits. From 1905 to 1911 he did more than forty portraits of people connected with art, music, and theater, a percentage consistent with his lifelong attraction to creative artists as subjects. The main characteristics of the late portraits are developments and refinements of his constant concern for compositional balance and the effect of spontaneity, along with complete finish, revealed in *Girl with Peaches* and *Portrait of Nikolai Rimsky-Korsakov*. But the later works also introduce new ways of handling paint or graphic media and radical simplification of composition, features related to Serov's illustrations and designs for the stage. In these areas, the artist was required to depart from natural appearances in order to use the qualities of each medium to the fullest. Serov's realization that painting and drawing were matters of perception and discipline rather than emotional expression allowed him to communicate the character of his subjects—and even convey the style of their art—without subordinating his own artistic character to the demands of the sitter.

The portrait of the tragic actress Mariia Ermolova (1905, Tretiakov Gallery), commissioned by the Circle of Literature and Art in Moscow, was one of Serov's most finished and successful works. It is rather formal, with its subdued gray, brown, and black color harmonies and narrow, vertical proportions, with the figure placed at an oblique angle to the picture plane, and framed by the mirror behind her. The portrait defines Ermolova's public role as a major artistic presence both on the Moscow stage and at her receptions at home (it was painted in the salon in which Ermolova received guests and gave readings). The quality of restraint and authority is all the more striking in comparison to the portrait Serov did the same year for the Circle of Literature and Art of the comic actress Glikeria Fedotova (1905, Tretiakov Gallery), shown facing the viewer directly and filling most of shallower, less angular, more intimate space.

For his portrait of Gorky (1905, Gorky Memorial Museum, Moscow), Serov used almost the same palette—the figure dressed in black, set against a light, yellowish-gray wall—but omitted all details of the setting. Instead of echoing the stance of the body by means of mirrors or door-frames, Serov related the figure's contours only to the picture frame and picture plane, implying a dimension of depth by the sharp torsion of the body. Although the paint is brushed on with wide, flat strokes, allowing no illusion of volume or shading, the figure is extremely sculptural.[39] The lack of pictorial space emphasizes the pent-up energy within the body, and the contrast between the inward-turning pose and the straight gaze outward.

Though Gorky was not an actor, he was accustomed to a public role, and Serov used his pose, as a director might, to emphasize both his intellectual complexity and his directness in action.

In contrast to these public images are two extraordinarily expressive portraits of artistic personalities in private settings. The *Portrait of Henrietta Girshman* (fig. 6-6) was initially meant to be a formal portrait of a society beauty, but it changed in progress. Henrietta Girshman was the wife of an important art collector, a patron of the arts herself, a friend of many artists, and an amateur painter. She and Serov were good friends; he had already drawn her portrait many times, and he was dissatisfied with the conventional appearance of his first study. Artist and model discussed the pose, choice of garments, and details of the setting. Girshman noted that the technique, tempera on canvas, was new for Serov at the time, and that the color scheme was partly due to Serov's recent trip to Paris, the dark grays, which Serov favored, enlivened by shining whites, the warm tones of Karelian birch furniture, and one bright red pincushion on the dressing table.[40] The pose was carefully contrived and difficult and, typically, Serov required Girshman to pose for several months. Very untypically, Serov included himself in the picture, through a fragment of his reflection in the mirror. The result is actually a dual portrait, a work that truly combines the aesthetic characters of model and artist.

In comparison with the superbly composed portrait of Girshman, Serov's portrayal of Nikolai Pozniakov (1908, Tretiakov Gallery) might seem casual. The subject, a young composer and ballet master of the Bolshoi Theater, appears here, not as an artist, taut with creative energy, but as a withdrawn youth lounging on a sofa. There are no straight lines in the picture, but every loosely curved contour of the body has its parallel in the back of the sofa, the hint of shadow on the wall, or the wrinkles of the fabric. The brilliant vermilion pillows and piping on the sofa pick up more subtle tones in the face and shirt. While seeming to abandon the tightness of his earlier compositions, Serov again adjusts brush strokes and contours to express the temporarily relaxed discipline of the musician.

His last important image of a performing artist, *Portrait of Ida Rubinstein* (fig. 6-7), is quite different in character. Unlike the portrait of Ermolova, and the less formal drawings of Anna Pavlova (1909, Tretiakov Gallery) and Tamara Karsavina (1909, Tretiakov Gallery), this work reveals not only a creative personality but a contrived spectacle. Serov saw Rubinstein perform in *Cleopatra*

6-7 Valentin Serov. *Portrait of Ida Rubinstein*, 1910. Tempera and charcoal on canvas, 147 × 233 cm. Russian Museum, St. Petersburg.

during the first Russian Season in Paris, and again in *Scheherazade*. He was attracted not so much to the sensual exoticism which she quite consciously projected, but to a "genuine, elemental quality of the East" and of antiquity. According to Igor Grabar', he talked about the qualities "of Egypt and Assyria, resurrected by some miracle in this unusual woman," and said, "there is a monumentality in every one of her movements, just like an archaic bas-relief come to life."[41] On another occasion Serov said that she had "the mouth of a wounded lioness,"[42] perhaps because he knew that she had been vacationing in North Africa on a lion-hunting safari just before coming to pose for him.

According to Serov's mother and his cousin Nina Simonovich-Efimova, Ida Rubinstein was a helpful sitter, understanding what effects Serov wanted, and perhaps sharing his attraction to the archaic.[43] Rubinstein posed nude; only the sinuous green scarf, the rich blue covering of the couch, the light tawny background, and the white gleam of diamonds on her fingers and toes identify her with the role of Cleopatra. There is no narrative, passion, or tragedy in the image, although her upturned face with slightly open mouth and oblique glance suggests mystery. Like the contemporaneous *Rape of Europa*, the image is overtly contrived, with the careful equilibrium of the pose and teasing play of the sand-colored body, outlined in black so as to deny an illusion of roundness, against the identically colored background.

Serov worked in tempera and charcoal on canvas, as he did for many paintings related to the theater. The previous year he had done a portrait of Anna Pavlova in the ballet *Sylphide* (1909, Russian Museum), also in tempera, as a design for a poster announcing the Russian Season in Paris. It probably came as no surprise that some of his friends at first thought *Ida Rubinstein* more like an advertising poster than a portrait. But when the more astute took a second look, they found that the "schematic contours" took on greater relief and a living body emerged, the apparently flat colors began to "breathe" and interact—"all without revealing the careful labor of the artist."[44]

Serov's labor was not so much in describing the appearance of his sitter (this seemed to come unusually quickly for him), but in maintaining the necessary balance among the elements of portrait, nude, and decoration. His refusal to restrict himself to the traditional definition of portraiture was consistent with his declaration over thirty years earlier that *Girl with Peaches* was not a portrait but a picture. Early in his career he was one of a few artists who were beginning to break down the rigid, hierarchical distinctions among historical painting, portraiture, landscape, and genre, upon which academic training had been based. Later, during his long association with the Abramtsevo circle and the World of Art group, Serov was less inclined than Korovin, Vrubel, and other friends to experiment with a range of styles and techniques; he concentrated on painting and drawing, on the basic problems of composing a picture to achieve the strongest effect. But the lively artistic, theatrical, and literary environment in which Serov was at home gave him opportunities to stretch the possibilities of his chosen media. What he learned from his illustrations, especially for the Krylov fables and the Royal Hunting series, and from theatrical work, with Shaliapin on Holofernes and with Bakst on Scheherazade, was the achievement of both variety and monumentality through economical means, often through stylization. He applied these ideas to portraits, sometimes to the point of departing from physical likeness in order to stress the stylistic elements—line, coloration, visual echoes between facial or body features and surroundings—which characterized a sitter. The late portraits, *Ida Rubinstein* most of all, represented, as one critic said, "Serov's stride into completely new territory—very close to the very latest explorations of contemporary modernism."[45] By drawing upon several disciplines, combining and composing elements of drawing, theatrical design, and even chore-ography with painting, Serov developed a new form of portraiture based not on representation but on visual equivalents for moods, ideas, and artistic personalities.

Notes

1. Aleksandr Benua, *Istoriia Russkoi zhivopisi v XIX veke* [History of Russian painting in the 19th century] (St. Petersburg: Znanie, 1902), 233.

2. Ibid., 233–34.

3. C. Baudelaire, "Salon de 1846" in Baudelaire, *Art in Paris 1845–1862*, trans. and ed. Jonathan Mayne (London and New York: Phaidon, 1965), 50. Aurier, in *Mercure de France* (1891), quoted in L. Nochlin, *Impressionism and Post-Impressionism 1874–1904* (Englewood Cliffs, N.J.: Prentice Hall, 1963), 162. On the *Mir iskusstva* group's knowledge of these critics see Janet Kennedy, *The "Mir Iskusstva" Group and Russian Art* (New York: Garland, 1977), 100–101.

4. Benua later wrote that the ideal of the *Gesamtkunstwerk* was achieved in Diaghilev's ballet *Scheherazade; Rech'*, 12 July 1910; quoted in Kennedy, *The "Mir Iskusstva" Group*, 343.

5. A. Benua, *Rech'*, 11 February 1909 and 19 October 1912, in I. S. Zil'bershtein and V. Samkov, eds., *Valentin Serov v vospominaniiakh, dnevnikakh i perepiske sovremennikov* [Valentin Serov in memoirs, diaries and correspondence of contemporaries] (Leningrad: Khudozhnik RSFSR, 1971), 1:409, 413.

6. Benua, *Istoriia*, 233.

7. Ibid., 232.

8. Leonid Pasternak, "V. A. Serov" (1911) in L. Pasternak, *The Memoirs of Leonid Pasternak*, trans. Jennifer Bradshaw (London: Quartet, 1982), 81. Bio-graphical data are in V. S. Serova, *Kak ros moi syn* [How my son grew up] (Leningrad: Khudozhnik RSFSR, 1968), in the commentary in *Serov v vospomi-naniiakh*, and in Dmitrii Sarab'ianov, *Valentin Serov* (New York and Lenin-grad: Abrams, Avrora, 1982), 266–76.

9. Igor Grabar', *Valentin Aleksandrovich Serov. Zhizn' i tvorchestvo* [Life and work] (Moscow: Knebel, 1913), 74.

10. Serov to I. Ostroukhov, 6 December 1888, quoted in N. Moleva, *Konstantin Korovin, zhizn' i tvorchestvo* [Life and work] (Moscow: Akademiia khudozhestv, 1963), 194.

11. Serov to O. Trubnikova, May 1887, in *Serov v vospominaniiakh*, 1:275–76. For a survey of Russian Impressionism see A. Hilton, "The Impressionist Vision in Russia," in N. Broude et al., *World Impressionism: The International Movement, 1860–1920* (New York: Harry N. Abrams, 1990), 370–406.

12. D. V. Sarab'ianov, "Reformy Valentina Serova" [The reforms of Valentin Serov], in D. Sarab'ianov, *Russkaia zhivopis' kontsa 1900–nachala 1910-rkh godov. Ocherki* [Russian painting at the end of the 1900s and beginning of the 1910s. Essays] (Moscow: Iskusstvo, 1971), 9–32, and Sarab'ianov, *Serov*, 12–13.

13. P. I. Neradovskii, "Kak Serov rabotal nad portretami" [How Serov worked on portraits], *Serov v vospominaniiakh*, 2:34.

14. *Serov v vospominaniiakh*, 1:33.

15. He taught there until 1909. See *Serov v vospominaniiakh*, for memoirs of colleagues and students. Further information on his professional work and membership in exhibiting groups can be found in Sarab'ianov, *Serov*, 270–75.

16. Benua and other contemporaries emphasized Serov's "conscience": *Serov v vospominaniiakh*, 1:406–7. Serov's concern with political issues was not new; through his mother and her friends, he had been involved with famine relief efforts in 1892, and he turned down commissions because of his political beliefs. See Serova, *Kak ros moi syn*, 15–50.

17. Serov had probably met Gorky in 1902; he took part in at least one meeting to work on the satirical magazine *Zhalo* [Sting].

18. Moleva, *Korovin*, 155.

19. Sergei Mamontov (the Mamontovs' eldest son) recorded these activities in "V.A. Serov v domashnikh spektakliakh Mamontovykh" [Serov in the Mamontovs' domestic theatricals], *Rampa i zhizn'* [Footlights and life], 1914, in *Serov v vospominaniiakh*, 1:169–72. See also Dora Kogan, *Mamontovskii kruzhok* [The Mamontov circle] (Moscow: Izobrazitel'noe iskusstvo, 1970), 97–98.

20. Mark Kopshitser, *Valentin Serov* (Moscow: Iskusstvo, 1972), 135.

21. A. Raskin, *Shaliapin i russkie khudozhniki* [Shaliapin and Russian artists] (Moscow, 1963), cited by Stuart Grover, "Savva Mamontov and the Mamontov Circle: 1870–1905. Art Patronage and the Rise of Nationalism in Russian Art" (Ph.D. diss., University of Wisconsin, 1971), 324.

22. F. I. Shaliapin, excerpts from *Maska i dusha* [Masks and souls] (1932), in *Serov v vospominaniiakh*, 2:277–82.

23. Ibid., 284.

24. V. Serova, letter to A. Simonovich, 20 April 1899, quoted in Serova, *Kak ros moi syn*, 21, 137–38.

25. *Serov v vospominaniiakh*, 1:456–57.

26. Kopshitser, *Serov*, 373.

27. N. Simonovich-Efimova, *Vospominaniia o Valentine Aleksandroviche Serove* [Memoirs of Valentin Serov] (Leningrad: Khudozhnik RSFSR, 1964), 123–24, and 173n. The curtain was sold at Sotheby's in London in 1968; its present location is unknown.

28. Serov, letter to M. Tsetlin, 29 June 1911, in *Serov v vospominaniiakh*, 1:456.

29. Sarab'ianov, *Serov*, 366–70.

30. Benua, from *Zhizn' khudozhnika* [Life of an artist], in *Serov v vospominaniiakh*, 1:392.

31. *Kartiny iz russkoi prirody i byta* (Moscow: A. Mamontov, 1898).

32. N. Kutepov, *Tsarskaia i Imperatorskaia okhota na Rusi. Istoricheskii ocherk* [Tsarist and Imperial hunting in Russia. Historical essay] (St. Petersburg, 1902). Several other artists including Vasilii Surikov took part; the works by Serov were reproduced in vol. 3, following pp. 30, 126, and 174.

33. S. Kniazkov, ed., *Kartiny po russkoi istorii* [Pictures from Russian history] (Moscow: Knebel, 1908).

34. Serov did not finish these paintings; the sketches cited are the most nearly complete and several others exist in the Russian Museum and Tretiakov Gallery.

35. See E. P. Gomberg-Verzhbinskaia, *Russkoe iskusstvo i revoliutsiia 1905 goda* [Russian art and the 1905 Revolution] (Leningrad: Izd-vo Leningradskogo Universiteta, 1960), 84–86.

36. See L. Bakst, "Serov i ia v Gretsii. Dorozhnye Zapisi" [Serov and I in Greece. Travel notes] (1923) in *Serov v vospominaniiakh*, 2:562–88.

37. *Serov v vospominaniiakh*, 2:611–12.

38. Ibid., 612.

39. Sarab'ianov, *Serov*, 21, 334–35, identifies a watercolor sketch of Michelangelo's Madonna in the Medici Chapel, Florence (1904, Serov family collection) as a possible source for the pose.

40. G. L. Girshman, "Moi vospominaniia o V. A. Serove" [My recollections of Serov], in *Serov v vospominaniiakh*, 1:328–39.

41. I. Grabar', *Serov* (Moscow: Iskusstvo, 1965), 233, quoted in *Serov v vospominaniiakh*, 1:74.

42. Simonovich-Efimova, *Vospominaniia o Serove*, 116–17.

43. Serova, *Kak ros moi syn*, 148–50. An afterword to this text, by editors I. S. Zil'bershtein and V. Samkov, 151–167, discusses the portrait, the documentation about it, and viewers' responses at the time of its exhibition in 1911 and later.

44. Sergei Mamontov, "Chego my lishilis' v Serove," [What we have lost in Serov], *Rampa i zhizn'* (1911), in *Serov v vospominaniiakh*, 1:174–75.

45. Sergei Glagol, "Novye raboty Serova na vystavke *Mir iskusstva*" [New works by Serov at the *World of Art* exhibition] (1911), in Serova, *Kak ros moi syn*, 163.

The Modernist Poetics of Grief in the Wartime Works of Tsvetaeva, Filonov, and Kollwitz

Antonina Filonov Gove

The artistic revolution of the twentieth century subsumed under the terms *modernism* or *avant-garde* includes numerous Russian painters, composers, and poets. Among the most innovative works of Russian twentieth-century poetry are the cycle "Wires" ("Provoda") and the long poems "Essay of a Room" ("Popytka komnaty") and "Poem of the Staircase" ("Poema lestnitsy") by Marina Tsvetaeva. Paradoxically, Tsvetaeva never belonged to a modernist group or movement, and her modern period began in the 1920s rather than in 1912 or 1913.[1]

In what follows I explore two propositions. The first is that Tsvetaeva became a modern poet in the process of developing a poetic voice responsive to the harrowing realities of life during the Russian Revolution and Civil War. Key stylistic innovations appearing in Tsvetaeva's poetry after 1920 are first found in concentrated form in the poetic cycle "Separation" ("Razluka"), written in 1921 and dedicated to her husband. This was the time when experiences of separation and loss reached a nadir in Tsvetaeva's own life. I propose that there is a close connection between the thematics of grief and loss in the poems of "Separation" and the introduction of new poetic features that transform the governing mode of Tsvetaeva's poetics from neoromantic to modern.[2]

The second proposition developed here is that Tsvetaeva's work is not unique in being aesthetically founded in experiences of grief and the profound psychological displacement of war. Tsvetaeva's modern poetics shares striking stylistic and thematic features with the work of the Russian painter Pavel Filonov and the German graphic artist and sculptor Kaethe Kollwitz. All three produced much of their major mature work during wartime and the post-Revolutionary and postwar period. It will be shown in the case of Kollwitz, and argued in the case of Filonov, that the modern features in their work are inscribed with the disorienting, death-laden experiences of the revolutionary and war years and offer thematizations of suffering and grief.

The changes in style identified in Tsvetaeva's verse beginning with the cycle "Separation" can be grouped under four headings.[3] First, there is greater *indirection:* the subject matter is more opaque and depersonalized; emblematic images and metonymy are favored over descriptive qualifiers; there is a sense of distancing of both speaker and reader from the text; and the reading of the text requires more interpretation than with earlier poems. Second, the poems display a new *economy* of means, especially a reduction in the number of verbs and the use of repetition (of words, syntactic constructions, metrical pattern, and rhymes). Third, the poems are marked by an effect of *fragmentation*, achieved by elision, a lack of overt connections between sentences, enjambement, the use of a short line (especially dimeter), a preference for masculine rhyme, and a prevalence of metonymic *pars pro toto* images. Fourth, there appears a technique of the *evolving image* with *associative* rather than logical, syntactic, or narrative connections in the poetic discourse. All these characteristics taken together contrast with the overall earlier manner of Tsvetaeva's verse, which tended to be discursive, easily interpreted, rich in descriptive qualifiers, abounding in a luxuriant lexicon and imagery, and provided with a complicated syntax and varied prosodic rhythms. Although the earlier qualities do not disappear from Tsvetaeva's verse, elements of the new manner shift her poetics in a radically new direction.

The terms introduced above—indirection, economy, fragmentation (including *pars pro toto* metonymy), and associative connection—refer to cognitive and aesthetic qualities that are not peculiar or limited to verbal material, but function equally well in describing works in the visual arts.[4] These terms of stylistic description are extended to a discussion of selected works of Filonov and Kollwitz in the second part of this essay.

Tsvetaeva's Emergence as a Modern Poet: The Cycle "Separation" and the Experience of Loss

Viewed chronologically, Tsvetaeva's poetic work exhibits a marked discontinuity. In her first creative decade, beginning in 1908, her verse consists of masterful extensions of existing literary modes, drawing generously on the Russian and European belles-lettres of the eighteenth and nineteenth centuries, the Russian Symbolists, and folk genres. Even as she develops a distinctive poetic voice of her own, her verse remains "accessible." In the second decade, beginning with the poems of the volume *Craft* (*Remeslo*), much of her poetry is concentrated, difficult, and sometimes cryptic, and clearly belongs to the innovative artistic creations of the twentieth century.[5]

While various characteristics of the "new poetics" can be found in isolation in earlier poems of Tsvetaeva, they first coalesce in the cycle titled "Separation." I believe this is not an accident but is closely bound with the thematics of this cycle. In the eight poems of "Separation," the motif of death, familiar from the beginning of Tsvetaeva's *oeuvre*, appears in a new guise as the motif of suicide. As the cycle progresses, a central theme is that the poetic "I" intends to die because this is the only adequate response to the separation from her dead beloved. The motif of suicide is stated in powerful imagery and undergoes a development in several of the poems of the cycle, with suicide being repeatedly presented as a process of transformation. As the speaker imagines her own death, she is translated into a new order of being where she and her beloved can no longer be separated. However, the motif of separation is reintroduced and the act of suicide replayed, for suicide as a means of redressing the separation from the beloved brings with it a new separation, that of mother and child. A third thematic development is that the speaker's courageous intention to achieve her own death in order to attempt an otherworldly reunion confronts a new danger—a threat that her beloved will be claimed by the gods of Olympus. At the conclusion of the cycle, the speaker's act of rebellion (whether by suicide or by means of the poetic imagination) rises to challenge the nature of being that is ordained by God, namely that everything that has existence is transitory.

The poems of "Separation" were written in May and June of 1921. What prompted the treatment of the theme of suicide as well as the emergence of a poetics of indirection, the new economy of poetic means, and the effect of fragmentation at this time? Tsvetaeva's biography informs us of three circumstances or events that profoundly marked her life. At the outbreak of the Civil War, she became separated from her husband, who was in the White Army in the Crimea. This meant that she was left on her own, with two small children and no income during the increasingly desperate conditions following the October Revolution.[6] In February 1920, at the peak of the famine, Tsvetaeva's younger daughter, Irina, aged nearly three, died in a children's home, of starvation. Intense grief and guilt over the child's death at a time when her older daughter was seriously ill was followed by yet another traumatic event—the defeat of the White Army in the Crimea ten months later, in December 1920. Now Tsvetaeva feared that her husband, Sergei Efron, with whom she had had no contact for nearly two years, might also be dead. The news of the defeat marked the beginning of a second period of mourning for Tsvetaeva in which she struggled with recurrent feelings of hopelessness and thoughts of suicide as she tried to transmute her pain into poetry.

A sense of Tsvetaeva's feelings and thoughts may be gained from several letters she wrote at that time. The first, addressed to Tsvetaeva's friends, the poet and translator Vera Klavdievna Zviagintseva and her husband, Aleksandr Sergeevich Erofeev, was written five days after Irina's death. The second, addressed to Vera Klavdievna alone, was probably written another five days after the first.[7] In these letters one hears the shock, grief, denial, guilt, low self-esteem, and thoughts of suicide that followed Irina's death. Especially terrifying was the thought that her husband would reject her because she had allowed their child to die   a thought that crystallizes her sense of isolation, her desperate need to have her husband back with her, and the fear that he would no longer love her.[8]

The letters most relevant to the topic of this essay were written by Tsvetaeva to another friend, the writer and translator Evgenii Lann, between December 1920 and September 1921, the period immediately following the defeat of the White Army.[9] The letter of June 1921 refers to the poems of "Separation" directly. (Remember that the cycle is dedicated to Efron.) Tsvetaeva writes: "Someday I'll pull myself together and send you the poems of the last few months— poems which are difficult to write and impossible to read (for me to others). I write them because, jealous of my pain, I don't tell anybody about S. [Sergei, her husband]—and there's no one to tell. Asia [Tsvetaeva's sister Anastasiia] has enough grief of her own, and *she never had an S*. These poems are an attempt to work my way to the surface, which succeeds for half an hour."[10] Previous letters give additional indications of Tsvetaeva's state of mind. On 9 December she writes:

I've finished that poem spoken over a dead man [a heart-rending "dialogue" of two women over a fallen soldier]. . . . My main concern at present is to kill time [*gnat' dni*]. A senseless occupation, because what awaits me is, perhaps, worse. Sometimes I think with dread that perhaps somebody in Moscow already knows about S., perhaps many people know, and I don't. Today I dreamed about him—repeated encounters and partings. We made plans to meet, we met, we parted. And the whole time, throughout the whole dream, above the whole dream—his beautiful eyes in their radiance.[11]

Here Tsvetaeva alludes to her fears that her husband may already be dead without saying it directly. Her dreams enact quite distinctly, however, the images of separation and parting. On 29 December she writes, "I'm also writing a lot, I live by my verse, by my dread about S., and my hope for reunion with Asia."[12] And in June (in the first letter quoted above): "I've just dreamed: first about Boris [her sister's husband], then about S. With B. I laughed (the customary path of my tenderness to him), but S. I only saw: he was in a hospital. I remember a nurse and wads of cotton. I dream about S. every night, and when I wake up I immediately don't want to live—not in general, but without him. The most exact thing I can tell you about myself is this: life has departed and laid bare the depths, or rather, the foam is gone."[13]

In light of these letters and of the thematics of "Separation," I propose that the new poetics that coalesces in "Separation" and characterizes some of the other poems in the collection *Craft*, as well as the long poem "On a Red Steed" ("Na krasnom kone") have their origin in the poet's attempt to find a new way of speaking in order to give voice to the experience of the chaotic, disrupted, grief-filled reality of her world "after the Revolution"—the famine and the killing cold of 1919 and 1920, the death of her child, a three-year separation from her husband, and the fear that he was dead.

Modernist Elements and the Poetics of Loss in the Cycle "Separation"

In what follows I look at poems 1, 2, and 6 of the cycle to illustrate the most salient elements of the new poetics and their connection to the thematics of separation. I focus in turn on the qualities of "indirection," "economy," and "fragmentation," and also point out examples of "evolving associative imagery."

One element of indirection consists of the degree of contextual interpretation invited by the text. The text of poem 1, taken by itself, is relatively obscure, offering few cues to the uninformed reader about the subject of the poem. For example, it reveals only in the very last line, "My abandoned one" (*"Broshennyi moi"*), that there is a poetic "other," a male persona who has been "abandoned." With regard to the four nouns in the phrases *"Krepost' moia, Krotost' moia, Doblest' moia, Sviatost' moia"* ("My strength, my meekness, my valor, my holiness") it is not obvious from just the language of the poem that the qualities named by means of the four feminine abstract nouns designate "the other," that is, the male beloved. This becomes apparent only gradually, first indicated by the last line of the poem, then further clarified by the whole cycle and by other poems addressed to Efron which contain similar epithets. The interpretation is thus contextual, not direct. The informed reader can also draw on the biographical context and infer with fair confidence that the real-life referent of the short, symmetrical noun phrases *"Gde na zemle, Gde— / Krepost' moia"* ("Where on earth, where— / [Is] my strength"), and so on, is the speaker's beloved, indeed the poet's husband, Seryozha Efron, to whom the cycle is dedicated. The reader who knows that some forty other poems written between 1911 and 1921 and bearing a dedication to Efron are addressed to him or written about him will be even more confident about including the biographical person in the interpretation.

Another element of indirection in poem 1 is that the reference to the male speaker is not in the second person of address, not a "you." This creates distance from the absent other. The speaker or poetic ego, too, is not named directly as "I," but in the third person, by reference to the speaker's condition, which is one of "being without": without a home, without sleep, without laughter, without light and, especially, without a trace of the presence of the beloved. Thus neither the poetic ego nor the poetic other is named directly, but only in terms of qualities or states of each from the vantage point of the speaker. These states are presented in the form of abstract or concrete nouns, dissociated from person or action. Indeed, the dominant category of nouns in this entire text is abstract. The complete absence of personal nouns results in a sense of depersonalization. In the context of the lexicon of abstract and concrete non-personal nouns, the single particular descriptive image that refers to the person of the beloved—"A trace of narrow footprints" (*"Uzkikh podoshv sled"*)—is poignant. All the other vocabulary serves to create a tone of distancing, which is broken only in the final exclamation—"My abandoned one!"

Yet another element of indirection is the image of the striking tower clock. In the context of the title "Separation" and the thematics of the entire cycle, this image can be interpreted as an emblem variously standing for the experience of separation, which is seen as a process in time; for the strokes of doom or fate that have brought about what the speaker fears is a final separation—the death of her loved one; and as an image standing for the speaker's imminent death by her own hand. The image also introduces the motif of iterativity (repetitiveness being a common characteristic of the psychological experience of grief) and the tone of dread and despair that emerges in the rest of the poem, especially in poem 2. The poet chooses not to provide within the text itself any explicit commentary to help us understand the image, leaving it as an image of multiple meanings, which requires the reader to infer an interpretation from the context. (The property of forcing the reader/viewer to make an effort at interpretation will be seen to be a principle advocated by Filonov and also by Kandinsky for communicating meaning on a deeper level.)

Further contributing to the sense of indirection is the virtual absence of verbs. The syntax of the poem consists of noun phrases which are either nominalizations, such as the apostrophe "My abandoned one!" (*"Broshennyi moi!"*), or parts of a statement or question with zero copula (*"Gde . . . moi dom"*). The absence of verbs means that no specific actions, events, conditions, or propositions are predicated as "new information" in this text. The states of the speaker and the qualities of the other are presented syntactically as givens, but as givens *in absentia*, present only as questions uttered by the poet. Indeed, the questions indicate either absence or nonexistence, implying though not stating the possibility of the death of the loved one. This verbless interrogative syntax expresses very well the emotional "limbo" of the woman left behind, whose husband is away at war "without news." (The Russian expression for "missing in action" is *propal bez vesti* ["lost without news"].) The questioning is as close as the speaker dares to venture in uttering her fear about the loved one's death (as in the letter to her friend, quoted above). In addition to verblessness, the poem is also marked by the complementary absence of agents, reflecting a sense of helplessness. (These characteristics are significantly modified in the second poem.)

Striking in poem 1 is the economy of lexical, grammatical, strophic, and prosodic resources. Morphemes and lexical categories are highly repetitive. The key word *boi* (stroke or striking; the word is homophonous with the word for battle) is repeated four times. *Bashennyi* (the tower's) is repeated twice and *broshennyi/sbroshennyi* (abandoned/cast down, paronomastically related to *bashennyi*) occur three times. The four qualities referring to the poetic other are all abstract nouns with the suffix *-ost'*. The words naming what the speaker lacks are the five monosyllables *dom, son, smekh, svet, sled* (house, sleep, laughter, light, trace), four of which begin in "s" and each of which rhymes with at least one of the others. The masculine personal possessive pronoun *moi* (my) occurs five times and the feminine *moia* four times (in succession). The phrase *na zemle* (on earth) is repeated twice.

The syntax of poem 1 is extremely symmetrical. Lines 2, 3–8, and 11–17 consist of three sentences beginning with *gde* (where), two of them questions. As can easily be seen, the relationship of lexicon and syntax to the line results in a high degree of parallelism.

The lines are as short as normally allowed by Russian versification—they are dimeters or lines where the number of metrical stresses is two. There are even four graphic lines with only a single syllable and a single stress.

Among the most remarkable innovative features of this poem is the prosody. It consists entirely of lines with the choriambic pattern ◡◡◡, except in those lines that contain a single stressed monosyllable (lines 4, 12, 13, and 16). This meter appeared in two poems written a short time previously: "Iaroslavna's Lament" ("Plach Iaroslavny"), written in December 1920, immediately after the news of the White Army's defeat five months earlier, which blends a lament for Efron with a lament for the husband of the historical-literary Old Russian princess; and "On a Red Steed" ("Na krasnom kone"), written in January 1921, four months earlier. In both "Iaroslavna's Lament" and "On a Red Steed," the meter is associated with themes of loss, as in the present poem. (It will become a key metric sequence of Tsvetaeva's logaoedic meters in her later verse.)

The economy of poetic resources extends to the rhyme of this poem, as well. All the rhymes are masculine and most of them occur more than once. The rhyme *boi/moi/rukoi* appears in seven lines; the rhyme *Kremle/zemle/gde* in four lines; the rhyme *moia* in four adjacent lines; the assonance *smekh/svet* and the rhyme *slet* occur in three lines. In addition, several of the lines violate the implicit rule of conventional rhyming, namely that the rhyming words not be identical. Prominent in this regard is the rhyme *moia*, which appears in all four lines of one stanza. Also noteworthy is the extensive internal rhyme. It is as if the poetic lexicon of Tsvetaeva had suddenly been reduced to a very small number of possibilities, resulting in recurring paronomastic connections and lexical repetitions.

The repetitiveness of lexicon, grammar, meter, and rhyme makes for a striking economy, producing a sense of iterativeness that creates a tone of unyielding insistence. The iterativeness functions as a formal correlate of the insistent, inescapable, and obsessive qualities of the grief and psychic pain that are the experiential ground of this poem. It also seems peculiarly appropriate that a poetry that expresses grief and loss not be too eloquent and resourceful, but rather repetitive and spare. (Simplicity as a correlate of the expression of grief will be observed in the work of and articulated by Kaethe Kollwitz, discussed below.)

One of the key devices contributing to a sense of fragmentation in the poem is the predominance of metonymy. Elements of synechdoche prevail in the imagery: the "strokes" of the tower, the list of the qualities of the beloved and states of the speaker, the trace of the beloved's footprints, and the strokes of the clock as if cast down by a disembodied hand. The sense of fragmentation is supported by the absence of connectives in the syntax of these lines. The lines, whose surface syntactic structure is that of noun phrases or of sentences with copula, are joined by being listed in sequence, by parallelism and by repetition. Another connection is by means of evolving imagery, that is, by association. The sentences are not connected by conjunctions, by syntactic subordination, or by elements denoting temporal or causal connection.[14] Further contributing to the sense of fragmentation is the surface verblessness of the syntax, resulting in a world of eventless qualities and objects. (Metonymy together with repetition will be observed along with fragmentation of images in the work of Filonov.)

Poem 2 modifies the array of poetic resources while maintaining some of the restrictions observed in the first poem. The most significant difference consists of the presence of the personal category and of verbs: in the form of first person verbs in lines 2, 5, and 7 referring to the poetic self and the third person verb with personal subject in the last two lines referring to the poetic other. Elements of action and desire as well as of agency are thus introduced into the text.

Indirection appears in lines 7/8 and lines 9/10 where the key verbs *brosit'sia* (jump or throw oneself off) or *upast'* (fall) are twice omitted. This elision avoids the overly specific quality of the verbs. The essential act imagined by the poet is, after all, not "falling" but dying—which the poet longs for as "going home" and describes in the rest of the cycle as a transformation. The desire for death by suicide is pointed to but remains unspoken, referred to indirectly by the phrases *domoi khochu, vniz golovoi,* and *ne o bulyzhnik ploshchadnoi* (I want to go home, head downward, not onto the cobblestones of the square). Indirection appears in the designation of the other by the cryptic "*nekii Voin molodoi*" ("a certain young Warrior"). His death, too, is unspoken but understood: he is winged (like the warrior saints of Orthodox iconography) and will meet her at the moment of death by spreading his wing to break her fall.

Emblematic imagery is again present, standing for absence, grief and death: "*pustye ruki,*" "*pustoe chernoe okno,*" "*ruki brosaiu v poluno-chnyi boi,*" "*domoi khochu*" ("empty hands," "the empty black window," "I throw my hands into the midnight striking of the tower clock," "I want to go home").

With respect to linguistic economy, this poem, too, features repetition: *pustoe/pustye, ruki/ruki, domoi/domoi* (empty, hands, home), and the verbs (present and elided) denoting throwing and falling.

As regards fragmentation, metonymy is used with even greater prominence than in poem 1. The metonymic *ruki* (hands) assumes the function of *pars pro toto* representing the speaker, as she at first only "throws her hands" into the empty black window, the "empty hands" into the "midnight striking of the clock." The image of the speaker's empty hands (or arms) is evocative of her isolation and grief; the striking of the clock and the empty black window, of her sense of abandonment and her suicidal despair. While in the first poem qualities of character and emotion were presented as abstract nouns, dissociated from persons or actions, in the present poem metonymic imagery is dominant in producing an effect of fragmentation. The imagery of dismemberment on the lexical level is echoed by the interaction of syntax and line in the enjambement at the end of lines 5 and 6.[15] (The metonymic imagery of dismemberment finds a parallel in the paintings of Filonov as well as in cubism in general.)

The second poem is connected to the first by the use of evolving imagery. The imagined abstract hand of the first poem reappears as the speaker's own hands, raised, outstretched, empty. The strokes of the clock continue, as the tower becomes part of the imagery of the suicidal impulse: the speaker will throw herself off the tower, head down. (The image of the tower appears once more in poem 8, the final poem of the cycle, in which it stands for the speaker's revolt against God.)

The prosodic signature of fate and grief—the choriambic ⌣⌣╱—occurs only twice in poem 2, but it appears in the thematically significant phrases that state the motif of suicide in lines 7 and 8:

> *vniz golovoi*
> —*S bashni*! —*Domoi*!
> (head down
> —Off the tower! —Home!)

That the choriambic metrical unit is well established as the signature of grief by the time "Separation" was written can be seen from the fact that it appears in this thematic connection six months earlier, in Tsvetaeva's "Iaroslavna's Lament," written on the occasion of the defeat of the White Army, when Tsvetaeva first feared the worst (see below).

A different prosodic motif is dominant in poems 5 and 6. These poems narrate the dreadful step that confronts the mother who considers suicide—abandoning the child. In poem 5, the meter is amphibrachic, a prosodic pattern that grows out of several key phrases of the lexicon of separation: "*ruchonki*," "*naprasno zovete*," "*mezh nami*," and "*struistaia lestnitsa Lety*" ("dear little hands," "you call in vain," "between us," "the streaming stairs of Lethe") that form the concluding three lines of the poem. However, the lines are irregular, varying from one to four metrical accents. The amphibrachic meter is continued in poem 6: "*Sedoi—ne uvidish'*, / *Bol'shim— ne uvizhu*" ("You won't see me gray / I won't see you grown"). But starting in the second stanza it is broken up by a series of short lines with hypermetrical stresses. There are six lines with the pattern ⌣╱╱ (*razzor—plach*) or ╱╱⌣ (*bros' ruku*) and three stanza-final lines of a single accented word (e.g., *Mat'*). As in poem 2, several of the lines are interrupted by enjambement. This percussive rhythm occurs in the heartwrenching passages that imagine the suicide of the mother who leaves behind her child. Equally striking is the formality of the nearly identical logaoedic sequences in the last three stanzas.

Poem 6 is a masterwork of anticipatory maternal grief. The speaker addresses her child in abbreviated dimeter sentences, saying that they will not see each other grow gray or grow up; the child will not weep a single tear: "*Sedoi ne uvidish'*, / *Bol'shim—ne uvizhu*. / *Iz glaz nepodvizhnykh* / *Slezinki ne vyzhmesh'*" ("You won't see me gray-haired, / I won't see you grown up. / From unmoving eyes / You won't squeeze a tear"). The reason the speaker believes the child will not weep is revealed in stanza five—the mother's death will be a relief. "—*O chem zhe* / *Slezam tech'*, / *Raz—kamen's tvoikh* / *Plech!*" ("What's there to / Cry about, / Since a stone has rolled off your / Shoulders"). The Russian expression for relief is "*kamen's plech svalilsia*" ("like a stone off my shoulders.") Although this belief that the child would not grieve the death of the mother reveals depths of pain as well as denial, the tone of the poem is one of stoic determination. The speaker refuses to linger in the feminine grieving attitude of classic statuary ("a stone-eyed cameo") to delay the separation, even as she realizes that it will be the "last earthly time" of feeling the "heaviness of blood, knees, eyes." Nor will she slink out like a wounded beast. Her exit will be that of a stone boulder. Even as she undergoes the transformation of death and rises into the azure heights, her cloak like eagle wings, she knows that the mother dare not take the child to that "shining city."

While continuing to display some elements of fragmentation, especially by means of the prosody, metonymy, and evolving imagery, this poem is not characterized by the same degree of indirection as poem 1. For example, there is a direct connection to the addressee in the second-person verbs, the second-person pronouns, and the imperative verbs addressed to the child. Lexically, the protagonists of this poem are named—*ditia, mat'* (child, mother). The sense of connection of the still-living mother with her very much present child is different from the sense of separation of a wife from a long-absent husband who she fears is dead. Suicide, while it would serve (in the world of the poem) to reunite the speaker with the dead beloved, would have the opposite consequence of forever separating the mother from the child, which poses an emotional and moral problem that the poem tries to resolve.[16] Thus the title of the poem "Separation" is seen to have more than one meaning.

Modernism: Aesthetic Means and Thematic Motivation in Verbal and Visual Art

Separation and grief as a thematics appear as early as 1918 in Tsvetaeva's poetry dedicated to the Civil War and her absent husband. Gradually the tone shifts from rhetorical pathos (*Sem' mechei pronzali serdtse* [Seven swords pierced the heart], May, 1918) to bitterness and pain (*Khochesh' znat', kak dni prokhodiat* [You want to know how the days pass], November, 1919) to an authentic tragic voice (*Ia etu knigu poruchaiu vetru* [I entrust this book to the wind], February, 1920). Two cycles, "The Taking of Crimea" ("Vziatie Kryma"), November–December, 1920, and "Iaroslavna's Lament" ("Plach Iaroslavny") December, 1920, draw on the medieval Igor Tale for imagery and structure while revising that lyro-epic tale to grieve and memorialize the defeat of the White Army and express the poet's personal anguish. At the time of writing the two cycles, Tsvetaeva depended on the Igor Tale and on folk lament to create a poetics for her poems of mourning.[17] The prosodic framework was traditional dactylic epic meter. However, in "Iaroslavna's Lament," written ten months later, the choriambic sequence (∼∼∕) emerges as her own prosodic signature of grief, combined with repetition as the intrinsic mode of lament.

It is not until a few months later that the more "abstract" verse of "Separation" makes its appearance. The thematics is no longer death and defeat on the battlefield, or even the grief of the woman as survivor, for which some existing literary models (the epic) and folk rituals (the lament) are offered by the culture and adapted by Tsvetaeva in "The Taking of the Crimea" and "Iaroslavna's Lament." Rather, the thematics arises out of a suicidal despair that is the poet's emotional response to the ultimate separation of death.

In trying to write out of this existentially displaced, disoriented condition, Tsvetaeva had no models.[18] In "Separation" she undertakes not only to express the inexpressible grief of the final separation of death but also to create a mythology transcending the separation. In the process of discovering formal means for expressing the grief of separation, Tsvetaeva created a poetics that has many of the characteristics that first appear in avant-garde verse and painting in the preceding decade.

The visual arts present striking parallels to the verbal in the work of two of Tsvetaeva's contemporaries, Pavel Filonov and Kaethe Kollwitz. Filonov has enough representational "expressionist" elements to make possible thematic as well as aesthetic observations about his work. Kollwitz, like Tsvetaeva, sought in her work to give expression to grief at the death of a loved one—her younger son, Peter, who was killed in battle in 1914.

Filonov shared the common tendency of modernist painters for distortion or fragmentation of represented objects. John Bowlt has written about his early work that "Filonov . . . expressed the fervor of a true Symbolist who believed in the need to distort surfaces so as to reveal the inner meaning beyond the world of appearances."[19] Bowlt adds that Filonov (and Vrubel, a Symbolist) "use the line telegraphically, dissecting and decomposing, freeing and activating the latent energy of the object. The uniform impression that we gain from works such as Vrubel's *Campanulas* . . . and Filonov's drawing of flowers from Khlebnikov's *Izbornik stikhov 1907–1914* (Selection of poetry) . . . is of fission and explosion."[20] From 1918 on, Filonov's work includes disquieting abstract compositions with fragmented images of human heads.[21] This distortion and fragmentation is parallel to Tsvetaeva's elision of verbs and other connections, which similarly breaks up appearances of continuity and the normality of everyday life, revealing chaotic inner experiences.[22]

Iterativity or repetition is used prominently by Filonov. Comparing Filonov's painting with his verse, John Bowlt points out that "to some extent, Filonov used a similar device [i.e., word association] in his paintings where he might take a primary 'syllable' such as a face or head and repeat it in many variations and convolutions, producing the effect simultaneously of familiarity and estrangement."[23] Even in the entirely abstract studies, repetition is prominent, as the same line contours or shapes appear over and over, covering the entire canvas. This quality draws the viewer into the work, through its rhythmical intensity and a "ritual" or hieratic quality. This is highly reminiscent of Tsvetaeva's repetitive rhymes and logaoedic prosodic repetitiveness, which lend an incantatory ritual quality to the verse.

Filonov believed it to be important to draw the viewer into being an active participant in the perception of the work of art.[24] This was also a concern of his influential contemporary, Kandinsky, who believed that "by forcing the spectator to decipher mysterious ambiguous images he would involve him in the process of replacing confusion with understanding. Kandinsky equated such participation in the creation of art with the creation of the world. If both content and form were too readable, and if the painting did not reflect the confusions of the present with which the people identified, the work would not be meaningful."[25] The last remark is especially significant with regard to Tsvetaeva, where one can argue that if the verse regarding suicide were too straightforward, it would diminish in power and in the ability to communicate the depth and disruption of the grief and the suicidal feelings of the speaker.

While Filonov in his written statements focused on painterly craft and intellectual analysis rather than feeling or "expression," his contemporaries perceived grief and suffering in his works. In 1916, the brilliant innovative Futurist poet Velemir Khlebnikov wrote of the painting *The Feast of Kings* (two versions, 1911–12 and 1913–14), "The artist had painted a feast of corpses, a feast of revenge. Majestically, importantly, the cadavers were eating fruits illumined by a fury of grief as if by moonlight."[26] The poet Kuzmin, in 1913, found in Filonov's works "suffering, twisted faces and figures, their skin flayed, looking like anatomical specimens—they made you shudder. When the First World War broke out, many claimed the role of prophet, divining the coming bloody misfortunes in their work. More than anyone else, Filonov merited the calling of prophet."[27] Likewise, in numerous studies titled *Heads* in the mid-twenties, the disembodied heads with large eyes, filled with fragmented patterns, and small downturned mouths convey an effect of dehumanization and pain. Particularly suggestive is the oil on paper titled *Beasts* and dated 1925–26. In an urban landscape, with hard-edged buildings that look empty and gutted, there stand or lie three cubistic animals (perhaps a cow, a horse, and a dog) with humanoid faces expressing profound suffering. While the burden of Filonov's work is apocalyptic rather than personal, both he and Tsvetaeva use analogous aesthetic modes to communicate existential disorientation and psychic suffering.

It is important to acknowledge that the paintings in question, especially the later ones, have minimal narrative content. As Bowlt puts it, Filonov's paintings "disturb us by their intensity of imagery [and] audacious combinations of many styles . . . but, ultimately, defy reading, i.e., a documentary or anecdotal explanation. . . . "[28] While Tsvetaeva's verse is, of course, relatively more narrative than the paintings, when compared to her own earlier verse, it is significantly less anecdotal and narrative, and in this way may be viewed as converging with the paintings in style.

The focus of Kaethe Kollwitz's work was always the human figure, with strong thematic content bearing on social justice, suffering, and the human condition. When the war began in 1914, her younger son, Peter, volunteered for military service and was killed within a few months. Kollwitz was forty-seven. Her diaries in the succeeding years reflect continuing grief and an evolving commitment to opposing war. Both grief and the opposition to war motivated much of her work for over two decades. Two months after her son's death she records her plans for a memorial for him that would "commemorate the sacrifice of all the young volunteers."[29] (This memorial was not to be completed until 1932, eighteen years later.) Two months later, she speaks of her son as "seed for planting which should not have been ground."[30] This quotation from Goethe becomes a motif for her famous studies of a woman protecting a group of children.

In this period, Kollwitz's work is marked by an increasing economy of means. Already in 1909 she articulated the principle of economy in representing grief: "I should like to do the new etching [very likely *Death and the Woman*] so that all the essentials are strongly stressed and the inessentials almost omitted."[31] The self-portrait in 1916 (the first after her son's death two years before) shows only the face, in silent grief. Eliminated are not only clothing but also the hair and even the ears and neck.[32] In a 1916 journal entry Kollwitz writes, "[I]n groping for the precious truth one falls easily into artistic oversubtleties and ingenuities into preciosity. I suddenly see that very clearly and must watch out. Perhaps the work on the memorial will bring me back to simplicity."[33] In 1917 Kollwitz is working on a small sculpture, *The Parents*, as well as on a new drawing. She writes, "I have the hope that this time something really new in drawing and etching will come into the work. It can happen only through greater simplicity. Just as I want to make these parents—simplicity in feeling, but expressing the *totality of grief*."[34] In 1920, in a charcoal sketch showing grieving parents, the bowed figures kneel, embracing each other. Only the father's face is shown; the mother is more deeply bowed and her face is hidden. The father's hands and one hand of the mother are roughly sketched in the embrace. The bodies and clothing are without detail. In a later version of the same subject (woodcut, 1923), even the father's face has been eliminated. The grief is expressed by the attitude of the bodies and heads and the large bony hand covering the father's face. This minimizes individualized characteristics and moves from a representation of personal pathos to a universal human attitude of grief (fig. 7-1).

7-1 Kaethe Kollwitz. *Parents [Die Eltern]*, 1923. Woodcut, 35 × 42 cm. Plate 23 in *The Diary and Letters of Kaethe Kollwitz*, ed. Hans Kollwitz (Evanston, Ill.: Northwestern University Press, 1988). Plate 108 in Otto Nagel, *Kaethe Kollwitz* (Dresden: VEB Verlag, 1963). Courtesy of Hamburger Kunsthalle, Germany. Photo copyright by Elke Walford.

The granite figures of the grieving parents in the memorial monument completed in 1932, when Kollwitz was sixty-five, are similarly advanced in economy of representation. (Already in 1919 Kollwitz had written in her diary, "As always only the total attitude and the face and hands speak to me.")[35] The figure of the father expresses grief in the lowered eyes, downturned mouth, and the drawn cheeks, the crossed arms with hands clasping his sides, and the kneeling attitude. In the mother's figure, for which Kollwitz used her own head as the model, much of the expression of grief is incorporated in the bowed attitude.

In comparing the resources of Tsvetaeva and Kollwitz, it is interesting to note that the metonymic use of hands plays an important role in expressing grief in the work of each. In Tsvetaeva's "Separation," *ruka* and *ruki* (hand, hands) appear in five of the eight poems of the cycle, in highly expressive lines. (In the last poem, the image changes to *nogi* [feet].) The image of hands serves as an emblem of grief especially in poems 2, 3, and 5. Kollwitz is famous for the large hands in her graphics, using them expressively and giving them special prominence in the presentation of her figures. In the context of death and grief, as Kollwitz draws and sculpts them, hands, which often are the instruments of human action and creativity as well as of love and intimacy in touching and holding, are seen as objects of empty helplessness and mute suffering. Tsvetaeva speaks of "empty hands" which she "stretches out" and "throws" into an "empty, dark window," and of a child's "small hands," which "call in vain." Like Kollwitz, she employs a bodily image laden with multiple existential meaning deeply grounded in the human psyche.

In the preceding comparison, modern poetic elements of Tsvetaeva's verse associated with a thematics of grief are shown to bear striking correspondences to aesthetic and thematic elements in the works of two stylistically and philosophically very different contemporary visual artists, the painter Pavel Filonov and the graphic artist and sculptor Kaethe Kollwitz. Each had a different history of artistic motivation, while sharing the tragic consciousness fostered by war and revolution. In the case of Tsvetaeva, the poetic quest of a twenty-nine-year-old bereaved mother, a woman whose husband was missing in action, and a veteran poet led to an artistic breakthrough as radical as that which had been produced by others in pursuit of an aesthetic revolution.

Разлука

Сереже

1

Башенный бой
Где-то в Кремле.
Где на земле,
Где—

Крепость моя,
Кротость моя,
Доблесть моя,
Святость моя.

Башенный бой.
Брошенный бой.
Где на земле—
Мой
Дом,
Мой—сон,
Мой—смех,
Мой—свет,
Узких подошв—след.

Точно рукой
Сброшенный в ночь—
Бой.

—Брошенный мой!

Май.

2

Уроненные так давно
Вздымаю руки.
В пустое черное окно
Пустые руки.
Бросаю в полуночный бой
Часов,—домой
Хочу!—Вот так: вниз головой
—С башни!—Домой!

Не о булыжник площадной:
В шепот и шелест...
Мне некий Воин молодой
Крыло подстелет.

Май.

6

Седой—не увидишь,
Большим—не увижу.
Из глаз неподвижных
Слезинки не выжмешь.

На всю твою муку,
Раззор—плач:
—Брось руку!
Оставь плащ!

В бесстрастии
Камешоокой камеи,
В дверях не помедлю,
Как матери медлят:

(Всей тяжестью крови,
Колен, глаз—
В последний земной
Раз!)

Не крадущимся перешибленным зверем,—
Нет, каменной глыбою
Выйду из двери—
Из жизни. —О чем же
Слезам течь,
Раз—камень с твоих
Плеч!

Не камень! —Уже
Широтою орлиною—
Плащ! —и уже по лазурным стремнинам
В тот град осиянный,
Куда—взять
Не смеет дитя
Мать.

15 июня.

Separation

To Seryozha

1

A tower's strokes
Somewhere in the Kremlin.
Where on earth,
Where [is]—

My strength,
My humility,
My valor,
My holiness.

A tower's strokes,
Abandoned strokes [or: battle].
Where on earth [is]—
My
Home,
My—sleep,
My—laughter,
My—light,
The trace of narrow feet.

As if by a hand
Cast down into the night—

My abandoned one!

2

I raise my hands
Dropped so long ago.
Out the empty black window
[My] empty hands
I throw into the midnight strokes
Of the clock, —I want [to go]
Home! —like so: head down—
Off the tower! —Home!

Not onto the pavement of the square:

Into the whisper and rustle . . .
A certain young warrior
Will spread his wing under me.

6

You won't see me gray-haired,
I won't see you grown up.
From unmoving eyes
You won't squeeze a tear.

To all your suffering,
Weeping is a frivolous response:
Let go the hand!
Release the cape!

In the impassive attitude
Of a stone-eyed cameo
I won't pause at the doorway
As mothers pause:

(With all the heaviness of blood,
Knees, eyes—
For the last earthly
Time!)

Not like a slinking wounded beast—
No, like a block of stone
I'll go out of the door
Out of life. What's there to
Cry about,
Since a stone has rolled off your
Shoulders!

Not a stone!—Already
With an eagle's breadth
[Soars] the cape!—and already in the azure steeps
[Winging] to that illumined city,
To which—a mother
Dares not take her
Child.

(May–June)

Notes

1. The year 1912 saw the publication in Moscow of the collection *A Slap in the Face of Public Taste*, which included the document of the same title, known as the Futurist manifesto. Another manifesto was published in *A Trap for Judges II* in 1913. Since Tsvetaeva began to publish her poetry in 1910, modernism in this paper is taken as post-Symbolist modernism rather than the Symbolist modernism dating from 1893.

2. Joseph Brodsky in his essay "Footnote to a Poem" makes the following claim and observation: "In terms of form, Tsvetaeva is significantly more interesting than any of her contemporaries, including the Futurists, and her rhymes are more inventive than Pasternak's. Most importantly, however, her technical achievements have not been dictated by formal explorations but are by-products—that is, natural effects—of speech, for which the most significant thing is its subject." Joseph Brodsky, *Less than One: Selected Essays* (New York: Farrar Straus Giroux, 1986), 201; Russian text "Ob odnom stikhotvorenii" [About a poem], in Marina Tsvetaeva, *Stikhotvoreniia i poemy* [Verses and poems] (New York: Russica, 1980), 1:43.

3. The characteristics presented here as modern or modernist are similar to some of the characteristics mentioned in George Gibian's introduction to *Russian Modernism: Culture and the Avant-Garde, 1900–1930*, ed. George Gibian and H. W. Tjalsma (Ithaca: Cornell University Press, 1976), 11–12.

4. The comparability of certain avant-garde literature and art is discussed by Juliette Stapanian in "*Universal War*   and the Development of *Zaum*': Abstraction toward a New Pictorial and Literary Realism," *Slavic and East European Journal* 29 (1985): 18–38.

5. Simon Karlinsky says, "Another paradox about *Craft* is that, with this book the poet who was a romantic conservative in her politics, became a full-fledged radical innovator in her art." Karlinsky, *Marina Tsvetaeva: The Woman, Her World, and Her Poetry* (Cambridge: Cambridge University Press, 1985), 111. In his introduction to the reprint of the 1922 edition of *Craft*, Efim Etkind speaks of the movement of Tsvetaeva's poetry from understandable, wholly transparent verse to verse that is mysterious and obscure. See Marina Tsvetaeva, *Remeslo* (Moscow/Berlin: Gelikon, 1923), xiv.

6. Karlinsky, *Marina Tsvetaeva*, 72.

7. Both are reproduced in Viktoria Schweitzer, "Stranitsy k biografii M. Tsvetaevoi" [Pages for a biography of M. Tsvetaeva], *Russian Literature* 9 (1981): 323–356.

8. Jane Taubman, in her book *A Life through Poetry: Marina Tsvetaeva's Lyric Diary* (Columbus, Ohio: Slavica Publishers, 1989), observes that Tsvetaeva appears to have felt alienated from her younger, slow-to-develop daughter, and may actually have abused her, that she bore a share of the responsibility for not doing a better job of providing for her children's needs, and that she was disingenuous in blaming conditions. While the evidence marshalled by

Taubman that Tsvetaeva was in many ways a shockingly poor mother is persuasive, a charitable and plausible interpretation would be that she was by temperament and upbringing truly unable to cope with the conditions. Whatever the case, the death of her child evoked grief and guilt, as well as denial, a defense mechanism against what the psyche finds "too bad" to acknowledge.

9. V. M. Volosov and I. V. Kudrova, "Pis'ma Mariny Tsvetaevoi Evgeniiu Lannu" [Letters of Marina Tsvetaeva to Evgenii Lann], *Marina Cvetaeva: Studien und Materialien*, Wiener Slawistischer Almanach, Sonderband 3 (Vienna, 1981): 161–194.

10. Volosov and Kudrova, "Pis'ma Mariny Tsvetaevoi," 187.

11. Ibid., 168.

12. Ibid., 171.

13. Ibid., 186.

14. This is similar to Anna Akhmatova's practice of "abrupt juxtaposition" of images, but without the semantic transitions characteristic of Akhmatova. See James B. Woodward, "Semantic Parallelism in the Verse of Axmatova," *Slavic and East European Journal* 15 (1971): 456–58, 460–62.

15. The imagery of dismemberment as a correlative of the pain of separation returns in one of the poems of separation in Tsvetaeva's great cycle "Wires"—*"Tochno ruki—vsled—ot plech! / Tochno guby vsled—zakliast'! / Zvuki rasteriala rech', / Pal'tsy rasteriala piast'* " ("It's as if the hands / arms—follow [you]—[having broken away] from the shoulders! / It's as if the lips follow [you]—to invoke a magic incantation! / My speech has lost its sound, / My hand has scattered its fingers"). The image of going home appears in the adjacent poem of "Wires"—*I domoi. / V nezemnoi— / Da moi* ("And home. / To an unearthly one— / But my own"). These lines were written in March 1923, when Tsvetaeva was grieving another separation—the departure of soul-mate and object of desire, Boris Pasternak, from Berlin for Moscow, while Tsvetaeva remained in the Czech countryside near Prague.

16. Sylvia Plath's poem "Edge," written five days before Plath's suicide, deals differently with the "impossible separation," imagining the death of the children together with the mother "with uncanny detachment." Cf. A. Alvarez, "A Poet and Her Myths," *New York Review of Books* (28 September 1989): 35.

17. The evolution of the poetics of grief in the verse of 1918 to 1920 is discussed in my unpublished papers "*Slovo o Polku Igoreve* as a Subtext of Marina Tsvetaeva's Cycles '*Vziatie Kryma*' and '*Plach Iaroslavny*,' " and "Marina Tsvetaeva: Developing Poetic Voice and Consciousness."

18. The suicide in *Axel* of Villiers de L'Isle Adam, which was a model for Tsvetaeva's juvenile verse, is ironically inappropriate. This Symbolist play relates a suicide pact by two lovers, who realize that their love will never again reach the height of bliss they are experiencing at their first encounter.

19. John E. Bowlt, "Pavel Filonov and Russian Modernism," *Pavel Filonov: A Hero and his Fate*, ed. Nicoletta Misler and John E. Bowlt (Austin: University

of Texas Press, 1983), 6. Unlike Tsvetaeva and Kollwitz, Filonov was a programmatic artist, publishing a manifesto on "Made Painting" in 1914 and lengthy programmatic pieces in the twenties.

20. Bowlt, "Pavel Filonov," 6–7.

21. Reproduced in *Pavel Filonov: A Hero and his Fate.*

22. I am indebted to Roger Anderson for this observation.

23. Bowlt, "Pavel Filonov," 15.

24. Ibid.

25. Rose-Carol Washton Long, *Kandinsky: The Development of an Abstract Style* (Oxford: Clarendon Press, 1980), 66.

26. Quoted in Bowlt, "Pavel Filonov," 10.

27. Ibid., 11.

28. Ibid., 7.

29. *The Diary and Letters of Kaethe Kollwitz*, ed. Hans Kollwitz, trans. Richard and Clara Winston (1955; reprint, Evanston, Ill.: Northwestern University Press, 1988), 63.

30. Kollwitz, *The Diary*, 64.

31. Quoted in Martha Kearns, *Kaethe Kollwitz: Woman and Artist* (New York: The Feminist Press at the City University of New York, 1976), 118; bracketed interpolation is Kearns's.

32. See Kollwitz, ed., *The Diary and Letters of Kaethe Kollwitz.*

33. Kollwitz, *The Diary*, 69.

34. Ibid., 86–87.

35. Ibid., 94.

EIGHT

Ironic "Vision" as an Aesthetics of Displaced Truth in M. Bulgakov's *Master and Margarita*

Juliette R. Stapanian-Apkarian

No! Not more light, but more warmth! We die of cold and not of darkness. It is the frost that kills and not the night.
Miguel de Unamuno, *Tragic Sense of Life*

Few works of twentieth-century Russian literature have captured more attention concerning literary parallels and real-life referents than *Master and Margarita* (1929–40) by Mikhail Afanas'evich Bulgakov. Scholarly studies have profiled the relationship of the novel to the author's life, the Bible, Faustian myth, Menippean satire, and reality in Stalinist Russia. Although mentioned frequently in analyses of Bulgakov's novel, the concept of irony often is discussed as an adjunct to the complex satire in the work, or as coloration to narration or to other aspects of the work. Yet, careful consideration of the text reveals that irony, far from playing a merely secondary role in the book, is a major component of its style and meaning. As irony penetrates the work, its essentially subversive "vision" offers a means for grappling with the cryptic nature of the novel, a nature arising specifically from the use of irony as a strategy to examine truth displaced by the very signs used to encode it. Rooted in the Greek word *eironeia* meaning "dissimulation," irony traces flux, or a confrontation of truths or realities. By means of irony as shift, the novelist questions "real" images and logocentric signs of truth to show Reality and Truth as primary texts that are persistently edited. As a result, absolutes are traced, ironically, from their continual potential for displacement. In this regard, then, *Master and Margarita* is a work about truth and art, Truth and the Word.[1]

Reinforcing an aesthetics of flux challenging apparent or codified truths, ironic vision suggests "all is not as it appears to be," in the visual arts as well as in literary texts. Although the concept of visual and verbal shift would be celebrated most vigorously in the art of the Russian Futurists in the twentieth century, a painting from the late nineteenth century offers a springboard from which to first examine the dynamics of irony in *Master and Margarita*. This painting, *What Is Truth?* (Chto est' istina?) (1890), by Nikolai Nikolaevich Ge (1831–94), shares with Bulgakov's later novel a pivotal moment from biblical accounts of Pilate's interrogation of Christ (Ieshua in the novel).[2] In 1913 Vsevolod Dmitriev wrote an article reevaluating the place of Ge in art history for the Russian art journal *Apollon*. According to Dmitriev, Ge had knowingly borne the label "crazy man" and had identified art with the sacrifice for truth. The article included many reproductions of Ge's paintings, and refers to the work *What Is Truth?* then hanging in the Tretiakov Gallery in Moscow (fig. 8-1).[3]

A Tolstoyan renowned for his depiction of historical and biblical themes, Ge developed a painterly style striking in its use of light. Although *What Is Truth?* may appear at first highly realistic in its depiction of Christ questioned by Pilate, consideration of shift reveals a powerful use of irony in the work which responds to the titular inquiry about truth. More precisely, this ironic vision involves interplay among coding systems, traditional loci for conveying "truths." Association of light with good and dark with evil codes an ancient artistic and biblical trope. Yet in Ge's painting it is Christ, the "Prince of Light," who stands bound and in dark shadow, while Pilate, representative of Rome, gestures authoritatively and walks confidently in the bright mideastern light. Pilate's hair lies smooth and unperturbed, while Christ's stands "crazily" disheveled.

Spatial enclosure by a frame articulated in the painting by the image of walls and floor is subverted by the encroachment of light and the open-endedness of the wall behind Christ. The lighting in the painting has a strong architectural quality, but, ironically, it is not clear in the work if the light, from which Pilate turns away, is the sun itself or its rays reflected from the moon. While this light seemingly falls directly onto the back of Pilate's head, it also gently captures Christ's unsettling eyes. This shift from back (Pilate) to front (Christ) takes yet another turn: because the intensity of light enveloping Pilate so severely heightens his silhouette, the trope of light-as-good is subverted by the extreme lighting itself. As a result,

8-1 Nikolai Nikolaevich Ge. *What Is Truth?,* 1890. Christ and Pilate. Oil on canvas, 233 × 171 cm. Courtesy of Tretiakov Gallery, Moscow.

the searing light negates any positive warmth emanating from the image of Pilate in the painting. The inversion of traditional symbols and tropes by light imagery is further complicated by the heavy shadow cast by Pilate that runs parallel to the darkness shrouding the tattered figure of Christ, at whose feet a leather thong crosses finger-like into the light. Although the picture is set near a corner of a room, space is not clearly contained in the painting. Yet the edge of Pilate's sharply articulated robe (in contrast to Christ's) appears to press against the confines of the frame. Christ, traditionally the Word, stands silent in the painting, while Pilate, posing the question, is in the act of speech. Nonetheless, the commanding presence of Pilate is undermined in the picture, for it is Christ who faces the spectator, while Pilate stands with his back to the viewer.

Signs of historic time and space in the painting give way to a fundamental timelessness, as biblical symbols confront the visual codes of "realism" depicting the interrogation. Use of foreshortened ground intensifies the questioning of appearances and heightens the sense of immediacy underlying truth revealed by ironic shift in the work: shadow is displaced light and untempered light is light without warmth. With deceptive simplicity, ironic vision serves as a mechanism in the painting to answer "what is truth?" in favor of Christ, the Truth. Later Bulgakov too would employ irony as a strategy to reveal the continual potential for displacement of truth/ Truth by the very signs which presume to describe, articulate, or identify it.

Irony in the context of displaced truth had tremendous appeal for artists in the early twentieth century. As an expressive and philosophic dimension of shift (*sdvig*), irony seemed particularly well suited to ideas in the emerging Age of Relativity. Although Bulgakov was not a proponent of radical modernism, his *Master and Margarita* does demonstrate modernist sensibilities regarding the device of shift. As defined by the Cubo-Futurists in the 1910s, such mechanisms as verbal and visual shift could provide new perspectives to unveil or expose a vital reality beneath the "ossified" vision of the past. By means of shift, artists disrupted distinctions between the conventionally rational and the irrational, and they permitted the prosaic to confound traditional boundaries with the mystical in order see the world anew. Artists considered the possibilities of a fourth dimension and called for dynamic art of multiple and simultaneous viewpoints with unexpected inversions and fragmented frameworks. Many Futurists heralded the value of words and forms in themselves, and they often created visual and verbal puns by means of realized metaphors. Some of these principles are illustrated in pictures like *Englishman in Moscow* (1913–14), a Cubo-Futurist work by Kazimir Malevich which utilizes the foreign perspective of the oddly colored Englishman to present a carnival-like, alogical vision of Moscow filled with displaced images, words and visual puns (fig. 8-2). Words take on a visual role as objects, and depictions of cutting tools such as a sword and scissors and the image of a ladder act as visual "abbreviations" for the spatial shifts and breakup of image-planes in the work. The motif of church cupolas in the painting is dominated by an adjacent fish, a signboard image used to play on Christian iconography. Because the fish overlaps or "eclipses" one side of the Englishman's face, the eye of the fish effectively displaces that of the man. The red arrow emanating from the word *chas*, which means "hour," a syllable from the words "partial eclipse" (*chastichnoe zatmenie*) in the work, acts as a clock hand in a vivid pun about time and space. Similarly, the words "riding society" (*skakovoe obshchestvo*) stand out like epaulets from the stylized figure of the Englishman.

Malevich works against assumptions of closed forms and traditional signs. By realizing metaphors and by violating conventional associations of size, space, time, and causality among objects, the painter magically opens a new logic and dynamic reality which cultural conventions and traditional logic have trained us not to see. Bulgakov, too, employs many devices of shift analogous to those in the overturned world of modernist painting; however, his continual use of shift in the text results in a self-reflexive irony: with an eye toward an absolute, Bulgakov demonstrates that it is not truth that is relative, but the signages which may mask or displace it. As Voland, embodiment of Irony, says, we do not need various points of view and proof—Christ simply existed (15).

The Bolshevik Revolution promised historic confrontation with Russia's past. Initially, many modernists as well as proletarian artists hoped that the revolution could bring about displacement of old values and fundamentally change human nature. Polemics were brutal as representatives from different artistic movements laid claim to their art as the only true voice for the new reality ahead. Debate ended as the principles of socialist realism were formulated. Harsh discrepancies between details of daily life in Stalinist Russia (where people really did suddenly disappear) and the optimistic vision portrayed in political slogans and official art became part of Soviet reality. This life of codified hypocrisy forms much of the context of the novel by Bulgakov. Although the author exposes deceptions specific to Stalinist Moscow, he also reveals that human traits like cowardice, greed, and superstition that promote shifts

8-2 Kazimir Malevich. *Englishman in Moscow,* 1913–14. Oil on canvas, 88 × 57 cm. Courtesy of Collection Stedelijk Museum, Amsterdam.

from truth or justice are as common on the streets of Stalinist Moscow as they were centuries ago in the Yershalaim of Pilate.

With reference points taken from artistic analogues and polemics in the visual arts, the pervasive use of ironic shift in *Master and Margarita* becomes readily apparent. The work represents a masterful study of changing and deceptive appearances and questionable identities and, ultimately, addresses "what is truth?" Like Ge, Bulgakov juxtaposes codes of both the mythic as well as the historicized Christ as Ieshua with Pilate, so that their displacement can describe moral Truth.

As in the painting by Ge, the interrogation of Christ by Bulgakov is set in a strong architectural setting with lines of intense lighting. Potential closure of space suggested by the covered colonnade between two wings of the building is displaced by the view of the garden plot (*ploshchadka*) and beyond from the balcony. Scenes with Pilate are scattered with sculptures, and Pilate comments negatively about the architecture of the city, an opinion reflecting both his foreign perspective and his feeling of estrangement. Like the painting, the novel presents Christ's hands as bound behind his back (16). While Christ stands in shadow in Ge's work with light capturing his eye, Ieshua in the novel smiles "luminously" (*svetlo*), screening himself from the sun with his hand (23). In another parallel to the painting, light crawls up to the worn sandals of the disheveled, beaten Ieshua, who deliberately moves away from the sun (*tot storonitsia ot solntsa*) (21). The Socratic posture of Pilate's boldly upraised arm in the painting finds variation in the book when Pilate "allows himself" to raise his arm, "as if screening himself from the sun's rays, and behind this hand, as behind a shield, to send the arrested man a certain telling look" (26). In the novel Pilate tries to assert his authority while helplessly suffering from a severe headache, heightened by the sun's light, echoing the undermining effect of harsh light on the back of Pilate's head in the painting by Ge. While the edge of Pilate's robe seems to press against the frame in the picture, Pilate utters at one point in the book, "I feel cramped . . . I feel cramped" (*"tesno mne . . . tesno mne!"*) (32).

To the question "What is truth?" ("Chto takoe istina?") in the novel, Ieshua answers that the truth is first of all that Pilate's head hurts so much that he thinks of death "faintheartedly" (the word play is even stronger in Russian, where *malodushno* literally means "little-soul-edly"). As a result, ironically, it is Ieshua the condemned who has involuntarily become Pilate's torturer (*palach*) (21). Along with this inversion from condemned to torturer, Ieshua takes on a position of dominance. Because conscience and light, like Ieshua, also torment Pilate, this effectively marks a place of moral dominance as well. Ironic displacement continues as Ieshua quietly, skillfully, and with disarming naiveté defuses questions and threats hurled at him. For example, when asked for his name, he counters, "My own?" Despite Pilate's warning that he can cut the hair by which Ieshua's life hangs, the accused responds that it can only be cut by the one who had hung it. The verbal expertise of Ieshua is, in fact, specifically acknowledged by Pilate, who says, "I do not know who hung your tongue, but it is hung well" (23).[4] As well as in the verbal parrying, irony is highlighted in deceptive appearance. When Pilate tells Ieshua not to "pretend" to be more stupid than he is (18) and to stop pretending to be "crazy" (19), Ieshua himself responds by asking Pilate if he looks like a "weak-minded person" (*slaboumnyi*) (23). In fact, rather than a prophet or a bearer of privileged knowledge (like a physician), Ieshua proves to be an exceptionally skilled interpreter or "reader"—complement of "writer"—of non-verbal signs. Seeing through the bold postures of Pilate, Ieshua is able to understand one gesture of the man of power as an unspoken wish for his dog. In contrast, although Pilate claims to the head of the secret service to "foresee" an attempt to kill Iuda (Judas), his words actually "write" a death sentence for Iuda; as a result, the purported foretelling acts as an ironic use of signs to displace causality in a murder prompted by Pilate's own words responding to his feelings for Ieshua. Ironically, then, Pilate becomes like Voland, able to predict death. In their interaction, Ieshua and Pilate present a confrontation of realities and "truths" to reveal the true. Although Ieshua says it is easy to speak the truth (*pravda*), he concedes that falseness now reigns by adding that one day the kingdom of truth (*tsarstvo istiny*) and justice will come to pass (28).

According to tradition, the Devil is the Spirit of Irony, and it is Voland, the Devil, who, by the device of framing, presumably shifts to the Master's voice to recount Master's story about Ieshua and Pilate in the second chapter of the work. Like the picture by Ge, Bulgakov uses the device of framing to undermine closure, for the last words of the epilogue are but a slight variation of the last words Master predicts would end his own novel (compare 134, 379, 392). In contrast to the subtle use of ironic shift shared by Ge's painting and the Jerusalem story line in Bulgakov's work, a much more colorful and dramatic use of shift emerges in the Moscow line, which strikingly echoes features of Malevich's "alogical" modernist style. Like *Englishman in Moscow*, Bulgakov places the "foreigner" Voland in the Moscow setting to overturn common expectations of reality. (Coincidentally, in the opening chapter Berlioz and Ivan even consider that Voland might be an Englishman.) Like Malevich's painting, the work by Bulgakov is filled with realized metaphors and with unusual displacements of color, proportion, and images. Reference is made to a "fifth dimension," and new perspectives make the familiar seem unfamiliar, as in Margarita's flight over Moscow, where a clock suddenly appears like a huge illuminated disk with an arrow drawn on it (230). As Malevich merges traditionally distinct spatial planes, Bulgakov too weaves the frames of Moscow, Yalta, and Yershalaim. Images are literally fragmented—decapitated, even, by Bulgakov—transformed and reassociated. Verbal and image play is rampant but not meaningless, for the alogical world unveiled by Voland is the logical world masterfully exposed. The very signs used to identify conventional reality turn upon themselves to reveal their displacement of truth. Analogous to examples from the pictorial arts, irony in the novel often is a function of the shifted codages themselves.

In his painting Malevich celebrates manipulation of visual images most succinctly as a realized metaphor of the eye of a fish eclipsing that of the Englishman. Few image types throughout the novel by Bulgakov are more extensive than those related to the eye, light, and looking. Eyes squint, gaze, glance, blur, reflect powers of perception, and link characters. For example, the mismatched eyes of the devil Voland (one is green and one is black) act ironically as a variation of those of the Christ figure Ieshua, who has a bruise under one eye. Stepa tries to unglue the lid of his left eye, Berlioz wears "supernaturally" large glasses, the Master gazes at the moon when he talks to Ivan, the loneliness never before "seen" (*ne vidannoe*) (135) in Margarita's eyes captures the Master's heart, and Pilate has a blinding headache. Significantly, the Master, who tells Ivan "we will look truth (*pravda*) in the eye," also declares that they are both "insane" (*sumasshedshie*) (132), literally "having stepped out of mind" or become displaced from socially codified norms. The issue too of witnesses in both the Moscow and the Jerusalem storylines repeatedly is undermined as a criterion for establishing truth, for false witnessing casts false "light" throughout the novel. Yet when

Ivan relates what he feels were unbelievable events that took place with Voland, the Master counters that they had indeed taken place "in reality" (*v deistvitel'nosti*) (132).

The symbol of perception—the eye—and the related symbol of reason or logic—the head—function literally (Berlioz and Bengalskii are decapitated, Pilate has a headache) and figuratively in ironic examination of what is real. Hallucinations, disappearances, dreams, mirages, and "strange" appearances mix with what seems at first to be the familiar or real world. At times people do not believe what they see, because it does not fit their expectations or accepted codes; or they believe what is illusory, often because of the distorting lens of greed or fear. In this regard, irony arises even in the etymology of common epithets in the work, as in the reference to the easily deceived audience at Voland's magic show, a group verbally encoded in Russian—unlike English—literally in terms of vision (*zritel'naia massa* ["viewing mass"]) (165). Because the Russian word for "glance" or "look" (*vzgliad*) peppers the text, one feels that the characters "look" more than they actually "see." Curiously, not until Margarita is invisible—i.e. not seen—does she actually feel herself to be "free" (*svobodna*) (230). This positive image finds variation in the erasure of presence by an African servant who "loses himself" (*rasterialsia*) under the gaze of Pilate; a slave, who—as Pilate notices—does not have the courage to look his master in the face, the African avoids further confrontation by standing out of sight. For Pilate, then, the servant has become forgotten, an invisible man (295–97). At the same time, however, the African also has become an unexpected witness. Voland, too, claims to have witnessed the first discussion between Ieshua and Pilate. Although Voland's presence need not be delineated by a single image in the scene such as that of the African, a variety of motifs like smoke, the swallow, and images related to the hippodrome (the novel was first called *Consultant with a Hoof*) could also suggest fragments of his figure. In Voland-the-Devil's role as a witness, predictor (as of Berlioz's death), and protagonist in the interplay of human life, the tradition of casting the "evil eye" is causally inverted in the novel.

Because human sight has physical constraints and is dependent upon light, limitations such as nearsightedness and references to light and its displacement in shadow are repeated motifs in the novel. Yet, in addition to its role in perception, light functions figuratively as a traditional trope for knowledge, goodness, and truth. Bulgakov manipulates this code too. As already noted, Ieshua is not consistently identified with direct light; nor is Voland, the Devil, strictly associated with darkness. Other instances of a sub-verted code, identifying good strictly with light and evil only with dark, fill the novel. For example, the sun displaced into the sun-flower oil kills Berlioz; and Margarita, whom the Master loves, carries sun-yellow flowers, a color the Master hates. As the novel demonstrates, in contrast to outward signs of "light" as knowledge, such as Berlioz's education, acts of courage and compassion—results of illuminated conscience—emerge as positive attributes which earn Light.

Like Malevich, Bulgakov explores the complex interplay of co-dages to reveal ironies both of perceptions and of expressions. In addition to the value of perceived imagery, Bulgakov questions the validity of a logocentric world by examining the word as a construct that can displace another truth or reality with its own. Instead of active "pursuit of signs,"[5] passive pursuit by signs can emerge. The ironic function of signage takes hold from the very title of the book, which announces characters not introduced until well into the body of the work, a work which in great part does not focus directly on the couple together. Morever, Bulgakov's text begins not with his own words, but with an epigraph from Goethe's *Faust:*

". . . so who art thou, in the end (*nakonets*)?"
"I am part of that force (*sila*) that eternally
wills evil and eternally accomplishes (*sovershaiet*) good (*blago*)."

As a snatch of conversation translated into Russian from a foreign masterpiece, the epigraph itself represents language codes dis-placed—first by fragmentation and then by shift from one language into another. Moreover, the ironic posture of a force that eternally shifts evil into good identifies a displaced presence, where good is defined by destabilized evil. This theme, embodied with variation in the figure of Voland, reverberates throughout the ironic action in the novel, and underlies Pilate's skepticism toward Ieshua's asser-tion that "there are no evil people on earth/in the light" (*na svete*) (24).

The very words labeling the first chapter, "Never Speak with Strangers," further promote a sense of ironic displacement. Indeed, action in the novel begins precisely because characters do speak with a stranger. But this ironic subversion is accomplished not just by the action in the text, but also by the verbal plane itself, for in Russian the word *neizvestnye* (strangers) literally means "the unknown."[6] This fluctuation between the figurative and the literal meanings of the word provides a paradigm for excursion in the novel into worlds where apparent lines between the real and the magical or mystical become blurred. Return to a more primal sense of the word manifests itself often in the work as ironic realization of epithets, or word "signs." For example, before Voland even fully appears, his identity is inadvertently revealed by Berlioz's curse about the Devil *"Fu ty chert!"* ("You damned devil!"). Similar epithets muttered by an irritated Ivan and others fill the book with realized metaphors about the Devil, and ironically reveal a wisdom exceeding the more reasoned commentary of many of the characters. At times shift among images involves concrete projections of psychological state or of metaphoric language, as when a "blunt needle" of seemingly irrational fear in Berlioz is transferred into a column of air from which a "citizen" appears.

Although realized metaphors often contribute to the humor or to the magical quality of the text, the device plays a serious role too in questioning the nature of reality. This role helps expose the matter of displaced truth integral to the work, for the very presence of epithets reflects a primal or literal reality that has long since been displaced by accepted codes of expression. The notion of language as symbolic placement and as physical dis-placement of concrete reality is associated in the text with the theme of editing. This theme, in turn, forms a dynamic line in the novel with the view of history as a construct and with the idea of identity or existence as a function of naming. Related but broader, Bulgakov's study of the realities of words parallels his interest in "the Word," represented in the contrast between biblical canon and the text of the Master; ultimately, linking irony to the theme of editing provides a strategy for discerning displacement of Truth in the novel. As Northrop Frye writes in *The Great Code*, "God ... may not be so much dead as entombed in a dead language."[7]

Although the word "ironic"[8] appears several times in the Moscow and Jerusalem story lines, the book is full of concepts related to the artfulness of writing as shift, including transcription, translation, transformation, and editing. Moreover, the manipulation of history and fiction or myth in the work enacts a masterful realization of the Russian word for history, *istoriia*, which also means "story" in Russian. Voland, a specialist in black magic; the Master, a writer; and Ivan, a poet; all are "historians" in the novel. In this regard, too,

Bulgakov's text functions to realize the Russian word for art, *iskusstvo*, which etymologically derives from "artifice." The word *iskusstvo* or *iskusstvenno* appears several times in the work. Ironically, "cultured" people dismiss events surrounding Voland as acts by a gang of hypnotists and ventriloquists who superbly mastered their "art" (*iskusstvo*) (380). In the Jerusalem storyline, Pilate is able "with great artfulness" (*s bol'shim iskusstvom*) to feign surprise at the High Priest's decision to release Bar-Rabban instead of Ieshua. The world of the theater is itself a world of shift from surrounding reality, but the author intentionally confounds the lines dividing this world from the "real" one. The tongue-in-cheek effect of a naive narrative voice who repeatedly assures the reader that he is "frankly speaking" is modulated in the Moscow line by a more omniscient voice, and this interplay represents a continual source of shift throughout the text. This device may not necessarily mean multiple narrators exist, for in the context of ironic identity in the work, multiplicity may arise from a single narrator's fluid guise, a changing of roles, so to speak, resulting in a polyphonic displacement of uniform narrative voice. In addition to the voices of narration, the book also has editors, who change or shift texts. While this theme reflects Soviet reality and Bulgakov's fate, the act of editing has broader meaning in the novel. The editor who first receives the Master's manuscript does not even focus on the text itself, but asks who had given the writer the idea to write such a novel. He then passes the decision about publishing the novel to an editorial board, and not surprisingly the editorial secretary's eyes permanently squint from constant lying. Berlioz wants Ivan to change his work, and Ivan, in turn, boldly exposes the hypocrisy of the self-editing poet Riukhin—a kulak who "pretends to be a proletarian." Scribes, like Pilate's secretary, also act as editors, for his record is a kind of powerful editorial displacement, since he does not (as the narrator notes) fully capture the interaction between Pilate and Ieshua. Matthew Levi (*Levyi Matvei*), another editor-scribe, has displaced "for a very long time" the original words spoken by Ieshua, words that have changed the world. When Pilate asks to see Matthew's parchment, it seems from Pilate's viewpoint to be a mix of incoherent ramblings. In a related theme, Pilate specifically asks if Ieshua got his ideas from some Greek books, to which Ieshua responds that he reached his conclusions "with his own mind" (24). In contrast, Berlioz is said to be "well read" (5).

Expression itself may involve a self-editing in codes, as the High

Priest warns, when he tells Pilate, "We are used to the Roman Procurator selecting [*vybiraet*] his words, before saying something. What if someone overheard us, Hegemon?" (33). When Pilate proceeds to passionately attack the High Priest, the narrator observes that with every word the Hegemon found it easier and easier, for he no longer had to "feign" (*pritvoriat'sia*), he did not have to "sort out his words" (*podbirat' slova*) (33). His "word" about the deception of the High Priest would go straight to the emperor himself, and his word should be remembered. After asking the Procurator if he believes what he is saying, the High Priest answers, "No, you do not believe" (34). Disciples carrying "the word" also act as editors, most clearly in the case of Matthew, but also, the reader anticipates, in the case of the Master's disciple Ivan.

Tellingly in this regard, the work ends with an image of Ivan's "perforated memory" (*iskolotaia pamiat'*) (392). While memory functions as a powerful editing force in the novel, the misunderstandings and rumors which abound in the novel also act to edit reality, often resulting in a compounding of codages far displaced from the original event or image. Bulgakov underscores the ability of words to disrupt or shift truth by repeatedly employing expressions like "in a word" (*slovom*) to summarize. An early example of this kind of ironic displacement occurs in chapter 1, when the narrator says that "for some strange reason" one of Voland's eyes is green, a strangeness undercut by his surprising conclusion that Voland must be "in a word—a foreigner." The Russian word for "foreigner" (*inostranets*) means literally, "one from another country," a sharp understatement when used to identify one who is the Devil. As packaging a concept in a single word can serve shift, so too the disturbance of verbal patterns can paint important ironic profiles. In contrast to the phrase repetitions marking frames between the Moscow and Jerusalem storylines, the work ends with a dramatic irony: as Bulgakov had earlier closed chapter 26, he writes his final lines of the book with words closely but not exactly echoing those the Master claimed to be the last words of his novel;[9] by this means, an editorial presence is established. As the text effectively avoids closure (cf. 134, 326, 392), distinctions between texts by the Master and by the author and narrator(s) become unclear. This blurring of boundaries parallels other transgressions of limits in the text, most broadly in the confusion between sane and insane and real and unreal, but more narrowly too: Voland's going abroad to Moscow (*za granitsu*, literally "beyond the border") and Ieshua's and Voland's roles as criminals (*prestupniki*), literally "crossers of lines" reflect this concept in word-labels themselves in Russian. Although scholars have noted that no foreign words (except for names) appear in Bulgakov's book, languages play an important role in the work.[10] Irony offers multiple "visions" as well as multiple "voices," and the matter of linguistic abilities of characters becomes a device of fluctuant displacement. At the magic show, Soviet citizens who know no French suddenly understand that foreign "babel." Voland, a polyglot, speaks at the beginning of the work in excellent idiomatic Russian colored with a foreign accent. Yet this accent miraculously disappears when he in effect takes on the Master's voice and embarks on narration of what we learn to be the Master's novel. The Master too is said to know many languages—five in addition to his own— and has worked on translation (133). Korov'ev the choirmaster-trickster is also a translator. Ieshua and Pilate are multilingual and not only shift among languages between themselves, but function in a society that utilizes more than one language. Pilate begins his conversation with Ieshua in Aramaic. Later, he asks the prisoner if he knows other languages. Ieshua responds that he knows Greek and begins to speak in Greek. Still later, only after Pilate specifically asks him, does Pilate find out that Ieshua also knows Latin. It is generally assumed by biblical scholars that Christ spoke Aramaic, but the gospels of the Christian Bible were written in a Greek translation, with almost all of the original Aramaic words lost, posing special problems of translation for biblical scholars. Because Bulgakov's Ieshua shifts among languages, there is no single language of revelation. Yet, because the narrator reports in Russian the multilingual exchange between Ieshua and Pilate, the reader too is reading a text in displacement (translation). Although Berlioz appears well read, his inability to target Voland's accent may either result from the atypical nature of Voland's language or from Berlioz's own lack of expertise in foreign languages. Linguistic range is an important theme in the novel, and it reflects the anti-cosmopolitan mentality, language policies (Stalin considered himself an expert in linguistics), and forced constraints upon expression and access to knowledge in the Stalinist era. The theme is emphasized ironically in the work by instances of comic inarticulateness and by contrasts such as Ivan's limited cultural vocabulary and therefore "vision" with that of the Master.

As the idea of accurate translation is tied to the notion of truth, recognition of authoritative texts is linked to the establishment of proof. Northrop Frye's reference to the Bible as "The Great Code" finds resonance in Bulgakov's approach toward truth and proof in his shifts from biblical accounts. As Frye notes, the Bible is a text written in a language different from the original, so the problem of translation is compounded by the "polysemous meanings" of the text itself.[11] In Frye's analysis of the Bible, he naturally confronts the issue of history and criteria of truth:

> The first thing that occurred to me was that the Bible itself could not care less whether anyone ever finds an ark on Mount Ararat or not: such "proofs" belong to a mentality quite different from any that could conceivably have produced the Book of Genesis. Similarly, if a historical record of Jesus' trial before Pilate were to turn up that corresponded in any detail to the Gospel account, many people would hail that as definitive indication of the truth of the Gospel story, without noticing that they had shifted their criterion of truth from the Gospels to something else.[12]

Put more simply by Voland, "Jesus existed [*Iisus sushchestvoval*] . . . no points of view. . . no proofs are needed . . ." (15). He then narrates nonbiblical accounts and shifts to the name "Ieshua."

Historical reality is traditionally quantified by elements of time and place. In *Master and Margarita* the broadest interplay of such frameworks involve the Moscow–Yalta timeline of the 1920s and 1930s and that of Pilate's Jerusalem. Yet because of artistic parallelisms, shifts take place, so that divisions of time and space between Jerusalem and Russia are obscured. Also, within frameworks, logical space and time are undermined. Stepa at one point has no idea what hour or date it is, and only remembers somewhere telling some woman he would visit her "the next day, precisely at noon" (71). Although the woman responds, "No, no, I won't be at home," Stepa, ironically, stubbornly holds to his word that he will come (71). The repeated motif of flight, too, blurs clear notions of space, and clock time at Satan's Ball is specifically suspended. Ambiguities of time and space in the novel are epitomized in a scene near the end of the book which brings members from the Moscow scene and Jerusalem frame together in a cosmic setting to decide the fates of Pilate and the Master. Ultimately, however, it is the act of writing itself which necessarily displaces time and space: the book itself is a physical presence embracing symbolically time and space; Master writes a manuscript about the past, which fire cannot destroy (in effect, a word expressed is a word that exists); Ieshua pleads in vain with Matthew to burn his inaccurate account; and the novel brings Master face to face with his own characters. Although breaks and inconsistencies in time often have been noted and interpreted by scholars, disruption of temporal planes extends to displacement of the very codes used to quantify time precisely. This disruption of codes begins at the very onset of the text, in a series of increasingly narrow time expressions: "One day in spring, at the hour of sunset" (*odnazhdy vesnoiu, v chas . . . zakata*). Ironically, despite this compounding of time expressions, the fixing of time remains elusive even when linked to "unprecedented" (*nebyvalo*) heat, for the etymology of the word *nebyvalo* is literally "un-being," or "imaginary." The device of deploying chains of words implying focus in order to unfocus appears throughout the novel. Similarly, the strikingly frequent use of the definite particle -*to* in Russian, although stylistic, also defeats the effectiveness of this code to delimit: words like "someone" (*kto-to*) or "somewhere" (*gde-to* or *kuda-to*), then, are exposed as constructs unable to bring precision to a world turned upside down.

The pervasive use and interplay of ironic shift to displace codified "vision" in *Master and Margarita* can be demonstrated further in the conflict among signages in the opening scene. It is said to be sunset, yet the incredible heat of the day still dominates; the characters sit in a place labelled Patriarch's Pond, but they represent the atheistic ideology of their state; the linden trees are "just turning green," but it is the weather of late summer that "terrible" (*strashnyi*) May evening. Even the assertion that "not a person" is in sight acts effectively as a kind of ironic erasure of the "two citizens," Berlioz and Ivan, already detailed by the narrator. In fact, their erasure anticipates the more serious questions regarding the existence of Christ and of the Devil and illustrates the power of editing. The narrator's matter-of-fact initial description of Ivan and Berlioz additionally serves the ironic edge. The rational Berlioz emerges in a series of unremarkable observations about his appearance, which is suddenly disrupted by mention of his black-rimmed glasses of "supernatural dimensions" (*sverkh" estestvennye razmery*). While the modifier "supernatural" may describe the narrator's own tendency toward hyperbole or suggest a distorting lens for perception, it also undermines the quantifiable codes for measuring reality.[13] Attention then turns to the younger companion, who has a mop of red hair and is dressed in a plaid cap and cowboy shirt.[14] Ironically, the very word used to describe the "alert" eyes of Ivan is undermined in Russian by its resonance with words to describe the cowboy shirt he wears (*boikie/kovboika*).

Subverting codages of apparent precision as an ironic device recurs throughout Bulgakov's work. The second paragraph of the text presents the narrator's claim that the first of the men is "none other than" Mikhail Berlioz. The marker "none other than," a colloquial expression from the narrator, also offers an ironic sense of disjuncture, for its exaggerated exclusivity ("none other") simultaneously implies the possibility of misidentification ("some other"). The author thus uses the very vocabulary of specificity to disorient. This takes an ironic twist, when, in response to Berlioz's inquiry—made with "natural irony"—about his death, Voland invokes an enigmatic formula which surprisingly names the precise form of Berlioz's death (12). Because numbers traditionally seem the most objective signs, they can play an effective ironic role.[15] By the time the narrator asserts in the first chapter that the "second strange thing" (*vtoraia strannost'*) (4) has occurred, the reader already has confronted numerous oddities and inconsistencies in the narrator's account. In addition to ironic enumeration, the novel also subverts numbers as the language of reason. When Ivan pursues Professor Voland, he is sure the professor was in house number 13 and in precisely apartment number 47, but he does not find him there. A later chapter heading announces Ivan's "splitting into two" (*razdvoenie Ivana*) (111), a process which suggests schizophrenia, a theme in the novel. And yet, in essence this notion acts positively instead of negatively in the novel, as demonstrated by Master's own mental acuity and by Ivan's increasing complexity, which makes him more human. Another important example of irony and numbers appears in Voland's assertion that in the realm of reason there can be no proof of the existence of God; not only did Kant disprove five proofs of God, he "as if to mock himself" created a sixth proof (9). This sixth proof becomes displaced in the novel with Voland's variation—there exists, he says, a seventh proof about the existence of the Devil, a proof which will be revealed to Berlioz (41). This proof ultimately is realized when, as Voland predicted, he literally displaces the editor from his apartment after meeting the bizarre death forseen by Voland. Mention has already been made of the often-noted discrepancy between clock time and natural sun time in the Jerusalem storyline. Yet here too emerges a challenge to precision: the call "it is time" (*pora*) is juxtaposed in the text with the claim that first it is getting "toward" (*k*) noon and then it is "around" (*okolo*) ten. Ivan's nighttime guest, the Master, who has lost his "name," is referred to only as "number 118" in the epilogue. In Russian, the number "one" (*odin*) also means "alone." This facet of the word is exploited in the ironic subtext drawn around Ieshua. Pilate asks the accused if he believes in any gods. Ieshua responds *"Bog odin, v nego ia veriu"* ("God alone [is one], I believe in him"), an answer echoed immediately in his response to the inquiry about his marital status: *"Net, Ia odin"* ("No, I am alone [one]").[16] The answer links Ieshua to God, to Pilate and his loneliness, and to a sense of personal integrity in contrast to the schizophrenic world around him. Indeed, too, the words tie all of these to Voland, who asserts "I am alone, alone, I am always alone" (40).

Modernists like the artist Malevich made use of signboards in their paintings, both as elements of urban iconography and as devices to realize visual puns. Signboards and labels are orientational codes which can effectively serve irony when displaced. Bulgakov too employs this device to comment effectively on illusions within the real world, or to mark the merger of different realities. In the opening chapter of the novel, the sign "Beer and Sodas" advertises falsely, since nothing but apricot soda is available. Voland specifically has the "Our Brand" (*Nasha marka*) cigarettes Ivan requests, but in a cigarette case marked with a black magic triangle. Details like Voland's poodle-headed cane, Master's cap with the letter *M* on it, and the ring with an identifying mark placed on Yeshua's dead body all serve as labels of sorts. Pilate's removal of the inscribed shields from the palace and of an insignia from the military uniforms reflects a conflict of his signage with the Judaic laws against graven images.[17] In contrast to the beer sign without beer, enticing advertisements for Voland's show prove shockingly accurate: the promised performances of black magic with complete "exposé" (100) are literally realized, when clothes disappear off the backs of unsuspecting citizens and an official's secret love affair is publicly exposed. Currency magically made at the performance is authenticated as "real" (*nastoiashchie*) because the right watermarks appear on it (119). The shift called black magic, then, is identified with human greed, cowardice, and hypocrisy.

While writers have questionable control over verbal signage, the very name of the building for the writers' organization involves ironic shift. As we are told, the domicile of MASSOLIT is named "Griboedov House" based on a highly questionable assumption compounded by a rumor by a known "liar" which results essentially in accidental reference to a famous Russian writer (51). The narrator pointedly notes, however, that everyone calls the place "Griboedov" rather than "Griboedov House." This abbreviation in effect displaces the writer with the building, a shift further realized by the building's primary identification with a restaurant, representing the literal meaning of *griboedov* ("mushroom eater"). While the word *griboedov* seems to dictate its own reality, another kind of verbal tampering occurs when the buffet manager of the Variety Theater uses the nonsensical label sturgeon "of second freshness" to mask his fraudulent practices (202). Throughout the novel, people make signs to each other and gesture, but the real communicative function is often unclear or multifaceted. In this regard, Pilate's gesture for his dog in the novel acts as a variation of the symbolic gesture of his washing his hands in the biblical account.

In a novel where ironic displacement of codes acts as a means to confront the notions of truth and the real, it is not surprising that the theme of names and identity is important.[18] Human beings are distinguished by their complex ability to signify and name. While names can be used to establish presence, the naming of abstract notions like gods or spirits can offer a means to organize or control the unknown.[19] Although scholars have done much work on the nature of the names used in *Master and Margarita*, the use of names as a shifting device has not yet been detailed. Words as both referents and as self-sufficient concrete entities (the *samovitoe slovo* of the Russian Futurists) offer a powerful source of irony in Bulgakov's novel. In this respect, displacement rather than placement of identity through names often arises in the work: names as concrete markers of presence or identity are challenged, offering a complex excursion into a metaphysics of presence.[20] Although the book's title presents the names Master and Margarita, we do not meet the characters themselves until well into the body of the novel. Although they have names, the question of whether Christ/Ieshua and the Devil/Voland exist is pivotal in the work. While Berlioz seems a strange name for a hard-nosed Soviet editor, it is the Master who must first tell the poet Ivan about the existence of the famous Romantic composer whose name Berlioz shares. Names of other characters like the doctor Stravinsky simultaneously recall names shifted from prominent composers. The character Fagot ("Bassoon") has two names, Ivan has three basic names, and when Berlioz dies, his name becomes nearly displaced by the label "the deceased" (*pokoinyi*). Unlike the French composer of the opera *Faust*, Berlioz is Russian, editor of an arts journal and a board member of a large Moscow literary association whose "shortened name" (*sokrashchenno imenuemaia*) only is given in the text. Ironically, this acronym MASSOLIT labels an organization which functions more as an exclusive eating club than a literary gathering. Significantly the oddly dressed Soviet "cowboy" Ivan Ponyrev writes under the pseudonym "Homeless" (*Bezdomnyi*), a label Ieshua will share. Master too is deprived of his home, and this idea of homelessness acts as a metaphor for displacement more generally in the text. In Russian, as in English, the name "pirate" in the Moscow story line curiously echoes the name "Pilate." *Begemot* (Behemoth), which means "hippopotamus," is a giant cat. Ivan has trouble remembering Voland's name and is surprised that Voland knows his—ironically, Voland claims, because of his public reputation from the pages of the literary journal. Hoods over heads act to conceal identity, and slowness or inability to recall names is a recurrent motif in the novel. In chapter 7 the narrator recounts that Anna Frantsevna de Fuzhere (an ironically foreign-sounding name in Russian) rented apartment number 50 to a person whose last name "it seems" was Belomut and to another with a "lost name" (*utrachennaia familiia*) (71). Although Bulgakov in this section playfully displaces naming of people who disappear, the overall effect is quite serious: not only does it parody Stalinist terror as an erasure of presence, but it also more broadly demonstrates that even precise naming cannot guarantee actual presence (72). In a reference again to the apartment dwellers, the narrator relates that one day a policeman appeared and asked for a resident "whose last name was lost"(71). Significantly, the Master himself claims no longer to have a name, his public presence denied by the editor's refusal to publish his work. Curiously, Ivan recalls the incident, but specifically says he cannot recall the Master's name. The Master, seeing for the first time a woman carrying yellow flowers, obeys the "yellow sign" (*znak*) and understands suddenly that he had loved "namely" (*imenno*) this woman all his life (135). As in English, *imenno* implies precision, a meaning often undermined in the book; but its tie to the concept "name" in conjunction with Margarita takes an additional twist when, in contrast, the Master cannot recall the name of his legal wife.

Margarita, his "secret wife," gives her love his new label "Master," ironically identifying him with the Soviet titular honor, "Master" of sport and culture, as well as with the unnamed craftsmen and masters of the cultural past. The letter *M* sewn on the Master's cap is a physical inversion of the letter *W* visible on Woland's passport. Ironically, however, this *W* must be indicated in the Russian account as *"dvoynoe V"* ("double *V*") (14), because the letter *W* officially marking Voland's identity does not exist in the Cyrillic alphabet. Although Margarita claims the Master's novel is her life, as a character named in Bulgakov's work, she indeed "lives" in a novel. Voland has several professional labels, or names, including "specialist in black magic" and "historian." Juxtaposition of these last two professions serves ironically to blur the distinction between them. Ivan, too, becomes a poet turned "historian," so that history and art continually share nomenclature in the novel. Playing with the housing chairman responsible for the apartment, Korov'ev questions what the difference between an "official" and "unofficial" person is and, when asked for his name, answers, "Let's say [*skazhem*] Korov'ev" (91–92).

A related theme in the novel is denunciation, or the terror of naming. Citizens unrestrainedly use this device to try to obtain Berlioz's apartment (90). Korov'ev maneuvers to "set up" the housing chairman so he can turn him in to the police. Yet, after reporting the bribe-taking chairman, Korov'ev asks the police not to reveal his name for fear the man might seek revenge (96). Margarita, whose name means "daisy" in Russian, carries flowers when she first meets the man whom she will name Master, and she is chosen by Voland to host his ball precisely because of her name.[21] Well, it seems, not quite so precisely, as Korov'ev reveals, for in Moscow there were one hundred and twenty-one Margaritas, none other of whom was suitable (247).

In the beginning of the novel, Ivan, who as a poet should represent culture, displays shocking ignorance of world culture. For him, the name of the philosopher Kant means nothing, and until Ivan is enlightened by Berlioz and Voland, Kant in effect does not exist for him. Names from a variety of sources like the Bible and Goethe's *Faust* emerge in the text. Although Voland is a name taken from the first part of *Faust*, Ivan does not make this connection. Later, when the Master identifies Voland, whom Ivan believes exists, as "Satan," Ivan declares that "he does not exist" (131). In "Seventh Proof," Voland himself asks if the Devil exists. When Ivan answers no, Voland's sharp response, in highly colloquial Russian, is telling: "What is this with you? Whatever you can't grasp doesn't exist" (*"Chto zhe eto u vas, chego ni khvatish'sia nichevo net!"*) (41). This erased presence emerges too in "By Candlelight" when the narrator, referring to Voland, the Devil, ironically says that the "nonexistent one" (*"nesushchestvuiushchii"*) was sitting on the bed (249).

The novel opens with a discussion concerning identity and existence. That conversation between Berlioz and Ivan is about Jesus Christ (*Iisus Khrist*) and his depiction in a poem by Ivan. Berlioz the editor criticizes the poem, not because it is a bad poem, but because Ivan's work suggests that Christ was born. Significantly, Berlioz attempts to prove to the poet that the main thing is not what kind of person Christ was, good or bad, but that Christ as a person did not exist "in the world" (*na svete*), *svet* in Russian also meaning "light" (5). Berlioz contends that Christians did not invent anything new, but simply used existing legends to create their Christ, that Christ's coming was spread by rumors. Ironically, not only does Berlioz himself refer to manifestations of the Christ-figure in other cultures to prove Christ as legend, the text itself employs several names for Jesus. Berlioz refers to Jesus as *"Iisus,"* while the Master in his novel employs the form *"Ieshua,"* *"Ga Notsri"* (Ha Nozri) and terms like "philosopher." Ultimately, just as the novel proves that the many precursors to the Christ myth and the proliferation of names for Christ cannot disprove His existence, the converse lack of traditional names for the Master likewise cannot serve to deny his existence. This relationship between name and figure holds for objects and actions as well. In the Moscow storyline, the financial director refers to a "really" (*"deistvitel'no"*) swinish trick, "for which there is no name" (*"net nazvaniia"*) (106).

Naming as shift forms a major dynamic in the Jerusalem storyline. During his interrogation of Christ, Pilate, the fifth Procurator of Judea, insists upon being addressed as "Procurator" or "Hegemon," the name of his station, and pointedly rejects the label "good man" offered by Ieshua, who in effect cancels the significance of the term "evil person," by saying "there are no evil people on earth" (*"zlykh liudei net na svete"*) (24). This notion reflects Christ's concern that Pilate has lost his faith in people. In contrast, Ieshua several times has to deny the label "physician" that Pilate attempts to apply to him. This denial of identity resonates in juxtaposition to the epithet of Christ as the Great Physician in biblical tradition, and contrasts with the negative attitude toward those in the medical profession in the Moscow storyline in the work. Reference by Ieshua to Pilate as a horseman (*vsadnik*) (34) after Pontius Pilate's self-reference as "horseman Golden Spear" (*"vsadnik Zolotoe Kop'e"*) (33) anticipates his association with the knights (*rytsari*) at the end of the work, a fairytale-like inversion of the horsemen of the apocalypse. Pilate's cold-blooded henchman Mark, nicknamed Krysoboi (usually translated "Ratkiller"), is called a good man by "criminal" Ieshua; and Bar-Rabban, rather than Ha-Nozri, is named by the Sanhedrin to be released in honor of the great holiday of Passover. Pilate claims to speak for Rome and pronounces the sentence "in the name of Caesar." The condemned men go to their deaths carrying signs reading "Outlaw and rebel" ("*Razboinik i miatezhnik*") in two languages, Aramaic and Greek (168). Curiously, although Matthew calls the man Ieshua a "dog," Ieshua says he "sees" nothing bad in that animal to warrant offense at such a "word" (19–20); conversely, Pilate's dog has a name, Banga, and it is to this creature that Ieshua says Pilate—who has little faith in people—feels closest. Later, at the execution of Ieshua, the only creatures not afraid of the merciless sun are two stray dogs. Matthew Levi, who considers himself Ieshua's most loyal disciple, fails to put Ieshua out of his misery and sits helplessly at the execution site, where he calls himself a "fool . . . coward . . . not a man" (172). Shocked that God would permit an innocent man like Ieshua to suffer, Matthew calls God a "black god" and "god of evil," ("*bog zla*") (175), whose eyes have been blinded by the smoke of incense burners from the Temple. The last word from Ieshua's lips at the execution is "Hegemon." Although the account of the execution says Ieshua drank from the sponge of water granted him by law before his death (177), the chief of the secret service creatively "edits" by reporting to Pilate that one of the criminals did not drink. When Pilate asks which one, the chief apologizes for not "having named" Ha-Nozri (301), whom Pilate proceeds to call a "crazy man" (*bezumets*) for not taking the water. In a telling moment of linked identities, Ieshua acknowledges that when his name is recalled, they will also recall Pilate ("*Raz odin—to, znachit, tut zhe i drugoi! Pomianut menia,—seichas zhe pomianut i tebia!*") (315), as in the painting by Ge.

One of the most important devices in the novel to demonstrate the ability of codes to displace the truth of identity and reality is the discrediting of documents as authoritative texts. Characters are often asked to reveal codified proof of identity, and when Ivan wants to know the identity of Voland, he asks for his passport documents, which mean little. MASSOLIT membership cards are no guarantors of literary skill. Ironically, Voland says he has come to Moscow to study historical documents on black magic. History is drawn from documents, but as the novel shows, these texts are artifacts which can be manipulated. Even when the narrator cites the lyrics to a song, he adds a possible disclaimer about their accuracy (127). At the magic show, a marriage license is called inadequate proof of marital status (a variation of Margarita's real "marriage" to the Master as opposed to her documented spouse.) Written contracts are overturned, and despite his own feelings, Pilate says that what is written about Ieshua is little, but enough "to hang him" (19). Issues of identity and authentication are tied closely to the establishment of concrete proof and documentation. Significantly, Ieshua's fate from Pilate's perspective results from words on more than one parchment. Ieshua claims that testimony to his allegedly expressed intentions was by uneducated people who had confused what he had said, a confusion that "would last a very long time." He then names Matthew, whose record includes words Ieshua claims he never said. Ieshua begged Matthew to burn his parchment; but, as he relates to Pilate, Matthew tore the parchment from his hands and ran away (19). Later, after the execution of Ieshua, Matthew attempts to remove (i.e., displace) the body. This action then lends an ironic ring to the words Pilate reads from Matthew's parchment (and after he catches Matthew in a white lie): ". . . there is no death" (324). Aphranius, in response to Pilate's inquiry whether he is certain Iuda was killed, says, "I do not have to see a corpse to say that a man was killed" (317).[22]

In the end, reality is holistic and signs of historical accuracy do not necessarily establish moral Truth. The Word exists in constant tension with the word. Bulgakov shows that human life and art are processes of editing reality, with intentional or unintentional displacements of truth. The heart is the noblest organ, and Truth is found in its wisdom, those "pricks of conscience" and courageous acts of goodness and compassion; for these, one earns not peace but light, a light with warmth. There is no relativity with truth, goodness, or justice.[23] They simply exist, like Christ with Satan, even in displacement. And although manuscripts, ironically, really can burn, their texts—even bad ones—in truth exist.[24]

Notes

1. The bibliography on irony is immense. But Wayne Booth suggests the connection between truth and ironic "vision," when he observes that "no other term used by critics, except possibly 'rhetoric' itself, has produced so many tracts about the nature of man, of the universe or all literature or all good

literature." Wayne C. Booth, *A Rhetoric of Irony* (Chicago: University of Chicago Press, 1974), ix.

For the purposes of the present study, citations and translations of Bulgakov's novel are taken from M. Bulgakov, *Master i Margarita* (Ann Arbor Mich.: Ardis, 1980). Page numbers from this Russian text will be referenced in parentheses in the body of the essay.

2. In addition to this compelling instance of artistic parallelism between the painting by Ge and the novel by Bulgakov, Bulgakov attended the same gymnasium that the painter Ge had attended decades earlier. See Ellendea Proffer, *Bulgakov: Life and Work* (Ann Arbor: Ardis, 1984), 5.

3. Vsevolod Dmitriev, "Nikolai Nikolaevich Ge," *Apollon*, no.10 (December 1913): 9–11. The painting *What Is Truth?* by Ge is reproduced in *Russkie pisateli ob izobrazitel'nom iskusstve* [Russian writers on art] (Leningrad: Khudozhnik, 1976).

4. In Russian, as in English, the word "tongue" (*iazyk*) also can mean "language."

5. That is, the critical examination of signifying structures. See Jonathan Culler, *The Pursuit of Signs: Semiotics, Literature, Deconstruction* (Ithaca: Cornell University Press, 1981).

6. Note that Bulgakov has chosen specifically the word "*neizvestnye*" ("the unknown") rather than "*neznakomye*" ("the unfamiliar"), another word used in Russian to mean "strangers."

7. Frye continues, "[A]ccording to Genesis 1:4, 'God said, Let there be light; and there was light.' That is, the word was the creative agent that brought the thing into being . . . and John's 'In the beginning was the LOGOS' is a New Testament commentary on the opening of Genesis, identifying the original creative word with Christ." Northrop Frye, *The Great Code: The Bible and Literature* (New York: First Harvest/HBJ, 1983), 17–18.

8. In the context of irony, a description by Bulgakov of his mental state in 1930 is telling: "I am poisoned by melancholy and my habitual irony;" M.O. Chudakova, *Arkhiv M.A. Bulgakova* [The archive of M.A. Bulgakov] (Moscow: 1976), 98, as cited by Kalpana Sahni, *A Mind in Ferment: Mikhail Bulgakov's Prose* (New Delhi: Arnold-Heinemann, 1984), 177.

9. Although one could speculate that this displacement of closure involves some lack of attention to detail on Bulgakov's part, the result works meaningfully from the standpoint of irony.

10. See B.M. Gasparov, "Iz nabliudenii nad motivnoi strukturoi romana M.A. Bulgakova *Master i Margarita*," [From observations on the structure of motifs in Bulgakov's novel *Master and Margarita*], *Slavica Hierosolymitana* (Jerusalem) (1978): 198–251.

11. Frye, *The Great Code*, 215, 220.

12. Frye, *The Great Code*, 44–45.

13. Curiously, the word "supernatural" occurs in inverse usage: the narra-

tor says that not a single telephone in a building is working, and although this is unpleasant, it is not a "supernatural" (*sverkh"estestvennoe*) event (114).

14. The physical contrast between the two "citizens" is striking and will parallel a subsequent contrast between the elegant Voland and his motley companion Korov'ev.

15. "[W]ithout accepting the fiction of logic, without measuring reality against the purely invented world of the unconditional and self-identical, without a constant falsification of the world by means of numbers, man could not live. . . . To recognize untruth as a condition of life . . . a philosophy that risks this would by that token alone place itself beyond good and evil." F. Nietzsche, *Beyond Good and Evil*, tr. Walter Kaufmann (New York: Vintage, 1966), 12. Bulgakov also appears to play in the novel with Russian folk incantations and beliefs, Russian Decadent and Symbolist ideas, and other understandings of evil. In this latter regard, see Paul Ricoeur, *The Symbolism of Evil*, tr. E. Buchanan (Boston: Beacon Press, 1967).

16. The concept of oneness implies a philosophical holism in the work. As Ieshua acknowledges, history will bind him to Pilate; and as the novel demonstrates, lives intertwine, and time and space overlap. The theme of oneness also is critical to the inversion in the novel regarding schizophrenia, an illness of identity involving changing truths.

17. Proffer, *Bulgakov*, 442.

18. In this regard, Northrop Frye has noted, "In Exodus 3:14, though God also gives himself a name, he defines himself (according to AV) as 'I am that I am,' which scholars say is more accurately rendered 'I will be what I will be.'" Frye, *The Great Code*, 17.

19. Ibid., 6.

20. In his study of Russian Formalism, Peter Steiner briefly discusses theories of proper names. These include a notion of traditional logic that a name is merely an index, Gottlob Frege's idea that proper names are telegraphic descriptions, and John Searle's notion that names serve pragmatically as loci from which to "hang descriptions." Paul Steiner, *Russian Formalism: A Metapoetics* (Ithaca: Cornell University Press, 1984), 40. Bulgakov appears to play with all of these concepts.

21. In view of the use of light imagery and other images in the novel, Margarita also appears as an inversion and displacement of motifs from Russian Symbolism, where Solov'ev's Divine Feminine finds contrast in Briusov's Harlot Astride a Beast and Belyi's Woman Clothed in the Sun. See Samuel D. Cioran, *Vladimir Solov'ev and the Knighthood of the Divine Sophia* (Waterloo, Ontario: Wilfrid Laurier University Press, 1977), 163–71. Also compare Blok's attack on the concept of Irony (*Ironiia*, 1908) as a disease of his generation which dangerously blurs distinctions between good and evil. See Cioran, 182.

22. By rendering the text in English as "to know" rather than "to say" that a man was killed, translators miss a valuable distinction in the Russian text that

underlines the power of words. (See, for example, M. Bulgakov, *The Master and Margarita*, tr. M. Ginsburg [New York: Grove Press, 1967], 336.)

More broadly, Bulgakov's work attacks the power of categories to conform to appearances. Whereas Hegel attempts to go beyond limits placed on reason as reflected in dialectical synthesizing of diversity, Bulgakov appears to reject the dialectic in favor of an absolute in continual displacement. In *Beyond Good and Evil* and *Genealogy of Morals*, Friedrich Nietzsche sees truth and morality displaced by the relational role of power. Language, then, is perceived as a mechanism maintaining social order by defining good and evil. For Michel Foucault in *The Archaeology of Knowledge*, trans. A. M. Sheridan-Smith (New York: Pantheon Books, 1972), documents are material entities from which history is reconstructed but which can never hold the complete truth; history, then, is full of discontinuities. Whereas the aspects of decentering in Foucault are curiously anticipated by Bulgakov's understanding of shift in history, knowledge, and language, Bulgakov does not share the God-less world of Foucault but turns shift upon itself to find a Center, a Truth or Absolute. (See the concise discussion of Foucault by C. Lemert and G. Gillan, *Michel Foucault: Social Theory and Transgression* [New York: Columbia University Press, 1982].) Bulgakov's philosophical view of language in his novel also seems to anticipate ideas somberly put forth about truth and language by Roland Barthes and Fredric Jameson. See Fredric Jameson, *The Prison-House of Language* (Princeton: Princeton University Press, 1972); this work begins with a quote by Nietzsche: "We have to cease to think if we refuse to do it in the prison-house of language; for we cannot reach further than the doubt which asks whether the limit we see is really a limit. . . ."

23. It is interesting here to compare Bulgakov's ideas on courage and justice with Plato's concept of four cardinal virtues: wisdom, courage, temperance, and justice.

24. The Russian poet Fedor Tiutchev once wrote the famous line "A thought uttered is a lie." Bulgakov, however, seems to remind us that once uttered, even a falseness truly exists.

Contributors

ROGER ANDERSON is professor of Russian literature, chair of Russian and Eastern European studies, and director of the Kazakh-American Studies Center at the University of Kentucky.

GARY COX is associate professor of Russian and director of Russian studies at Southern Methodist University.

PAUL DEBRECZENY is Alumni Distinguished Professor of Russian literature and director of the Center for Slavic, Eurasian and East European Studies at the University of North Carolina in Chapel Hill.

ANTONINA FILONOV GOVE is professor of Slavic languages and literatures at Vanderbilt University.

ALISON HILTON is associate professor of art history at Georgetown University.

PRISCILLA R. ROOSEVELT is a research associate at Georgetown's School of Foreign Service and the George Washington University Institute for European, Eurasian, and Asian Studies.

JULIETTE R. STAPANIAN-APKARIAN is associate professor and chair of the Russian Studies Department at Emory University.

JAMES WEST is professor of Slavic languages and literatures at the University of Washington.

Index